Could You Live This Way?
Would You Live This Way?

An Illustrated Compilation of Idyllic Experiments in North America

John W. Friesen, Ph.D., D.Min., D.R.S
Virginia Lyons Friesen, Ph.D.
University of Calgary

DETSELIG
ENTERPRISES LTD
Calgary, Alberta, Canada

© 2011 John W. Friesen and Virginia L. Friesen

Library and Archives Canada Cataloging in Publication

Friesen, John W.
    Could you live this way? would you live this way? : an illustrated compilation of idyllic experiements in North America / John W. Friesen, Virginia Lyons Friesen.

Includes bibliographical references.
ISBN 978-1-55059-419-5

    1. Utoias--North America. 2. Collective settlements--North America. 3. Communal living --North America. I. Friesen, Virginia Lyons, 1952- II. Title.

HX652.A3F748.2011   335.'02097   C2011-903507-3

Detselig Enterprises Ltd
210, 1220 Kensington Rd NW
Calgary, Alberta
T2N 3P5

www.temerondetselig.com
temeron@telusplanet.net
Phone: 403-283-0900
Fax: 403-283-6947

All rights reserved. No part of this book may be produced in any form or by any means without written permission from the publisher.

Detselig Enterprises Ltd. acknowledges the financial support of the Government of Canada through the Canada Books Program for our publishing program.

Also acknowledged is the financial assistance of the Government of Alberta, Alberta Multimedia Develpment fund for the support of our publishing program.

Photos in this book are by the authors.

ISBN 978-1-55059-419-5   Printed in Canada

Aberrent, Abnormal, Alienated, Absurd, Animated, Ambitious, Apparition-oriented, Anticipative, Ardent, Bizarre, Bohemian, Atypical, Chimerical, Capricious, contrived, Committed, Aggressive, Astonishing, Captivated, Anomalous,

Creative, Dissident, Earnest, Estranged, Curious, Disoriented, Determined, Dogged, Dubious, Dreamers, Eager, Enthusiasts, Enamored, Erratic, Exraordinary, Fake, Eccentric, Delusionary, Distinct, Expectant,

Fanciful, High-flown, Idyllic, Inauthentic, Fantasists, Farfetched, Fervent, Hopeful, Idiosyncratic, Idealists, Imaginative, Incomprehensible, Implausible, Intractable, Impassioned, Irrational, Fallacious, Hallucinatory, Illusionary, Inconceivable,

Inflexible, Kooky, Nirvana, Otherworldly, Mirage-oriented, Irregular, Mysterious, Ludicrous, Melodramatic, Mawkish, Obdurate, Optimists, Offbeat, Outrageous, Passionate, Paradise, Intentional, Nonconformist, Outlandish, Lofty,

Peaceful, Purposeful, Peculiar, persevering, Persistent, Phantom-oriented, Quixotic, Romanticists, Remarkable, Shangri La-oriented, Sanguine, Phony, Preposterous, Put on, Resolute, Sentimentalists, Perfectionists, Quaint, Philosophical, Seventh Heaven

Labels They Had to Live With: Critics' Descriptives of Utopian Dreamers

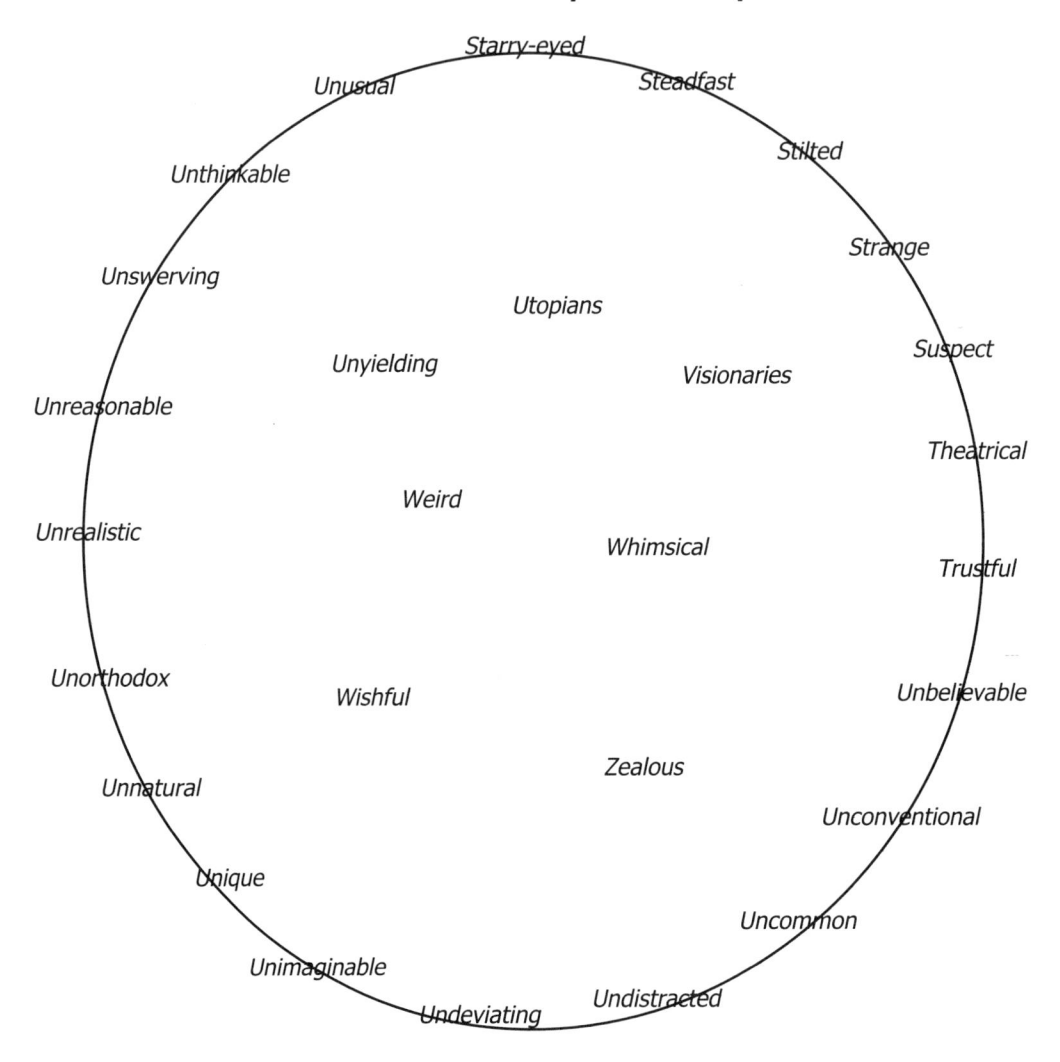

- Starry-eyed
- Steadfast
- Unusual
- Stilted
- Unthinkable
- Strange
- Unswerving
- Utopians
- Suspect
- Unyielding
- Visionaries
- Unreasonable
- Theatrical
- Weird
- Unrealistic
- Whimsical
- Trustful
- Unorthodox
- Wishful
- Unbelievable
- Unnatural
- Zealous
- Unconventional
- Unique
- Uncommon
- Unimaginable
- Undeviating
- Undistracted

To Keigan John Keian deVries

Our first great grandchild

*May you grow to appreciate
study and travel
as much as we do.*

LAL MOHAN JENA

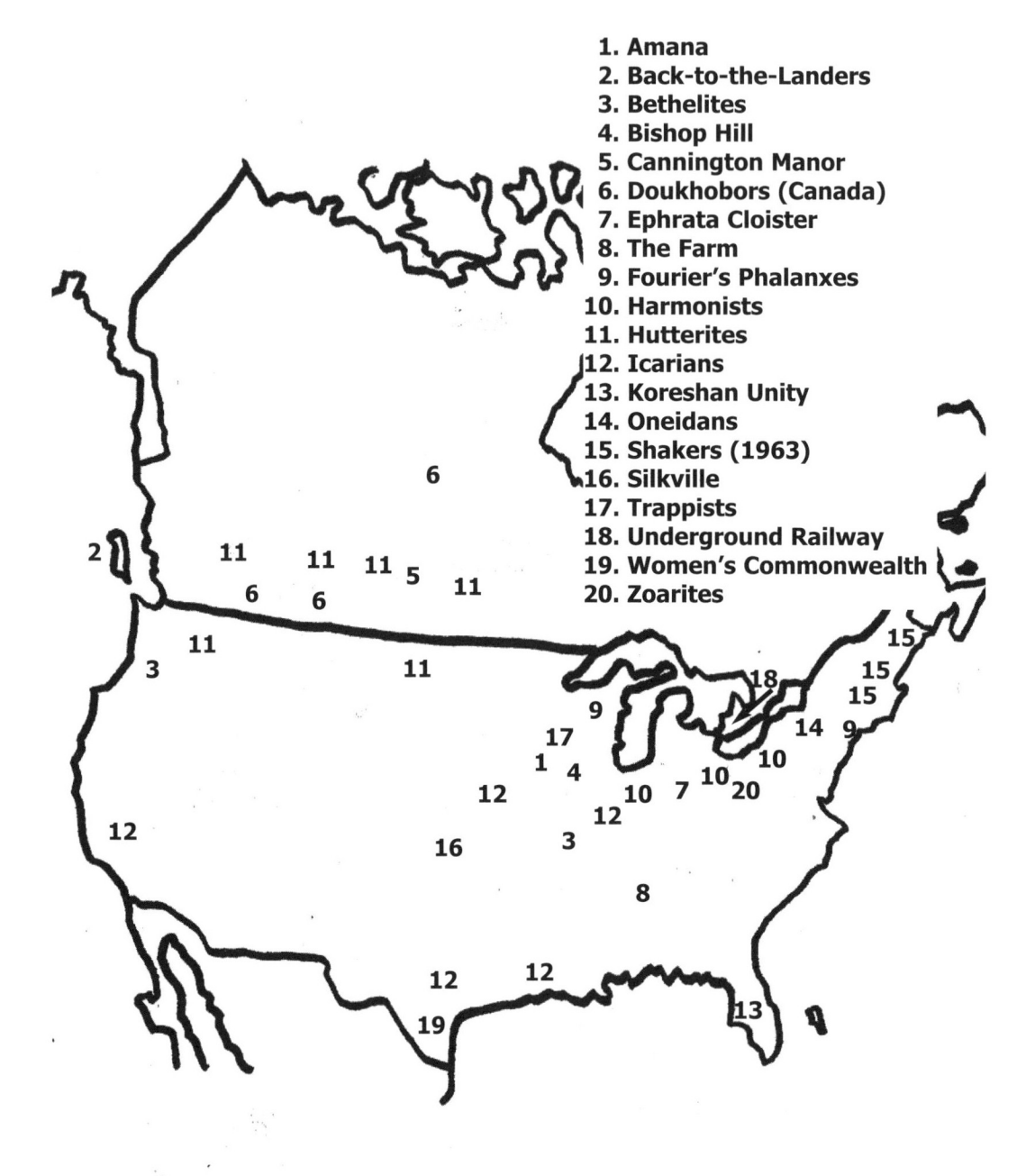

1. Amana
2. Back-to-the-Landers
3. Bethelites
4. Bishop Hill
5. Cannington Manor
6. Doukhobors (Canada)
7. Ephrata Cloister
8. The Farm
9. Fourier's Phalanxes
10. Harmonists
11. Hutterites
12. Icarians
13. Koreshan Unity
14. Oneidans
15. Shakers (1963)
16. Silkville
17. Trappists
18. Underground Railway
19. Women's Commonwealth
20. Zoarites

Preface

Thus ever at every season in every hour and every place visions await the soul on wide ocean or shore...
— Robert Bridges, 1844-1930 (Cohen and Cohen, 1985: 66)

One of the unique things about human beings is their innate desire always to hope for better things. Some individuals actually do something about it; we call them dreamers, inventors, or composers, and sometimes even radicals. This book relates the stories of some of the idealistic experiments developed by these folk.

This volume is the result of many research trips across Canada and the United States over the last dozen years. During our travels from one coast to the other, we visited a wide variety of historical communal sites, and always we were impressed with the extent to which the developers of these idyllic experiments went in pursuing their dreams of a better life. We marveled at their vision, their energy, and their drive. Many of them proved their willingness to give up individual pursuits for the greater good of the community. Sadly, most communities ceased to exist after a few generations with only the Hutterian Brethren continuing to grow. It seems logical to conclude that while it is relatively easy to conceive of living together and sharing all things, it is a much greater challenge to actually do so.

During the past several centuries since North America was "discovered" by European explorers, a significant number of individuals and groups acted on their dreams for a better life, and they did this for a number of reasons. Some groups that migrated to this continent during the 17th and 18th centuries believed that the best way for them to adjust to frontier conditions was to band together and form communal societies. Others formed communal societies when inspired to do so by the visions of charismatic leaders. Often these groups had religious reasons for stepping away from mainline society with their plans to form idealistic ways to live out their convictions. Still others, either dissatisfied or disillusioned by societal developments believed they could improve conditions for their compatriots by isolating themselves from the world and creating their own version of utopia.

The honeymoon period for building utopian societies in the United States occurred just prior to the 1900s, most of them designed by middle class contingents who sought to escape what they perceived to be severe economic conditions elsewhere. Another intense desire to create utopian conditions occurred during the latter part of the 20th century, perhaps in response to the idealistic portrayals of family life on television. A parallel form of social response developed in the form of the hippie movement in the 1960s, many of whose adherents were American draft dodgers. The post 1960s era has also witnessed the growth of utopian experiments, many of them motivated by the spiritual quests identified by proponents of New Age philosophies.

The effect that visiting the various historic sites identified in this book had on us was one of admiration for the courage and idealism manifested by these societal entrepreneurs. Thankfully, many provincial and state historical societies have seen fit to preserve these vestiges of past dreams, and we are all the richer for it. Human societies have always needed people who think ahead of the times and act on their dreams.

We are deeply indebted to Dr. Ted Giles and the staff of Temeron/Detselig – Devon Bates, James Dangerous, and Aaron Dalton for undertaking the arduous task of publishing this work. These individuals have all been encouraging, helpful, and efficient, and we owe them a special debt of thanks.

If the readers of this volume experience only a measure of the admiration that we garnered while visiting these commemorative sites of past human visions, the effort of collecting these historical gems will have been well worth it.

J.W.F.

V.L.F.

2011

Reference

Cohen, J. M, and M.J. Cohen. (1985). *Dictionary of Quotations.* New York: Penguin Books.

Contents

Introduction 11
    PART ONE
A Potpourri of Utopian Dreams – Successes, Failures,
and Continuing Quests 15
  1. Amish: A Dream Fulfilled 17
  2. Barr Colonists: Utopia in Conflict 23
  3. Bloc Settlements in Western Canada: Parallel Utopias 27
  4. Chinese in North America: In Pursuit of Happiness 31
  5. Hull House: Utopian Welfare 37
  6. Kemano, British Columbia: Sudden Death Utopia 40
  7. Japanese in North America: A Continuing Quest for Utopia 42
  8. Manitoba Mennonites: Utopian Dreams Compromised 45
  9. Maryhilll, Washington: An Unfulfilled Dream 48
10. Metlakatla, British Columbia: An Aboriginal Communal Utopia 51
11. Mormon Trek to Utah: Utopia at Long Last 54
12. Old Believers: Utopia in Motion 57
13. People of the Plains: Utopia Was Never Their Goal 60
14. Pueblo Invasion: Delivering an Uninvited Utopia 63
15. Puritans in America: Utopia Was a Very Serious Pursuit 66
16. Quakers: Sharing the Utopian Dream 69
17. Route 66: An All American Utopian Dream 72
18. Sikhs in Canada: A Perpetual Quest for Utopia 75
19. Utopia, Ohio: Utopia for Real! 78
20. Western American Trek: Determined Interlopers 80

PART TWO:
Communal Utopias .... .85
  1. Amana .... .91
  2. Back-to-the-Landers .... .96
  3. Bethel .... .96
  4. Bishop Hill .... .103
  5. Cannington Manor .... .109
  6. Doukhobors .... .114
  7. Ephrata Cloister .... .122
  8. Farm, The .... .128
  9. Fourier's Phalanxes .... .133
10. Harmonists .... .140
11. Hutterites .... .150
12. Icarians .... .157
13. Koreshan Unity .... .164
14. Oneidas .... .170
15. Shakers .... .178
16. Silkville .... .188
17. Trappists .... .193
18. Underground Railroad .... .197
19. Women's Commonwealth .... .203
20. Zoar .... .208

Epilogue: What Can We Learn From These Idealistic Pursuits? ...... .213

PART THREE:
An Encyclopedia of Utopian Pursuits .... .219

About the Authors .... .249

Introduction

Where there is no vision, the people perish (Proverbs 29:18a KJV).

Your sons and daughters will prophesy, your young men will see visions, and your old men will dream dreams (Acts 2:17b NIV).

Utopias are realizable, they are more realizable than what has been presented to us as "realistic politics" and what has simply been the calculated rationalism of armchair politicians. Life is moving toward utopias. – Edmund Clerihew Bentley (1885-1956) in *New Middle Ages*, 1924: 122.

Poet Robert Browning stated it this way; "A man's reach should exceed his grasp, or what's a heaven for?" The implied striving of humankind implied in Browning's observation seems to be borne out in people's actions. People tend by their very nature to be dreamers and visionaries – always reaching out – and this is a good thing. Dreams that are put into action often generate great social benefits. Visionaries often come up with new ways to do things, or they invent ways to revamp outdated practices. Many visionaries have a knack for making things happen – including designing new ways to live.

Not surprisingly, the notion of trying to create a Shangrila or Garden of Eden-like community is never far from anyone's mind. In the past, leaders of distinctive social movements with utopian characteristics forged into previously uninhabited areas to realize their dreams. Today many of the physical ruins of their creative developments are still recognizable by individuals who take time to visit these places. Some of these unique historic experiments have been transformed into state parks or heritage sites. As one wanders the grounds of these sites, one can only marvel at the zeal of these utopians, many of whom came from across the ocean to plant new communities. They often arrived in North America with little more than the threadbare clothes on their backs, but with the desperate dream that there was something better for them out there in the North American hinterlands.

Indeed, most of the time this turned out to be true, and their experiments did not fade away for lack of either energy or resources. When these experiments *did* fail, it was for other reasons. Sometimes individual egos or hero worship got in the way. Other times it was simply the case that a charismatic leader may have had the gift for attracting a following, but was not able to follow through with fiscal management. There were also instances when modernism caught up and bypassed the framers of a social experiment and they were technologically left in the dust. Finally, as always, the human factor was sometimes at play and disagreements resulted in the formation of competitive communities which brought the organization to its knees financially.

It is doubtful that anyone could catalog completely the many utopian experiments that have dotted the North American landscape throughout its history. There have been literally dozens of such attempts in the past several centuries, and only a few have prevailed. The longest lasting is that of the 60 000 plus Hutterites, seconded by several remaining Shakers.

It is not our intention in this book to catalog all of the many attempts to build a better society, but instead to offer brief descriptions of a potpourri of idyllic quests undertaken by a wide variety of groups in different time frames and in locations across North America. We also offer a pictorial commentary of some of the larger, more successful utopias that endured for an inordinate length of time.

In section one we outline a series of unrelated and quite diverse utopian dreams that were being pursued when North America was being populated by immigrants mainly from Europe. The discussion will elaborate some reasons why these utopias were built, and why they attracted followers. Most of the utopian attempts described in this section have left visible ruins and their dreams have been kept alive by a variety of historical institutions, museums, and alumni organizations.

The major section of the book (section two) will provide a commentary and pictorial portrayal of twenty of the better-known utopias in Canada and the United States. The third section contains an encyclopedia of utopian pursuits offering quick reference to highlights, characters, and groups discussed in the previous two sections.

The first question readers may want to ask it, "Why another book on utopian experiments when there are already several on the market?" We would like to think that three reasons may explain our motivation in completing this project.

First, this book is the result of personal experience and resultant insights accumulated from many years and many miles of travel. We have had the privilege of visiting at least one site of every commune described in the second section. We feel somewhat of a bond with many of the idealistic groups who built these settlements because we have traversed the soil they tilled, entered their schools, homes, and churches, wandered through their garden plots, and even sat in some of their chairs. There is one exception. Unlike the other communes in section two, The Farm at Summertown, Tennessee, is of fairly recent origin, but we felt that it was still an approprate fit. We hope that some of the feelings and impressions we gathered as a result of our field-work will provide a more appreciative stance towards these unique people of the past.

Second, as we toured these sites, we carried cameras with us – at first the old 35 millimetre type in three motifs – color, black-and-white, and slides. Then we became modern and purchased a digital camera and scanner whose capabilities enabled us to make copies of pictures we had previously taken with our 35 millimeter cameras. As a result, all of the photographs in this book were taken by ourselves.

There is a third feature of the book to consider, offered in part one of the book. This discussion cuts a wider swath than specifically discussing communal experiments. Not all dreamers conceived communalism to be the best route to achieve utopia. Thus a variety of idealistically conceived patterns of living are summarized to include experiments promoted by a variety of groups – European immigrants with both secular and religious orientations, western agrarian-minded settlers, route 66 migrants, and even Trappist monks!

Finally, although both of us are academically trained, we tried as much as possible to explain the history and nature of these experiments in non-academic language in order to make the book more appealing to readers representing other sectors.

We hope we have been successful.

John W. Friesen
Virginia Lyons Friesen
Calgary, Alberta, Canada,
May, 2011

Part One
A Potpourri of Utopian Dreams – Successes, Failures and Continuing Quests

Did you ever feel like launching out and starting life all over again in a new location? Many people felt that way in the past and if our observations are correct, some still do. Some even act on these impulses. This section will outline a few examples of individuals and groups who were determined enough to make fresh starts. They set out in pursuit of their dreams with few resources, and persisted even when things got tough. Some of them were successful in their quest for a happier and more fulfilling lifestyle, while others failed.

Academic scholars prefer to use the terms utopias or intentional communities when they discuss idyllic-oriented social movements. These communities were/are deliberately planned communities, but usually with a twist, depending on the perspective of their originator(s). Our purpose in this section is to describe a fairly wide scope of intriguing utopian pursuits to support the thesis that following a dream is unique to human nature. Everyone likes to think that somehow a better world can be developed. As the following brief accounts will illustrate, many people have been willing to risk a great deal (even persecution or ridicule) by relocating to newly planned lifestyles to fulfill their idyllic dreams.

Amish: A Dream Fulfilled

Let's start (alphabetically) with the Amish, a religious group of Swiss Anabaptist heritage who migrated to the United States during the early part of the 18th century, beginning around 1727. Like other eccentric cultural minorities, the Amish have had to put up with their share of contrived stereotypes, in this case black bonnets, kerosene lamps, roadside food and craft stands, one-room schoolhouses, and horse-and-buggy rides. Truth be told, there is actually a fairly wide range of Amish groups in North America, but to the untrained eye, they all appear the same. In this discussion we shall address our attention to the Old Order Amish. They are the largest of the various Amish groups and most closely represent the classic Amish way of life.

"The Amish Way" has remained remarkably unchanged for hundreds of years.

Although the Amish try to live a non-communal, yet secluded way of life, they often find themselves in the public spotlight, perhaps because of the curiosity their lifestyle evokes. A huge cultural gap exists between their way of life and that of most North Americans, mainly because they now live the way most North Americans used to live. The Amish also attempt to follow the edict of the Holy Scriptures quite literally, which leaves them with a relatively unsophisticated lifestyle. Many books and movies have targeted the Amish, often penned or promoted by individuals and companies who possess little knowledge of Amish ways. For the most part the Amish have ignored these onslaughts, based on their interpretation of pacifism. They regard themselves as being in the world, but not part of it.

For a farming community like the Amish, America offered the fulfillment of their dreams.

The Amish originated from within the Mennonite Church, a Protestant group in Switzerland in 1693, thanks to the efforts of one Jacob Amman (also spelled Ammann or Ammon). A Swiss Mennonite preacher, Amman became concerned that the Mennonite church had lost its spiritual vision and needed to go back to some of the old ways. Three of his major concerns were these: (i) Amman wanted to celebrate the ritual of Holy Communion (the Eucharist), twice a year instead of annually; (ii) he wanted to bring back the ritual of foot-washing, a simple act that took place just before partaking of Holy Communion; and, (iii) he insisted that congregations exercise a more stringent form of church discipline, so that deviants would be excluded from any form of church fellowship when they broke the rules. Amman also insisted that a more conservative form of dress be adopted to differentiate Mennonite Christians from the rest of the community. Men were to wear beards, and substitute a hook-and-eye device on clothing instead of what were sometimes ostentatious buttons. Women were to wear dark colored clothing with near floor length skirts. A conference session was called to discuss Amman's concerns, and as a result twenty-seven of sixty-nine Mennonite ministers present sided with Amman. The die was cast; another Anabaptist group was born.

> On weekends, tourists often flock to Amish communities to admire and purchase Amish made goods, including quilts, handmade wooden toys, fresh vegetables, and baked goods.

Like other Anabaptist groups, the Amish were severely persecuted for their beliefs, essentially because they refused to swear allegiance to the state. As pacifists, they declined to serve in the armed forces, or engage in acts of violence. At Tun, Switzerland, in what is now Tun Castle, some 500 Amish were imprisoned and drowned at night so as not to attract the attention of would-be joiners. Drowning was done by having two men force the head of an adherent into a large barrel of water until he or she drowned. Nearly one thousand Amish were killed in this fashion before the practice was finally stopped.

With the situation in central Europe increasingly unstable politically and religiously intolerant, the Amish were forced to look for more promising living conditions. The Catholic princes, who up to this time had tolerated Protestant groups like the Amish, suddenly turned on them. Only individuals who belonged to a form of state church were safe from their vindictive behavior. Many groups, such as the Amish, were labelled sectarians, and if they refused to recant, were punished in a variety of ways. Many of them were imprisoned, some were sold as slaves, and others were killed. Sometimes men were taken to the border of the country, branded with hot irons, and warned not to return.

News of political freedom and economic opportunity in mid 17th century America greatly excited Amish leaders, so they eagerly made plans to sail the seas to the new land. For a farming community like the Amish, America offered the fulfillment their dreams. Land being made available comprised areas of rich soil, regular rainfall, and climate that was ideally suited for growing a variety of crops. Land prices were low, and at first there seemed to be a limitless amount of it, even though this later turned out not to be the case.

The Amish prospered in America, and despite their pacifism, which was often criticized during times of war, they were viewed as good neighbors. There were minor political skirmishes from time to time, many of them having to do with the fact that the Amish liked to run their own one-room schools – featuring grades one through eight only. These schools used only an Amish-written curriculum (which omitted science and social studies), and their school administrators refused to allow students to participate in state-sponsored examinations. They also hired young Amish women as teachers who usually had only a grade eight education. Following a test case in Oelwein, Iowa, on November 19, 1965, the United States Supreme Court ruled that Amish schools posed no threat to American society and described them as a legitimate option to public education.

When promised amounts of land became scarce in Amish occupied areas of the United States – particularly Ohio and Pennsylvania – Amish groups migrated to as many as eighteen other states as far west as Montana. Today there are more than 100 000 Amish in the United States and in Ontario, Canada, but there are no Amish in Europe, not even in their homeland of Switzerland.

Amish beliefs have always been a source of intrigue to outsiders. Visitors to Amish communities often ask these kinds of questions; Why do the Amish still travel with horse-and buggy? Why do they wear such outdated clothing styles? Why do they insist that their youth try to take up an agricultural way of life? Is there something particularly sacred about that?

> *For the Amish in North America, life is good; their migration to America has fulfilled their wildest dreams.*

The Amish response to these kinds of questions is that Christians must make themselves responsible to the body of Christ. This requirement is mandatory for individuals after they are baptized. Baptism and church membership are required before individuals can be married, and behavioral rules are actually a bit lax before baptism. For this reason, many youth put off baptism until just before they decide to enter the state of matrimony. Even then, they require permission from the church board before a wedding ceremony can be performed. Matrimony notwithstanding, there are many regulations pertaining to daily behavior required of Amish believers. Authority to determine whether or not an individual is obeying the ordinances of the church is grounded in the local church board (Ordnung) which consists of a group of elderly men. Each Amish congregation makes its own rules, and these sometimes contradict those in other Amish jurisdictions. One thing that all Amish congregations agree on is that traditional ways of doing things, particularly those in practice at the time of the origin of the Amish, are perceived as best. This applies to apparel, ways of making a living, means of travel, and sex roles. Amish congregations generally have rules about everything from acceptable worship practices to the kind of harness one puts on a horse to pull a plow.

Obviously, "traditional" ways of doing things – like those laid down in the 17th century, and practiced by the Amish – will often come into conflict with modern practices. A case in point is the telephone. Some Amish businessmen now find it necessary to have a telephone in their place of business, but severe restrictions are in place about its location and use. Sometimes a telephone is deliberately located away from an office building or home so the temptation to use it is reduced. Congregations vary regarding regulations pertaining to the telephone; it all depends on the mood of the *Ordnung*. Similar observations can be made with regard to the use of tobacco. Some congregational members are allowed to both grow and use tobacco, while others may grow the plant and sell the product, but not engage in smoking. Still other Amish groups are not allowed either to grow tobacco nor engage in smoking.

Perhaps the most severe Amish practice pertains to excommunication and shunning. This applies specifically to individuals who have taken their church vows and then deviate from the rules. Although perceived as a gentle people, and often called "the quiet in the land," the Amish can be quite mean when it comes to punishing deviants. Any baptized individual engaging in an activity judged by the Ordnung to be worldly or deviant – that is, a rule has been broken – is targeted for excommunication. When that happens, and the individual is discharged from the congregation, he or she will be shunned by members of the Amish community. This means, depending on the congregation, that the individual may not be seen with nor addressed in conversation by other baptized members. In more strict congregations, the practice is that members who are married to excommunicated mates, are not permitted to eat with them or even sleep with them. Outsiders may not readily appreciate the purpose of Amish shunning, but Amish leaders will be quick to point out that the practice works to conserve traditional Amish values. They will insist that the practice is designed to encourage deviants to repent, and when they do, they will be welcomed back into the fold.

For the most part the Old Order Amish have managed to struggle successfully with modernity and maintain their cultural and spiritual identity. In areas where their agricultural pursuits have been hampered by industrial development, many Amish families have switched to small cottage industries that have enabled them to employ their own children. On weekends, tourists often flock to Amish communities to admire and purchase Amish made goods including quilts, hand-made wooden toys, fresh vegetables, and baked goods. Amish cottage industries sell virtually every kind of product from A to Z, including the manufacture of farm equipment, furniture, and playground equipment as well as garden produce. Many Amish women have entered various household trades and offer for sale a full range of home-sewn items including tablecloths, tea towels, napkins, potholders, and even dolls. Opportunities in this socioeconomic arena, plus the scarcity of farmland, have pulled many young Amish away from agriculture by the magnetic force of modernization.

For the Amish in North America, life is good; their migration to America has fulfilled their wildest dreams. Their population has experienced remarkable growth, doubling in size almost every twenty years. Their congregations continue to fellowship in peace and maintain their membership. Amish individuals may sometimes be inconvenienced by public displeasure, but they do not suffer from religious persecution. Amish private schools continue to flourish, and Amish economic status is parallel in many ways to that of the American middle class. This is not to say that the Amish way of life is poetically idyllic, for it is not. Like other North American families, they often struggle with raising children and keeping them in the fold. There are instances of family violence in Amish communities, and some of their young people yield to the allure of alcohol and other kinds of substance abuse. At times when markets are down or farm and garden crops do not materialize, Amish farmers have to work very hard to sustain themselves economically. They do this without fanfare or complaint.

Does the plain and simple Amish lifestyle satisfy everyone who participates in it? By no means. There are always individuals who stretch the boundaries outlined by the Ordnung. Locals call them "fence jumpers" or "fence crowders." When new technical gadgets become available, those who like to test the limits of disapproval often experiment with them until they are told not to do so. If they find the rule of the Ordnung too strict, they may leave the church and affiliate themselves with another religiously conservative (usually Mennonite) congregation. If they do not repent of their ways when called upon to do so, they will be excommunicated and shunned. However, to their credit, there are times when "fence crowders" are also effective in introducing technological change to the Amish community.

The Amish experience illustrates that it is possible to experience fulfillment in the American dream, but its attainment may come at a very high cost. The Amish have had to endure generations of persecution, and escaping from them involved arduous long distance migration. The Amish have had to adjust to an entirely different socioeconomic milieu. They have often been the target of criticism, prejudice and discrimination, and misunderstanding on the part of the public. Despite these factors, the record will show that they have met these challenges with determination and dignity.

Surely they deserve what will hopefully turn out to be a very happy future.

For Further Reading

Claeys, Gregory, and Lyman Tower Sargent, editors. (1999). *The Utopian Reader.* New York: New York University Press.

Friesen, Bruce, and John W. Friesen. (1996). *Perceptions of the Amish Way.* Dubuque, IA: Kendall/Hunt.

Friesen, John W. (1983). *Schools With A Purpose.* Calgary, AB: Detselig Enterprises.

Hostetler, John A. (1980). *Amish Society.* Third edition. Baltimore, MD: The Johns Hopkins University Press.

Kephart, William M., and William W. Zellner. (1994). *Extraordinary Groups: An Examination of Unconventional Life-Styles.* Fifth edition. New York: St. Martin's Press.

Kraybill, Donald B., editor, with Marc A. Olshan. (1994). *The Amish Struggle with Modernity.* Hanover, MD: University Press of New England.

Kraybill, Donald B. (1989). *The Riddle of Amish Culture.* Baltimore, MD: The Johns Hopkins University Press.

Nolt, Stephen. (1992). *A History of the Amish.* Intercourse, PA: Good Books.

Weaver-Zercher. (2001). *The Amish in the American Imagination.* Baltimore, MD: The Johns Hopkins University Press.

Barr Colonists: Utopia in Conflict

Individuals who share a utopian dream with their peers may not always agree about how to attain it. In fact, sometimes differences may arise even as these individuals are on their way to their destination of promise. The story of the Saskatchewan Barr Colonists is one such example.

With ox carts carrying what possessions they had, the Barr Colonists walked to their new home.

> Individuals who share a utopian dream with their peers may not always agree about how to attain it. In fact, sometimes differences may arise even as these individuals are on their way to their destination of promise.

Canada has long been viewed as a land of promise, and nowhere was this more pronounced than at the turn of the 20th century with regard to Canada's western region. Many descendants of the brave settlers who migrated to that region of the country a century ago, and who know their family history, can attest to that. The Barr Colonists were a group who endured excessive hardship on their journey to "the promised land," but they prevailed. Background to their story begins with the end of the Boer War of 1902 when English troops returned to Britain to face a dismal economic future. A clergyman, the Reverend George Exton Lloyd, had travelled in Canada and was therefore familiar with the landscape of the western prairies. He saw the Canadian West as a potential utopia and determined to lead a group of optimistic immigrants to the new land.

Lloyd pursued his dream by publishing a letter in the *London Times* inviting volunteers to form a party of English immigrants who would be interested in settling Canada's western plains. One individual who replied to Lloyd's letter was also a minister, namely the Reverend Isaac Barr. Barr had farmed previously for fifteen years in Canada and then returned to England. He had become disappointed with what he perceived to be limited opportunities in England, and wanted to return to Canada. The would-be settlers who joined Lloyd were promised fertile farming land that was located near a railroad depot. Lloyd warned his followers that it would be a very difficult challenge to settle the territory, and only the brave should apply to be part of the venture. In 1903, a group of 2 000 English dreamers followed Reverend Lloyd to Canada first by ship to the east coast, and then by railway to Saskatoon, Saskatchewan. They then took up additional means of travel, including on foot, before finally reaching their destination.

As the plan for migration unfolded, Lloyd took Isaac Barr into his confidence with the latter being made responsible for handling finances and making practical arrangements for the newcomers. Barr was to see to it that when the group reached Saskatoon, funds would be available to purchase groceries, lumber, farm implements and other machinery, oxen and wagons, and cattle. Barr agreed to take on this responsibility, but his lackadaisical attitude proved to be more magnanimous than pragmatic. When the settlers arrived in Saskatoon it soon became apparent that few of the promised provisions were on hand. Barr also seemed to think that when the settlers finally developed their community, buildings such as schools, churches, stores and other needed buildings would somehow emerge.

This company of stalwarts left England on March 31, 1903 and on April 10 of that year, landed at St. John, New Brunswick. Their voyage was anything but pleasant with many succumbing to sea sickness. Everyone was relieved when they finally boarded the train to Saskatoon, but even more difficult days lay ahead. The plan was that shortly after arrival, the group would leave Saskatoon for a northwest location, travelling by wagon train. It was expected that seed oats, supplies, and wagons would be ready for purchase. After all, Reverend Barr would be looking after this responsibility. In addition to facing a very rugged journey, the would-be farmers were in for some unpleasant surprises. Barr, it seems, had inflated prices for supplies by purchasing seed oats for twenty-five cents a bushel and then charging colonists five times that amount! Anger and near bedlam broke out, and Reverend Lloyd was called upon to make peace. Barr was fired from his position and Lloyd was asked to take his place. He was reluctant to do so, but consented if it could be found that his election was unanimous. He also insisted that an elected board of twelve members assist him in making decisions. Armed with the results of this decision, Isaac Barr apparently disappeared, later showing up in Australia.

The Barr Colonists were a group who endured excessive hardship on their journey to "the promised land," but they prevailed.

The journey to what is now the Lloydminster area of Saskatchewan was anything but pleasant. Picture a wagon train of heavily laden, ox-drawn vehicles slowly making their way through heavy prairie grass, wet marshlands, and watered sloughs, many times bogging down in soggy soil. Wagons were so overloaded that most people, including women and children, had to walk. A location just thirty miles from their final destination was nicknamed Starvation Camp because at that point the colonists ran out of supplies. No one had very pleasant thoughts about Rev. Barr during those days.

The historical record will show that various utopians have a way of connecting with one another regardless of philosophical or religious differences. While travelling through what is now the Blaine Lake area of Saskatchewan on the way to Lloydminster, the Barr Colonists were provided with supplies by friendly Doukhobors who had settled there four years earlier. They too had followed a utopian dream. For the colonists, the nearby Doukhobor village seemed like an oasis on an otherwise bleak prairie plain. Armed with everything they needed, thanks to the generosity of the Doukhobors, the colonists finally reached their intended goal.

The Barr Colony never did materialize as envisaged. Instead of a tightly knit community of common heritage and experience, the newcomers distributed themselves over some twenty townships. Many settlers of other national backgrounds soon occupied nearby lands, giving the community a very multicultural flavor. In 1953 the town of Lloydminster, Alberta, celebrated its fiftieth anniversary with appropriate tributes to the settlers who followed their dreams and made the community possible. The many agricultural awards won by Lloydminster residents in the past half century of their history were acknowledged as part of the heritage initiated by the Barr Colonists. Despite hardships, fraud, and personality conflicts, the dream has persisted to this day.

Lloydminster, Saskatchewan is a unique city, and is located on the North central border of Saskatchewan and Alberta. Half of the city is located in the Province of Alberta and the other half lies in the Province of Saskatchewan.

Its friendly citizens warmly welcome visitors.

For Further Reading

Bowen, Lynne. (1994). *Muddling Through: The Remarkable Story of the Barr Colonists.* Vancouver, BC: Greystone Books.

Burnet, Jean R., and Howard Palmer. (1988). *Coming Canadians: An Introduction to a History of Canada's Peoples.* Toronto, ON: McClelland and Stewart.

Palmer, Howard. (1972). *Land of the Second Chance.* Lethbridge, AB: The Lethbridge Herald.

Peake, Frank. (1983). Anglicanism on the Prairies: Continuity and Flexibility. *Visions of the New Jerusalem: Religious Settlement on the Prairies.* Benjamin G. Simillie, ed. Edmonton, AB: NeWest Press, 55-68.

Wetton, C. (1979). *The Promised Land: The Story of the Barr Colonists.* Lloydminster, SK: The Lloydminster Times.

Bloc Settlements in Western Canada: Parallel Utopias

Usually when people plan to build an ideal form of community in a new location, they prefer to live in close proximity to one another in their new neighborhood. A big part of their utopian plan is to move together, and then live together. In Canada, such communities were historically known as bloc settlements.

Statue of the Rev. Father Bruno Doerfler.

When western Canadian expansion flourished in the latter part of the 19th century, a myriad of European ethnic groups leaped at the chance to own land they could call their own. Most of the would-be settlers who migrated to the prairies during this time had been pushed off their lands in Europe by overpopulation, impoverishment, political discontent, or persecution. Those who simply relished the opportunity for adventure also seized the chance to make a new start, lured by Canada's generous immigration policies and promises of agricultural lands. As the 19th century came to a close, Canada was looking for cheap labor, so it seemed that there was something in it for everyone. For many European immigrants the most appealing feature of western Canadian immigration was the promise to occupy land in one specific area. That way they could establish distinct communities similar to those back home.

Bloc settlements, as it turned out, were both bane and blessing. The United States, at this time, had set quotas on immigration, and so the number of newcomers who arrived in Canada swelled proportionately. Clifford Sifton, Minister of the Interior, at this time was anxious to populate the west, and he willingly compromised Canada's dream of building a unified nation by allowing bloc settlements to develop and flourish. As a result, even today one can identify distinctive rural communities comprised of French, German, Scandinavian, Ukrainian, and other national descendants. Provinces like Saskatchewan, whose politicians wanted only British immigrants, reluctantly gave in to Sifton's policies lest they be bypassed in development.

Three main processes were in play with developing bloc settlements, the first being comprised of groups of people banded together by national, religious, or political ideals who wanted to or had to leave their homelands. These people arrived as socially intact groups who settled in specific geographic areas. Second, there arose what were called "chain" settlements, many of which came into being rather slowly. They consisted of a string of localities or villages, bound together by a road or a series of railway depots. Third, were gravitational group settlements comprised of people who arrived at different times but became bonded with those already resident through some force of common interest or cause such as use of a common language. The pros and cons of this kind of immigration patterning are still being debated by analysts.

There are numerous examples of bloc settlements on the western Canadian prairies. One of the first was the St. Laurent-de-Grandin Métis settlement at Batoche, Saskatchewan. Many Métis settled here following the defeat of Louis Riel's army during what historians still call the Northwest Rebellion. French-speaking immigrants also settled in the area, thus forming a significant francophone community. A series of bloc communities were established with the assistance of the Roman Catholic Church, for example, St. Albert in Alberta, and St. Joseph's and St. Peter's in Saskatchewan. St. Joseph's was the dream child of the Reverend Bruno Doerfler, a Benedictine priest. Initially seventeen families from the

United States followed Father Doerfler to the new location, some of them anxious to obtain land they could call their own. One family, the Henry Herman Tegenkamp family, had been tenant farmers in America, and when their house burned to the ground, they lost everything. Father Doerfler's offer seemed to be too good to be true. Soon the Tegenkamp family would be able to build another house on their own land. Three years after the Bruno Colony was begun, the railroad arrived. The following year a school was built and the population began to thrive. Even today the family names of the original settlers are commonplace in the Bruno area.

Those individuals who like to refer romantically to the "good ole days," are usually members of the older generation who grew up in rural areas. They often recall with fondness the social and religious events that tied communities together – albeit usually along religious or ethnic lines. These included the annual spring picnic, perceived as the first "official" outdoor activity after winter was finally over. The event included a softball tournament, foot races for younger children, and lots of food and drink. The old-timers rallied to the occasion, partially to get some sun, and the more active tillers of the soil exchanged information about grain and beef prices, or gathered to admire a neighbor's new horse, truck, or tractor. The younger set made the most of what was often an excellent opportunity for courtship, as the day ended with a traditional country dance.

Rural communities also featured pig butchering, threshing, and woodcutting bees, community thanksgiving dinners, box socials, and the observance of Sunday as a day of rest. Before the advent of the telephone, a family might simply go over to a neighbor's house for an evening visit – unannounced. If that neighbor was not at home, another would be sought out and on arrival it might even happen that the first neighbor would be at that location. Some evenings it might require several stops to find a neighbor at home. Community members did things together and this reinforced their unique cultural identities. At the same time this form of in-house camaraderie inhibited the development of outside ties.

Residents of bloc settlements usually tried to maintain strong community ties through the maintenance of religion,

Residents of bloc settlements usually tried to maintain strong community ties through the maintenance of religion, language, and social customs.

language, and social customs. They attempted to influence their children to marry members of the same ethnic background. Their outlook on life could best be described as conservative. This combination of factors assured a certain amount of segregation from other ethnic communities and slowed or hindered the development of national patriotism. Ironically, the characteristics of "the good life" that they attempted to create in their segregated societies, were matched by those of their ethnically different neighbors on the other side of the road.

One might conjecture that these developments created a series of parallel utopias of sorts.

For Further Reading

Anderson, Alan B. (1977). Ethnic Identity in Saskatchewan Bloc Settlements: A Sociological Approach. *The Settlement of the West.* Howard Palmer, ed. Calgary, AB: The University of Calgary, 187-225.

Brown, Craig, ed. (2002). *The Illustrated History of Canada.* Toronto, ON: Key Porter Books.

Friesen, John W. (1989). The Human Side of Prairie Settlement, 1809-1914. *Multicultural Education Journal, 7*(2), 28-36.

Friesen, John W., and Alice L. Boberg. (1990). *Introduction to Teaching: A Socio-Cultural Approach.* Dubuque, IA: Kendall/Hunt. Chapter twelve.

Hébert, Raymond, and Jean-Guy Vaillancourt. (1971). French-Canadians in Manitoba: Elites and Ideologies. *Immigrant Groups.* Jan Leonard Elliott, ed. Scarborough, ON: Prentice-Hall, 175-190.

Jones, David C., and Ian MacPherson. (1985). *Building Beyond the Homestead.* Calgary, AB: University of Calgary Press.

Lower, Arthur. 1983). *Western Canada: An Outline History.* Vancouver, BC: Douglas & McIntyre.

Owram, Doug. (1993). *Promise of Eden: The Canadian Expansion Movement and the Idea of the West, 1856-1900.* Toronto, ON: University of Toronto Press.

Rasporich, A.W., ed. (1975). *Western Canada: Past and Present.* Calgary, AB: University of Calgary Press.

Chinese in North America: In Pursuit of Happiness

Not everyone who pursues a utopian dream does so because they are unwavering idealists. For example, the first Chinese to arrive in North America were influenced by both push and pull factors. They did not like the way things were going back home in China, and Canada's invitation featuring near utopian opportunities, simply sounded too good to pass up. By now both Canada and the United States had established fairly positive reputations as countries offering freedom and opportunity, and Chinese immigrants soon sought out both locations.

A quick background check will reveal that between 1839 and 1900 China had engaged in unsuccessful wars with Austria, France, Germany, Italy, Japan, Russia, and the United States. With each defeat, citizens grew increasingly unhappy with conditions in their homeland, and as the generations unfolded, the prospect of moving away seemed more desirable. The hope of a better life abroad appealed to many families, and North American immigration loomed like a golden opportunity. The word on the street was that anyone who wanted to work hard in North America could become wealthy. As history will demonstrate, the Chinese certainly felt up to the challenge, and succeeded. Unfortunately, on arrival in North America, the Chinese did not get the warm welcome they had anticipated.

The skills and techniques used in making Chinese lacquered furniture pieces have been handed down for thousands of years.

Between 1876 and 1884, 17 027 Chinese were admitted to Canada at the Port of Victoria, where they joined about 3 000 Chinese already resident in British Columbia. These folk had moved north when the California Gold Rush had abated and anti-Chinese sentiment had erupted. The first Chinese – sailors and merchants arived in the United States in the early

1800s, lured by the rumor of "gold in them thar hills." However, they were soon banned from participating in that event, so many of them stayed on to develop coastal fisheries and reclaim swampland for agricultural purposes. Although often trained for better professions, many of them took them took menial jobs just to keep bread on the table.

A number of Chinese men joined the northern army during the American Civil War, but when the war was over, they were regarded as unwanted immigrants. Chinese workers often hired on for jobs that no one else wanted and the reward they got for doing so was to be labelled "cheap labor." The arrival of the Great Depression in the 1870s did not help. Now, because of prejudice and discrimination the Chinese found it difficult even to find menial employment, and in many neighborhoods they were targetted for cruel treatment. The American government did little about this. In fact, in 1882, Congress passed the *Chinese Exclusion Act* to suspend Chinese immigration and deny the rights of citizenship to those already resident in the country. Sixteen years later through action of the United States Supreme Court, the American government granted citizenship rights to Chinese born in the country.

Even though Chinese immigration to the United States was prohibited, some individuals found loopholes by which to enter the country. Because most of the Chinese population in North America was male, illegal smuggling of young women became quite commonplace. President Franklin D. Roosevelt repealed the *Chinese Exclusion Act* in 1943, but the government quickly established a quota system for Chinese immigration. The following decade thousands of Chinese students came to study in the United States, but found it difficult to remain there when their studies were completed. Those who did find employment after graduation were allowed to stay in the country. It was not until 1965 that Chinese immigration was changed to parity with other countries. Despite this ill treatment, members of the Chinese community kept their dream alive; someday they would be accepted in North America and their contributions would be appreciated. As it turns out, after several generations of having to endure prejudice and abuse, it indeed did happen to some extent.

> *Not everyone who pursues a utopian dream does so because they are unwavering idealists.*

The atmosphere for Chinese in Canada in the latter part of the 19th century was little different than that in the United States. Anti-Chinese sentiments were high and many acts of violence were committed against them. However, there were a few positive developments. In the early 1880s, the Canadian government was planning to build a national railway, stretching from coast to coast. Prime Minister Sir John A. Macdonald, himself not particularly given to making kind remarks about Chinese people, insisted that employing Chinese labor was the best guarantee to get the job done. He knew that the Chinese would work hard for low wages, and their work camps could be set up with less fanfare and contain few extras. As Macdonald put it, "Either you must have this labor or you can't have the railroad." It is not certain whether the nation heeded Macdonald's advice or if he simply proceeded regardless of public opinion.

"Either you must have this labor or you can't have the railroad."

The Canadian Pacific Railway was completed in 1885, the same year that Canada followed America's example and passed its first anti-Chinese legislation. Chinese persons were still allowed to immigrate to Canada, but they would have to pay a head tax of fifty dollars each. Six years later the amount of the head tax was increased to one hundred dollars, and then to five hundred dollars in 1905. This action was followed by the passing of the *Chinese Immigration Act* in 1923, which allowed only Chinese students or merchants to immigrate. As a result, during the years 1925 to 1946 only seven Chinese individuals immigrated to Canada. The *Chinese Immigration Act* was repealed in 1947 and subsequent changes in legislation allowed Chinese to immigrate through a family sponsorship program.

In many ways the Chinese value system represents traditional Canadian ideals. Education and hard work are highly praised in the Chinese community, elderly people are respected, and a significant percentage of the population is involved in professional occupations such as teachers, physicians, lawyers, and accountants. Family loyalty is prized and esteemed values are taught in the home without relying on schools to do the job. At a time when North American families face an impending obsolescence, the Chinese family stands as a monument to the high status of that institution, and serves as a positive example to other communities.

Perhaps the Chinese commitment to achieving happiness finds its root in their religious and spiritual background. Unlike most North Americans, the Chinese find it perfectly logical to draw values from a variety of persuasions including Buddhism, Confucianism, Islam, Taoism, and Christianity. In searching for a principle by which to explain the nature of the universe, and even of life itself, it is helpful to examine the two fundamental forces of nature – yin and yang. Yin is the negative force in nature, and observable in darkness, coolness, and shadows. Yang is the positive force, and observable in light and warmth, dryness, and the sun. When these two forces work in cooperation, as they do on occasion, harmony is achieved. Life, therefore, comprises both negative and positive forces. No one is put out by that reality; life is fundamentally the pursuit of harmony. Therein lies true happiness.

Elderly people in North American society constantly complain that they are not respected by youth, but such is not the case in orthodox Chinese communities. If anything, Chinese venerate old age to the extent that observers sometimes accuse them of engaging in ancestor worship. Historically, it was the aged grandfather, father, grandmother or mother who dominated home life. It was the obligation of children to provide for their parents and grandparents – even to the extent of looking after their graves after they had passed on. Even today many Chinese homes have a small shrine or altar at which the names and deeds of previous generations are remembered with small sacrifices. With age comes wisdom.

Two related concepts central to traditional Chinese philosophy (borrowed from Confucianism), are *jen*, translated to mean goodness, benevolence or human-heartedness, and *i* which stands for justice, loyalty, and integrity. Thoroughly intended to be comprehensive in application, Confucious followed up these principles by outlining four arenas in which to practice them – the past, the family, the economy, and the development of a community culture. There is no respite from these obligations; they must be practiced in every activity of one's daily sojourn and indeed throughout life. The achievement of orderly life requires strategies to maintain order in the face of disorder. To face disorder, as the Chinese have done in North America requires autonomy, that is, belief in *jen* and *i*. Adherence to that code may help to explain Chinese tenacity in the face of adversity.

During the 1880s, public discrimination against the Chinese forced them into building exclusive neighborhoods and developing local industries. Chinatowns rose up in both Canada and the United States, particularly on the west coast. A series of canneries sprang up, either run by members of the Chinese community or by nonChinese entrepreneurs who mainly hired Chinese workers. Even today, Chinatowns in Vancouver and San Francisco are well known, and boast excellent reputations for tourism.

Racism is only one reason for the development of Chinatowns. In many cases landlords would not sell or lease their properties to Chinese merchants unless the premises were located at the edge of town where no one else wanted to establish a business. Discrimination, racism, and violence incited by outsiders erupted in many Chinatowns and many Chinese were forced to leave their homes. Those who remained tried even harder to safeguard their cultural borders for the sake of the children. Many of the older people who had immigrated to North America did not speak the English language and were ignorant of western ways. If they stayed in the safety of their cultural enclave they could speak their own language, eat their own kinds of food, and engage in valued ceremonies.

Acceptance of Chinese immigrants has been a slow process in North America and assimilation, if it has been a goal, has also been hindered. At times it has been a two-way street; the Chinese have kept to themselves in order to avoid the onslaughts of racism, and the nonChinese population has invented a mythology about the Chinese that justifies their prejudice toward them. Many nonChinese like to eat Chinese food and perhaps feel that they are engaging in some form of meaningful multicultural interaction when they do so, but they deceive themselves. There is always much more to a culture than its food, fashion and finery, fads, and festivals.

The last quarter century has witnessed a gradual acceptance of immigrating minority groups, but both Canada and the United States are far from having reached the goal where minority citizens can practice their unique cultural and religious customs and feel that they are accepted on par with those of their fellow countrymen.

One thing seems certain; the Chinese quest for an improved standard of living will continue in North America, and it will be propelled by a strong sense of identity, family loyalty, and hard work.

For Further Reading

Bramadat, Paul, and David Seljak. (2005). *Religion and Ethnicity in Canada.* Toronto, ON: Pearson Longman. Chapter five.

Burton, Pierre. (1974). *The National Dream: The Last Spike.* Toronto, ON: McClelland and Stewart.

Evasdottir, Erika E.S. (2004). *Obedient Autonomy: Chinese Intellectuals and the Achievement of Orderly Life.* Vancouver, BC: UBC Press.

Dawson, J. Brian, with Patricia M. Dawson. (1991). *Moon Cakes in Gold Mountain: From China to the Canadian Plains.* Calgary, AB: Detselig Enterprises.

Elliott, Jean Leonard, ed. (1971). *Immigrant Groups.* Scarborough, ON: Prentice-Hall. Chapter Nine.

Fleras, Augie, and Jean Leonard Elliott. (2007). *Unequal Relations: An Introduction to Race, Ethnic, and Aboriginal Dynamics in Canada.* Fifth edition. Toronto, ON: Pearson Prentice Hall.

Friesen, John W. (1983). *Schools With A Purpose.* Calgary, AB: Detselig Enterprises. Chapter Seven.

Friesen, John W. (1995). *Pick One: A User-Friendly Guide to Religion.* Calgary, AB: Detselig Enterprises.

Hopfe, Lewis M. Edited by Lavinia R. Hopfe and Lewis M. Hopfe, Jr. (1994). *Religions of the World.* Sixth Edition. Englewood Cliffs, NJ: Prentice-Hall.

Lai, David Chuenyan. (1988). *Chinatowns: Towns Within Cities in Canada.* Vancouver, BC: University of British Columbia Press.

Lan, Sheung-King. (1993). The Chinese in Calgary: Schooling for Cultural Identity. *When Cultures Clash: Case Studies in Multiculturalism.* Second edition. John W. Friesen, ed. Calgary. AB: Detselig Enterprises, 167-188.

Pryke, Kenneth G., and Walter C. Soderlund, eds. (2003). *Profiles of Canada.* Third edition. Toronto, ON: Canadian Scholars' Press.

Hull House: Utopian Welfare

The story of Hull House is a unique communal-like experiment that was planned and instigated by a woman who wanted its benefits to accrue to individuals other than herself. The woman often given the most credit for co-founding Hull House was Jane Addams (1860-1935). Born in Cedarville, Illinois, and graduating from Rockford Female Seminary in 1881, Addams consistently pursued a lifelong concern for the down-and-out citizens of America. Although born with Pott's disease, which caused a curvature of Addams' spine and gave her lifelong health problems, she never deviated from her goal of improving things in America. To accomplish this she was co-founder of an institution dedicated to delivering an overwhelming series of social welfare programs to needy people in Chicago. Hull House was never really a communal institution, but its staff and other occupants shared a mutual concern for social reform. Jane Addams had a dream, the fulfillment of which meant that every American citizen would have their physical, social, economic, and psychological needs met.

The Women of Hull-House – Pioneers of social work – Chicago, Illinois.

In 1889, Addams worked with a colleague, Ellen Gates Starr, to develop a settlement dwelling in Chicago known as Hull House. Thanks to their efforts, Hull House became the prototype for the settlement house movement in America. By 1900 there were more than one hundred settlement houses across the United States.

The purpose of settlement houses, which were mostly occupied and/or operated by educated middle class women, was to elevate the educational and socioeconomic status of poor people and newly arrived immigrants. Programs offered by these institutions included daycare and kindergarten classes, an employment bureau, an art gallery and library, English language and citizenship classes, meeting places for trade union groups, and clubs of all sorts. A series of cultural events representative of local minority cultures were also on the program. Culturally speaking, thanks to Hull House, "no one was ever needy."

At Hull House specifically, Jane Addams and her colleagues launched the Immigrants' Protective League, the Juvenile Protective Association, the first juvenile court in the nation, and a Juvenile Psychopathic Clinic – later known as the Institute for Juvenile Research. Although deeply involved in establishing such an effective vehicle for alleviating human needs, Jane and her staff were not completely responsible for such turn of the century reforms as the abolition of child labor, the regulation of working hours and conditions for women, enforcement of safe working conditions, and improving juvenile laws. Addams was a leader in the Consumer's League and served as the first woman president of the National Conference of Charities and Corrections. She was chairperson of the Labor Committee of the General Federation of Women's Clubs, vice-president of the Campfire Girls, and a member of the board for the National Child Labor Committee and the National Playground Association. The list goes on.

As a dreamer and practical social reformer, there was hardly a dysfunctional aspect of American life that Addams did not address. Although she never designed a fully functional physical utopia, the social and psychological assistance that thousands of Americans received because of her efforts, had a far greater impact than any communal empire might have accomplished. In fact, Addams inspired utopian dreams in the people she touched.

That was not all. Addams decided that it was not enough to provide for the needs of the poor and underprivileged. She believed that public awareness was the key to convincing lawmakers and politicians to improve living and working conditions by passing the right laws. Addams soon found herself lobbying politicians at the Illinois state legislation for

> *The purpose of settlement houses, which were mostly occupied and/or operated by educated middle class women, was to elevate the educational and socioeconomic status of poor people and newly arrived immigrants.*

the enactment of a child labor law and other similar reforms. Much of her lobbying was successful.

During her final years of service Jane Addams continued to spread her message of hope and equality for all Americans by speaking at conferences and gatherings of national leaders, always upholding the idea that meeting human needs must take priority over economic advancement. As a pacifist she and a group of women met at the International Congress of Women in 1915 in an effort to convince national leaders to stop World War I. Addams was probably the last one-person female campaigner for justice and equality in America. Her inspiration motivated similar actions across the nation, although it is doubtful that anyone could keep up with her. She was one of the first women to be awarded the Nobel Peace Prize which was bestowed upon her in 1931. She died on May 21, 1935, and was buried in her childhood home town of Cedarville, Illinois.

Jane Addams added a special social twist to the concept of utopia. She developed a unique experiment with human concern for people of all socioeconomic levels.

For Further Reading

Addams, Jane. (1990). *Twenty Years at Hull-House: With Autobiographical Notes.* Chicago, IL: University of Chicago Press.

Elshtain, Jean Bethke. (2001). *Jane Addams and the Dream of American Democracy.* New York, NY: Basic Books.

Farrell, John C. (1967). *Beloved Lady: A History of Jane Addams' Ideas on Reform and Peace.* Baltimore, MD: The Johns Hopkins University Press.

Polikoff, Barbara Garland. (1999). *With One Bold Act: The Story of Jane Addams.* Chicago, IL: Boswell Books.

Kemano, British Columbia: Sudden Death Utopia

Now and then everyone dreams about living in a utopia with the characteristics of Shangrila or the biblical Garden of Eden. Believe it or not, for some fifty years a community in northern British Columbia had just such an experience – at least they thought so.

Kemano, British Columbia, was a town built in the 1950s to house workers of the Alcan Company which controlled and maintained the local hydroelectric plant. The station at Kemano on the Nechako River, still serves one of the biggest aluminum plants in the world. The plant is located at nearby Kitimat, British Columbia. Long, narrow lakes are found throughout the interior of this area of British Columbia, that supply vast backwaters for nearby dams. Williston Lake Dam, on the Peace River, is the largest of these.

A half-century after Kemano was constructed, Alcan's cost-cutting process brought an abrupt end to the town which residents perceived as an idyllic place to live. At its peak, only 220 people lived in Kemano, but they enjoyed all of the amenities of a fulfilling lifestyle. Although the population was small in size, locals enjoyed the benefits of a much larger community. Alcan provided residents with a variety of cultural and social facilities – stores, a school, daycare, restaurants, a bowling alley and golf course, and other recreational and educational facilities. Residents of Kemano thought they had it all; it was a safe and peaceful place to live.

At the peak of its existence, Kemano had all the earmarks of a social utopia. The town offered stability because Alcan took care of all resident needs. In fact, those individuals who were born and raised in Kemano had never lived anywhere else. As landlord, Alcan provided low rents, and served as mayor, security guard, and grocery supplier. No one locked

Kemano is located 75 km (47 mi) southeast of Kitimat, in British Columbia's rugged mountain territory.

their doors at night and women and children were safe on the streets – even late in the evening. Virtually everyone knew everyone else in town and the familial setup was such that every child had dozens of grandparents and aunts and uncles to look after them.

A major outing for residents of Kemano was a boat ride to the northern town of Kitimat, British Columbia. The one-and-one-half hour trip was available twice a week and constituted a "big deal" for locals. The trip offered residents an opportunity for out of town shopping and access to services not locally available. In Kemano, life was good. Then, without warning, one day the residents of the town received notice that their idyllic society was to end, and that very quickly.

Alcan's announcement came without warning; due to financial concerns the town of Kemano was to be shut down – immediately. The citizens of Kemano were in shock. They were given little time to proceed through the various stages of grieving from shock to anger to denial and gradually to sad reality. Further pain was inflicted when the company announced that at least half of the town's houses would be burned to provide training to firefighters in British Columbia. Only twenty-four individuals were left on site to manage the Alcan plant.

A lesson learned by the people of Kemano might be this; "Enjoy what you can of the good life if you have it; you may not always have it." The residents of Kemano could readily testify to that.

Their utopia suddenly disappeared.

At the peak of its existence, Kemano had all the earmarks of a social utopia. The town offered stability because Alcan took care of all resident needs.

For Further Reading

Britannica Concise Encyclopedia: *British Columbia.* http://www.answers.com/topic/british-columbia

Laird, Gordon. (November/December, 2000). Closing Kemano: Pulling the Plug on a British Columbia Small-Town Utopia. *Canadian Geographic, 120*(7), 82-96.

Japanese in North America: A Continuing Quest for Utopia

New Denver, British Columbia was the site of an internment camp for approximately 2000 Japanese Canadians displaced from their West Coast homes during World War II.

Most North Americans probably consider Japanese culture a vital part of the continent's makeup, but this was certainly not always the case. Although Japanese immigrants to Canada and the United States were not warmly welcomed when they arrived, students of history are also aware of the atrocities committed against them after the bombing of Pearl Harbor in 1941.

Japanese immigrants, mostly from the peasant class, began migrating to North America in 1869, partially to escape very limited economic opportunities and unstable conditions in their homeland, and also because they heard that North America was the land of opportunity. They dreamed of getting jobs, planting gardens, and building their own homes. They wanted to assure a better future for their children. Sadly, they were in for some surprises. Shortly after they arrived they discovered that North Americans were not ready to grant them their utopian wish. In fact, it took a century for the Japanese to achieve the rights and privileges afforded to their neighbors. In the meantime they had to settle for menial jobs with low pay and put up with an inordinate amount of adversity and suffering.

The first arriving Japanese immigrants to North America were men who left their wives and families back home hoping to get established before they sent for them. Because marriages were arranged, unmarried men often sent home for brides who, when they arrived, found themselves placed in detention barracks where they were processed and given medical exams. Many Japanese women met their husbands for the first time at the detention homes. After a very brief "courtship," they would be married and commence to establish themselves economically. When the couple became economically self-sufficient they were welcomed into a local Japanese community. There they could join their neighbors in establishing schools, places of worship, and business organizations.

Japanese dreamers who migrated to Canada and the United States brought a number of precious agricultural items with them – silk cocoons, tea plants, mulberry trees, and bamboo roots. It took some years, but eventually many of these items were added to the Canadian cultural milieu. Japanese immigrants also brought elements of the Buddhist religion with them, which often targetted them for discrimination by Christian groups. In order to gain a financial footing, many Japanese men obtained work as cooks and dishwashers in restaurants, or as workers in farmers' fields or in coal mines. Some of the more fortunate families started small businesses of their own and thus managed to survive. Between 1886 and 1911, more than 400 000 Japanese men and women entered the United States and American possession lands, and this trend continued for several years following.

Continue on in your journey and make a contribution to family, community, and loyalty.

Everything changed for North American Japanese after December 7, 1941, when Japanese planes bombed the American navel base at Pearl Harbor. Within a very short time, everyone with Japanese ancestry in both Canada and the United States was under suspicion. Both countries were now officially at war with Japan and the governments of both countries panicked. Everyone started to believe that every individual of Japanese heritage was a spy for the Japanese government. The Canadian government immediately closed all Japanese language schools, impounded Japanese fishing boats located on the British Columbia coast, and forbad Japanese people from leaving their homes after dark. The Canadian Pacific Railway fired all Japanese workers, and many other businesses did the same. A total of 21 000 Japanese were forced out of their homes and sent to the British Columbia interior and to Alberta. It did not matter to government leaders that many of the Japanese they interred were born in Canada or that some of their number had served the country during World War I. When World War II eventually ended, restrictions on where Japanese people could live remained in effect until 1949. Similar conditions were in effect in the United States.

After the bombing of Pearl Harbor, Americans were angry, but some of their anger was misdirected. Claiming concern for internal security, American government officials took similar action to that taken in Canada. American Japanese citizens were taken from their homes and placed in work camps located in relatively uninhabited areas from California to Arkansas. Life in the work camps was particularly hard on Japanese children because they did not understand why their families were being relocated. Japanese Canadians were forced to take loyalty tests to prove that they were committed to upholding the Government of Canada, but nonJapanese citizens did not have to take these tests.

When the remains of the highly decorated 442nd Combat Team were returned to the United States after World War II, they were refused gravesites in some cemeteries because of their Japanese ancestry. In the immediate period after World War II, very few Japanese migrated to North America, but their numbers have increased since.

Thus the quest for idyllic living continues, even though scholars can point out that Japanese Americans continue to endure discrimination in housing, shopping, dining, and recreational activities. Discrimination toward Japanese Americans may be subtle, but is still very much in existence, as can be shown in recent legal cases involving discrimination in employment promotion. Despite this, the Japanese spirit remains strong. Perhaps it is the Buddhist mandate of "following the path" with its inherent mandate to release oneself from the tyranny of materialism and attachment to the world that pushes them on.

The Buddhist mandate is this: Continue on in your journey and make a contribution to family, community, and loyalty.

That motto could well comprise a continuing search for everyone, regardless of religion or cultural affiliation.

For Further Reading

Adachi, Ken. (1976). *The Enemy That Never Was*. Toronto, ON: McClelland and Stewart.

Buell, Raymond Leslie (1970). *Japanese Immigration*. Boston: World Peace Foundation, 1924. Reprint, Ann Arbor: University Microfilms.

Chuman, Frank, F. (1976). *The Bamboo People: The Law and Japanese-Americans*. Del Mar Publisher's Inc.

Palmer, Howard. (1972). *Land of the Second Chance: A History of Ethnic Groups in Southern Alberta*. Lethbridge, AB: The Lethbridge Herald. Chapter Eight.

Ramacharan, Subhas. (1982). *Racism: Nonwhites in Canada*. Toronto, ON: Butterworth.

Ruether, Rosemary Radford. (June, 1995). Story of Japanese Haunts U.S.: Racism of Interment Camps Thrives Today. *National Catholic Reporter,* 21.

Sunahara, Ann Gomer. (1981). *The Politics of Racism: The Uprooting of Japanese Canadians During the Second World War*. Toronto, ON: James Lorimer and Company.

http://www.edukits.ca/multiculturalism/student/immigration_japanese_e.html

http://www.nps.gov/history/online_books/5views/5views4a.htm

Manitoba Mennonites: Utopian Dreams Compromised

Purusing the next utopian dream takes us back to Central Europe and to the left wing of the Protestant Reformation. This is the story of Mennonites in Manitoba.

Mennonites are an ethnic/religious group that originated from within the Protestant Anabaptist movement in the 16th

A Russian Mennonite house-barn located in Hague, Saskatchewan. A northern European tradition of house-barn architecture was brought to North America by the Mennonites.

century. Included in the list of their radical beliefs the original Mennonites denounced militarism and taking of oaths, and declared themselves pacifists. They rejected infant baptism and confirmation, and substituted adult baptism. They declared the Christian church to be an independent, voluntary organization made up of believers banded together for the purpose of worship. They rejected the Sacraments, declaring that Holy Baptism and the Eucharist were to be regarded only as symbols. Not surprisingly, the Mennonites were persecuted for their faith, many of them being imprisoned and burned at the stake. The best option for them was to leave their European homeland and migrate elsewhere. Catherine the Great of Russia had the answer; her country was badly in need of farmers and the Mennonites fit the bill.

When the Mennonites arrived in Manitoba they were assigned large tracts of farmland (known as reserves) on both sides of the Red River.

Like many other ethnic and religious European groups, the Mennonites (followers of an ex Roman Catholic priest named Menno Simons), migrated to Russia in the 1770s at the invitation of Catherine the Great. In 1707 their Swiss counterparts chose America as a place to live and so started the flow of immigrants that brought thousands of Anabaptists to the new world.

Meanwhile back in Russia, their government promised free land to incoming religious European groups with few stipulations. Basically the new settlers had to promise to farm the land awarded them and guarantee that they would not try to overthrow the Russian government. Specifically, the Mennonites were given the right to run their own language schools, maintain their own form of self-government, and be excused from participating in military conscription. Everything went well for a hundred years until Russian leaders decided to become a world power through militarization. Military exemption for Mennonites was cancelled, the Russian language became mandatory for all citizens, and independent forms of self-government were abolished. The Mennonite honeymoon was over.

As the 19th century was drawing to a close, Canada was experiencing the urge to develop the west and badly needed farmers. Clifford Sifton, Minister of the Interior, was bent on populating the west with experienced farmers. In 1873 a delegation of Mennonite leaders negotiated with Sifton for lands in southern Manitoba then occupied by members of the Métis Nation. The American west was also being targeted for development, specifically Kansas, Minnesota, Nebraska, and South Dakota. American government authorities representing the west made similar offers to Russian Mennonites. Between 1874 and 1880, a total of 18 000 Mennonites arrived in North America with two-thirds of them settling in Manitoba. A contingent of some 100 000 Mennonites chose to remain in Russia, but because of continuing Russian oppression, during the 1920s many of them also sought refuge in North America.

At first the Canadian government was generous to the Mennonites who arrived in Manitoba during the 1870s. They were promised freedom from conscription, and the right to operate their own schools in which the German language and Bible lessons could be taught. Alas, this honeymoon was also short-lived. In 1890 the government of Manitoba passed the *Manitoba Public School Act*, forcing closure of Mennonite schools and relegating the teaching of Bible to a half hour after public schools closed. Also, the Union Jack flag was to be flown over every school in the province, a travesty to Mennonite beliefs about a strict separation of church and state. When World War I was in progress, the federal government of Canada passed a secret Order-in-Council mandating military conscription for all Canadians. In 1921, with guarantees similar to those promised by Russia and Canada, over 5 000 Old Colony Mennonites (a subsection of the mainstream) moved to Mexico. Another 1 700 settled in Paraguay.

When the Mennonites arrived in Manitoba they were assigned large tracts of farmland (known as reserves) on both sides of the Red River. There the Mennonites prospered, making societal compromises as time and conditions dictated. From time to time small numbers of Mennonites relocated to other countries to avoid regulations concerning schooling, but for the most part, the majority of Manitoba Mennonites, as well as those in other provinces, assimilated into the Canadian mainstream. Today their lifestyle is not unlike that of other mainline Christians across the country. Mennonites in Canada may support churches that bear their ethnic designation, but many of their numbers have also aligned themselves with both mainline and evangelical denominations. Their high schools and colleges enroll students from a variety of ethnic and religious backgrounds, and many of their members serve as lawyers, businessmen, teachers and professors, and politicians. Two outstanding missionary and welfare inter-Mennonite organizations remain clearly identifiable in North America – the Mennonite Central Committee and Mennonite Disaster Service.

For Mennonites in Manitoba and indeed across North America, life is probably as good as it can get.

For Further Reading

Epp, Frank H. (1982). *Mennonites in Canada, 1920-1940: The History of a Separate People.* Toronto, ON: Macmillan.

Francis, E.K. (1955). *In Search of Utopia: The Mennonites in Manitoba.* Altona, MB: D.W. Friesen & Sons.

Friesen, John W. (1993). *When Cultures Clash: Case Studies in Multiculturalism.* Second edition. Calgary, AB: Detselig Enterprises. Chapter eight.

Friesen, John W. (January, 1988). Concepts of Mennonites in School Curriculum. *Mennonite Quarterly Review, LXII:1*, 56-77.

Regehr, T.D. (1996). *Mennonites in Canada, 1939-1970: A People Transformed.* Toronto, ON: University of Toronto Press.

Smith, Henry C. (1957). *The Story of the Mennonites.* Fourth edition. Newton, KS: Mennonite Publication House.

Maryhill, Washington: An Unfulfilled Dream

Maryhill, Washington.

Yes, there is a replica of England's Stonehenge in The United States. It is located in the State of Washington and built in 1918 by a man named Sam Hill.

Sam Hill (1857-1931), was born in Deep River, North Carolina, and when he was eight years old, the family moved to

Minneapolis, Minnesota. Hill was raised in the Quaker tradition and trained as a lawyer at Harvard University. He was a man of great energy who followed an unusual dream; he wanted to build a Quaker commune in the American northwest.

In 1888, Hill married Mary Hill, the daughter of James J. Hill who worked for the Great Northern Railway. Sam Hill also took employment with the railway, but later involved himself in many different lines of work. Sam and Mary had two children and eventually moved to Seattle, Washington. Mrs. Hill did not enjoy life in the northwest so she took her children and moved back to Minneapolis. Her husband Sam Hill remained behind and involved himself in a myriad of unique activities.

In the early days of settlement, Hill spent much of his time targetting the improvement of roads in Oregon, even to the extent of launching a public relations campaign calling for paved roads through the Columbia River Gorge. After picking up the cost for a ten-mile stretch of the road, he attracted the attention of the governor of the state who visited the area to see things for himself. The result was a newly paved road through the Columbia River Gorge supervised by Sam Hill and an engineer named Samuel Lancaster.

In 1907, Hill purchased 6 000 acres of land located one hundred miles east of Portland, Oregon, with the intention farming it. The project failed, due to a lack of rain and unsuitable farming conditions. This did not deter Hill from going on to other ventures. He now turned his attention to building a Quaker community on the site and designed an entire village to accommodate future dwellers. The village plan was to contain a store, a blacksmith shop, a post office, an inn, a stable, and a Quaker church building. What later transpired (in 1914) was the building of a large mansion that Hill named Maryhill after his wife, Mary (who never saw it), and his daughter, Mary (who never actually lived there). Perhaps it was his overambitious concern to finish the project that Hill may have forgotten to inform the Quaker community about his venture. When his construction of facilities was complete, only a few families came to live there, and so the utopian dream never really materialized. Although a bit depressed by his failure to

Although Sam Hill's dream of building a Quaker communal utoia did not materialize, he made a significant contribution to the cultural life of the Columbia River Gorge and to the American northwest.

develop the intended community, Sam Hill moved on to other concerns.

Sam Hill's mansion is like no other. Built entirely out of concrete, the rectangular structure is long in style and faces east and west. Guests who used to arrive by car could literally drive their automobiles into the lower floor of the house from the east end, drop off passengers, and exit through the west side. The building stands four stories tall, and is 400 feet in length.

With community dreams unfulfilled, and with the advice of two of his friends, in 1918, Hill decided to turn his mansion into an art museum. Two individuals who encouraged him to do so were Loîe Fuller, a pioneer of modern dance in Paris, and Queen Marie of Romania, granddaughter of Britain's Queen Victoria. Queen Marie was living in exile at the time she collaborated with Hill. Although unfinished, the museum was dedicated with a lavish ceremony in 1926 with Queen Marie of Romania present for the occasion. More then two thousand people attended the event, but since it was still incomplete, the museum could not be opened to the public until May 13, 1940. In the meantime, another of Hill's friends, Alma de Bretteville Spreckels, wife of San Francisco sugar magnate Adolf Spreckels, took up the task of finishing the museum. She was later elected to the board of trustees and donated several pieces of artwork from her private collection.

Loîe Fuller, through her acquaintance with artists in France, was instrumental in convincing Hill to obtain an impressive collection of French sculptor, August Rodin's work. Today the museum includes more than eighty of Rodin's works in its inventory. Queen Marie's throne is on view as well as her crown jewels, wedding dress, and icon collection. As though to add a local flavor, there are also Indian baskets on display as well as one hundred unusual chess sets, and art from the Belle Epoque.

In 1918, Hill began the construction of a replica of Stonehenge as a memorial to the men who lost their lives in World War I. He also built a peace arch where the present day Interstate Highway No. 5 crosses the border into Canada.

Hill's grave is located on a hillside just below the Stonehenge memorial.

Although Sam Hill's dream of building a Quaker communal utopia did not materialize, he made a significant contribution to the cultural life of the Columbia River Gorge and to the American northwest.

The Sam Hill Memorial Bridge, which carries U.S. Route 97 across the Columbia River near Maryhill, is named after him.

For Further Reading

http://www.maryhillmuseum.org/
http://www.maryhillmuseum.org/exhibits.html
http://www.maryhillmuseum.org/history.html
http://www.nwcouncil.org/history/Maryhill.asp

Metlakatla, British Columbia: An Aboriginal Communal Utopia

Although not known by many people, there was once an authentic commune of Native North American Indians in British Columbia. Due to some unusual political maneuvering, however, it was later moved to Alaska where it eventually met its demise.

For the record, the Indigenous people of the Americas have always been known as a sharing people, that is, traditionally they looked after their own tribal members if they were in need. To be accurate, however, the traditional First Nations way of life could not really be called communal in the true sense of the word.

A photo of a replica Tsimshian-painted housefronts in The Museum of Anthropology collection, British Columbia. The original screen would have measured 5.5 metres (18 feet) high by 18 metres (50 feet) across.

> Metlakatla was an immediate success, supporting its population with sawmills, a fish processing plant, soap and textile factories, and stores.

The particularly unique communal experiment described here was the dream child of William Duncan (1848-1918), who was born in England to a very poor family. Somewhat theologically trained, he eventually immigrated to Canada with the Church of England Missionary Society nurturing the goal of starting a mission among the Indians of British Columbia. Duncan arrived in Vancouver in June 1857, then travelled to Fort Simpson, some 500 miles north where the Church of England had already selected a site for his mission. Some 2 300 potential converts awaited Duncan, one of the largest gatherings of Tsimshian Indians in the province. Several Tsimshian tribes had earlier moved to Fort Simpson to be closer to the flourishing fur trade in that area.

At first Duncan was a bit overwhelmed with the potential size of his congregation, but he quickly set about learning the Tsimshian language, establishing a school, offering Bible studies, and conducting worship services. Within a year, Duncan managed to attract a congregation of fifty worshippers and began making plans to build a communal utopia of First Nations. He shared his dream with the governor of the territory, who concurred with the idea, and a site named Metlakatla was selected near Fort Simpson, British Columbia. A settlement was established in May 1862, by a company of 300 Aboriginal men who agreed in advance to abide by Duncan's rules. Soon thirty houses were completed and located next to a large church with a 600-seat capacity. Adherents were divided into companies governed by elders, councillors, and constables. The primary governing body consisted of hereditary chiefs and Duncan himself.

Metlakatla was an immediate success, supporting its population with sawmills, a fish processing plant, soap and textile factories, and stores. Native handicrafts were traded, shipped, and marketed further south using a boat Duncan obtained for that purpose. Moving products directly down coast with one's own means of transportation effectively eliminated the middleman. In 1874 the commune became home to St. Paul's Church, the largest cathedral west of Chicago, and North of San Francisco. It was equipped with a vestibule, gallery, belfry and spire, groined arches, and a solid timber frame. The church had a seating capacity of 1 200, but it unfortunately burned down in 1949 and a smaller one, called the William Duncan Memorial Church, was built to replace it. It remains to this day.

Happy ending? No. Duncan ran into church politics. Although active in missionary work, Duncan said he did not feel called to the ministry and therefore refused to be ordained when asked to do so. Duncan's decision did not sit well with the local bishop, William Ridley, who then divided Metlakatla into several districts and appointed a new missionary to take over the mission. Duncan appealed to the Canadian federal government, but to no avail. Duncan then contacted American President, Grover Cleveland, about starting a new Indian settlement in Alaska, some 75 miles north. His request was granted because the American government was impressed with Duncan's success in "civilizing the Indian." Eight hundred Tsimshian people followed Duncan to Alaska, and within a few months, a new village emerged, partially built of materials salvaged from Metlakatla. Then trouble brewed.

Up to this point, William Duncan was manager, trustee, and sole shareholder of the Metlakatla commune. The move to Alaska brought a new awareness to community members who wanted more than a token voice in deliberations and a more meaningful share of communal holdings. Duncan resisted any form of change, and conflict arose. As members began to fade away, Duncan grew more possessive. In 1915, ownership of the new colony was transferred to the local Indian band. Duncan died in 1918, a lonely and disillusioned man. He was buried in front of his new church.

Today Metlakatla continues to thrive as a community, with several religious denominations operating mission churches in the settlement. To some extent these religious organizations are in competition with the renaissance of Native spirituality which has recently gained a stronghold in most First Nations communities in North America. Only a few village buildings of the old Metlakatla in British Columbia remain as a testimony to a once successful, all Aboriginal utopian commune.

Visitors to the area are welcome.

For Further Reading

Arctander, John W. (1909). *The Apostle of Alaska: The Story of William Duncan of Metlakatla.* New York: Fleming H. Revell Co.

Scott, Andrew. (1997). *The Promise of Paradise: Utopian Communities in BC.* Vancouver, BC: Whitecap Books.

Usher, Jean. (1974). *William Duncan of Metlakatla: A Victorian Missionary in British Columbia.* Ottawa, ON: National Museums of Canada.

http://www.clan-duncan.co.uk/rev-william-duncan.html

Mormon Trek to Utah: Utopia at Long Last

The Mormon Temple dedicated in 2002 is located just north of Highway IL-96 in Nauvoo, Illinois. The temple is positioned in the same location as the original structure that was dedicated in 1848.

It is unequivocally an insurmountable task to describe the history and beliefs of the Church of Jesus Christ of Latter Day Saints (Mormons), since so much has been written about it. Although this denomination grew out of the great religious and intellectual movement of the 1920s in New York, the significance and outreach program of the Church of Jesus Christ of Latter Day Saints is virtually second to none. For our purposes, the relocation of Mormons in 1846 from Nauvoo, Illinois to the State of Utah may be described as an ultimate experience for the group.

The founder of Mormonism was Joseph Smith (1805-1844) who claimed to have received special Divine revelations that enabled him to establish a new church. The new revelation came in 1823 when Smith was only eighteen years old, apparently in the form of a set of golden plates given to him by an angel in the desert. Smith claimed to have been able to translate the plates and the result was *The Book of Mormon: Another Testament of Jesus Christ.* Adherents to the faith claim that The Book of Mormon is the key to their faith because it describes the story of a group of Israelites, part of the ten lost tribes, who migrated to the new world before the birth of Jesus Christ.

The Mormons managed to establish colonies in Illinois, Missouri, and Ohio, but soon faced bitter persecution because of their unorthodox beliefs and the practice of polygamy. Smith and his brother Hiram were imprisoned at Carthage, Illinois (a short distance from Nauvoo), and killed by a mob that broke into the jail where they were imprisoned. Unable to withstand the opposition that continued, four years later the next Mormon leader, Brigham Young, led an exodus of Mormons to what later became the state of Utah. This migration is known in history as the Great Mormon Trek. As the group left their homes they had to face the reality of the road ahead – nearly one thousand miles of open prairie and bush country, and more than one treacherous mountain pass. After the Mormons left Nauvoo, a group of communal Icarians (discussed later in this book) established themselves in homes previously occupied by Mormons.

As the group left their homes they had to face the reality of the road ahead – nearly one thousand miles of open prairie and bush country, and more than one treacherous mountain pass.

Prior to embarking on the Great Mormon Trek the group had to adjust to the death of their leader, Joseph Smith. A few factions arose, one led by Samuel Rigdon who led a group of followers eastward. Most of the people remained loyal to Brigham Young who ruled the church for thirty years. Young saw that persecution of his followers was continuing in Illinois and decided that the group should move away. Heading west seemed to be a particularly good idea. Land was available and the climate was suitable for their purposes. The Great Trek began on February 4, 1846. Five months later the group reached Council Bluffs, Iowa, from where an advance party was sent west. Headed by Brigham Young and Heber Kimball, the route that the search party took to Utah is identical to that later followed by the Union Pacific Railway and US Highway 30. The advance party included 140 people, 93 horses, 72 wagons, 66 oxen, 52 mules, 19 cows, 17 dogs and a few chickens. On July 24, 1847, having reached the site of where Salt Lake City is located today, Brigham Young is said to have lifted his hand and said, "This is the right place."

Anyone visiting Salt Lake City today will be unaware of the dangerous adventures faced by participants in the Great

Mormon Trek. Picture, if you can, a long train of creaking wagons led by horses and mules with hundreds of people in tow. Between 1846 and 1869, more than 70 000 Mormons headed towards Utah, following the path set by their leader, Brigham Young. Some people could not afford wagons and so traversed the entire trip on foot. Some pushed two wheeled carts capable of carrying up to 500 pounds of goods. Many Mormon travellers kept diaries and wrote in journals so we have a fairly accurate picture of what they endured. Journal entries included references to tired feet and sprained ankles, suffocating dust, violent thunderstorms, swollen creeks and rivers, and poor food, all of which often meant sickness, and death.

Other challenges faced the weary travellers after they reached their destination. It was late in the year when they arrived, but they still planted crops, laid out streets, built temporary dwellings, and prepared for winter. Some 1600 people spent their first winter in the valley. The rest is history. Today a few traces of the original Mormon Trail still exist in the Salt Lake Valley. Ruts from wagon wheels may be seen, but that part of the trail is on private land.

Today the Church of Jesus Christ of Latter Day Saints is one of the largest, most wealthy religious denominations in the world with branches in many countries. Their status in North America is politically acknowledged and respected, and the socioeconomic wellbeing of many of their members is well above average.

The Mormon utopian dream has indeed become reality.

For Further Reading

Barlow, Philip L. (1991). *Mormons and the Bible: The Place of the Latter-Day Saints in American Religion.* New York: Oxford University Press.

Friesen, John W. (1995). *Pick One: A User-Friendly Guide to Religion.* Calgary, AB: Detselig Enterprises.

Kephart, William M., and William W. Zellner. (1994). *Extraordinary Groups: An Examination of Unconventional Lifestyles.* Fifth edition. New York: St. Martin's Press. Chapter Seven.

May, Dean L. (1997). *One Heart and Mind: Communal Life and Values among the Mormons.* American Communal Utopias. Chapel Hill, NC: The University of North Carolina Press, 135-158.

Mullen, Robert. (1966). *The Latter-Day Saints: The Mormons Yesterday and Today.* Garden City, NK: Doubleday.

Palmer, Howard. (1972). *Land of the Second Chance.* Lethbridge, AB: The Lethbridge Herald.

Persuitte, David. (1985). *Joseph Smith and the Origins of the Book of Mormon.* Jefferson, NC: McFarland & Company.

Old Believers: Utopia in Motion

If ever there were wandering minstrels with utopian dreams, the Russian Old Believers certainly qualify!

The origins of the Russian Old Believers date back to the beginning of the 17th century when Nikon, Patriarch of the Russian Orthodox Church decided to reform the denomination. Nikon was appointed to office by Tsar Alexei and at first no one objected to the appointment. Soon it became clear, however, that the Orthodox Church was going Greek, and objections to Nikon's actions began to emerge. Nikon insisted that Greek themes in architecture be imitated and Greek rituals and furnishings be adopted. In addition he mandated a revised prayer book, the making of the sign of the cross with three fingers instead of two fingers, a sun-wise direction for processional marches, a ban on shaving, a change of name for Jesus from *Isus* to *Iiusus*, and the repetition of alleluia to be three times instead of twice during services. The conservative factions of the church became exceedingly angry with Nikon, but he had little patience with them. Often he had his opponents flogged or exiled, and even burned at the stake. It has been estimated that between 1672 and 1691, more than 20 000 Old Believers were put to death by their persecutors.

Nikon's changes were quite radical, and he would probably have been better off introducing them one by one over

Old Believers Church located in Lac La Biche, Alberta

time. Because he was in a hurry, Nikon was blamed for the origin of literally dozens of new sects that arose from within the ranks of the Russian Orthodox Church. Although the Russian government tried to dissuade these groups, they strongly desisted. The Russian government quickly grew impatient and it soon became obvious that the dissidents were no longer welcome in Russia. Thus began a continuing exodus of Old Believers (one of the emerging sects) to Siberia, central Asia, northwest China, Hong Kong, Australia, New Zealand, and Brazil. Migrations continued as late as 1972 when a group of Old Believers migrated to northeast Alberta after short stays in Alaska and Oregon. Their elusive utopian dream, it seems, was always on the move.

> The Old Believers' interpretation of an idyllic lifestyle would probably not satisfy many people.

The Old Believers' interpretation of an idyllic lifestyle would probably not satisfy many people. Old Believers do not recognize a priesthood of any sort. They believe in a life of simplicity, abstinence from "worldly" habits, and strict adherence to their unique interpretation of Christian prescriptions. Every aspect of daily life is supposed to reflect one's Christian beliefs including attitudes towards property, marriage relationships, interaction with nonbelievers, and leadership. If members of the faith "marry out," they are shunned by loyal adherents. There is no record of any outsider ever converting to the faith, probably because of the strict lifestyle new converts would have to adopt.

The move to Canada was probably the best choice the Old Believers made. At least there they can live somewhat in isolation and practice their religion unmolested. Their move to northwest China, for example, put them up against unconscionable roving groups of bandits who roved the area and plundered all of the unprotected communities they encountered. About one thousand Old Believers eventually escaped to Hong Kong where, thanks to the kind intervention of several charitable organizations, they were given the option of relocating to Australia, New Zealand, Argentina, Brazil, Paraguay, or Uruguay. Most of them chose Brazil and Australia as destinations. Today there are still small groups of Old Believers in Brazil and Australia.

Life in Brazil was challenging from the start. The first anticipated harvests of grain were total losses. When the Old

Believers finally did manage to grow crops they discovered that markets were extremely limited. Illegal tax collectors were another problem. These imposters often stopped Old Believer farmers on the road as they travelled and demanded "tax money" from them. When the trusting Old Believer farmers paid up, they were not provided with a receipt. The Tolstoy Foundation finally intervened and arranged for the Old Believers to migrate to the United States. The first move was to New Jersey, and then to Oregon. Some groups even went on to Alaska. After arriving in Oregon the newcomers again faced a difficult situation. Even though they managed to gain a financial foothold, they decided to share their earnings with their former neighbors in Brazil. This self-imposed commitment kept them in the poorhouse for a long time.

In 1972 a group of thirty households of Old Believers from Oregon purchased a large tract of land near Lac La Biche, Alberta, Canada, and formed the settlement of Berrezovka which exists today. There these stalwarts of conservatism struggle to keep their children in line with their beliefs and practices, and "keep themselves unspotted from the world."

Have the Old Believers finally attained their unique concept of utopia? Only time will tell.

For Further Reading

Crummey, Robert O. (1970). *The Old Believers and the World of Antichrist,* The University of Wisconsin, Milwaukee.

Friesen, John W. (1995). *Pick One: A User-Friendly Guide to Religion*. Calgary, AB: Detselig Enterprises.

Gerhart, Genevra. (1974). *The Russian's World, Life and Language,* San Francisco, CA: Harcourt Brace Jovanovich, Inc.

Kach, Nick. (November, 1984). The Acculturation of the Old Believers. *Multicultural Education Journal, 2*(2), 19-26.

Scheffel, David. (1998). *In the Shadow of the Antichrist.* Peterborough, ON: Broadview Press.

Wigowsky, Paul J. (January, 1978). http://www.reocities.com/Athens/Agora/2827/collection.html

People of the Plains: Utopia Was Never Their Goal

There are not many people around today who would be content to live in sync with the rhythms of nature. However, this was undeniably the goal of Native North Americans for many centuries before European contact. And it worked.

A great deal of misunderstanding about traditional Indigenous cultures in North America still exists in the public mind. For too long people have had to rely on misguided historical accounts of the European domination of First Nations. Now, thanks to a renewed look at history, often provided by Indigenous writers, the public perspective is slowly changing.

Pow wow dancers, Stoney First Nation, Morley, Alberta.

Utopia is not a term that exists in the traditional languages of the various North American Indian tribes. The traditional Indigenous philosophy of daily life does not include longing for better days or a better place. Life is to be lived in the "perennial now," that is, every aspect of each moment is to be perceived, absorbed, and analyzed in terms of its possible implications for one's individual spiritual journey. That journey is designated by the Creator, and it is up to each individual to seek its meaning for his or her life. Once the direction of the journey is realized it is to be followed up daily with each thought and action.

Many of the first accounts describing Indigenous cultures were written by well meaning, but ill-informed explorers, fur traders, missionaries, and representatives of the state. These writers were either French, Spanish, or English, not Aboriginal. The first European visitors to this continent who initially encountered the First Peoples, did so from the perspective of their own cultural perspectives without bothering to learn why the resident First Nations chose to live completely in harmony with nature. Of course the newcomers did not have the benefit of having studied cultural anthropology, which today places heavy emphasis on the notion of cultural sensitivity, that is, cultures should be explored and interpreted on the basis of their internal rationale. Members of every cultural configuration have their own reasons for living the way they do. Usually these reasons have been developed over time and formulate distinct but consistent patterns. These prescribed regulations for living include means of livelihood, social governance, forms of caring for children, aged, the sick and needy, and regulations about property.

The original inhabitants of North America developed societies that were quite complex in terms of social structure and individual and group roles, expectations, and obligations. All of these structures and responsibilities were based on one undeniable truth – the universe exists and unless its rhythms and cycles are respected and obeyed, human cultures will cease to exist. The universe, of course, includes gifts brought into being by the Creator through the auspices of Mother Earth. Life on earth is never intended to be constantly improved, but is to be lived in cooperation with the processes of nature. Everything in the universe is perceived as interconnected, which means that every entity, creature, process, and item are to be respected as gifts from the Creator.

Aboriginal spirituality is a topic that has yet to be explored on any large scale by nonAboriginals, and there are signs that this may be happening. Living in complete harmony with the universe implies a very here and now orientation. Native elders play a huge role in this respect, often acting as interpreters of spiritual searches. Elders are respected for their knowledge, experience and wisdom, and like grandparents in the extended family, will be expected to assist with child-raising. Decision-making is designed to be a group process because, after all, decisions made affect everyone. All aspects of tribal life need to be talked through to consensus by duly appointed councils. As mentioned earlier, living in harmony with nature implies living in the "perennial now." Perhaps that is the best attitude by which to live; it is, of itself, a form of utopia.

Utopia is not a term that exists in the traditional languages of the various North American Indian tribes.

One only has the moment at hand to respond to the gentle spiritual proddings one receives through nature; the future cannot be predicted.

Since it is virtually impossible to deal with such a vast subject in the short space allotted here, it is advisable that literature on the topic be consulted by those interested in this topic. Therefore, this section offers a longer list of references than the others.

For Further Reading

Dickason, Olive Patricia. (2006). *A Concise History of Canada's First Nations.* Toronto, ON: Oxford University Press.

Cajete, Gregory. (1994). *Look to the Mountain: An Ecology of Indigenous Education.* Durango, CO: Kiva Press.

Couture, Joseph E. (1991). Explorations in Native Knowing. *The Cultural Maze: Complex Questions on Native Destiny in Western Canada.* John W. Friesen, ed. Calgary, AB: Detselig Enterprises, 53-73.

Dickason, Olive Patricia. (1984). *The Myth of the Savage and the Beginnings of French Colonialism in the Americas.* Edmonton, AB: University of Alberta Press.

Dion, Joseph F. (1979). *My Tribe, The Crees.* Calgary, AB: Glenbow Museum.

Friesen, John W. (1997). *Rediscovering the First Nations of Canada.* Calgary, AB: Detselig Enterprises.

Friesen, John W. (1999). *First Nations of the Plains.* Calgary, AB: Detselig Enterprises.

Friesen, John W. (2000). *Aboriginal Spirituality and Biblical Theology: Closer Than You Think.* Calgary, AB: Detselig Enterprises.

Friesen, John W., and Virginia Lyons Friesen. (2005). *First Nations in the Twenty-First Century: Contemporary Educational Frontiers.* Calgary, AB: Detselig Enterprises.

Harrod, Howard L., (1995). *Becoming and Remaining a People: Native American Religions on the Northern Plains.* Tucson, AZ: University of Arizona Press.

Henlin, Calvin. (2006) *Dances with Dependency: Indigenous Success Through Self-Reliance.* Vancouver, BC: Orca Spirit.

Hungry Wolf, Beverly. (1982). *The Ways of My Grandmothers.* New York: Quill.

Josephy, Alvin M., Jr. (1968). *The Indian Heritage of America.* New York: Alfred A. Knopf.

Kennedy, Dan (Ochankugahe). (1972). *Recollections of an Assiniboine Chief.* Toronto, ON: McClelland and Stewart.

Lowie, Robert. (1963). *Indians of the Plains.* New York: The American Museum of Natural History.

Ross, Jeffrey Ian, and Larry Gould, eds. (2006). *Native Americans and the Criminal Justice System.* Boulder, CO: Paradigm Publishers.

Ross, Rupert. (1992). *Dancing With a Ghost: Exploring India Reality.* Markham, ON: Reed Books.

Snow, Chief John. (2005). *These Mountains Are Our Sacred Places: The Story of the Stoney People.* Calgary, AB: Fitzhenry and Whiteside.

Underhill, Ruth M. (1953). *Red Man's America: A History of Indians in the United States.* Chicago, IL: University of Chicago Press.

Warry, Wayne. (2007). *Ending Denial: Understanding Aboriginal Issues.* Peterborough, ON: Broadview Press.

Pueblo Invasion: Delivering an Uninvited Utopia

Travellers to the southwest part of the United States will be intrigued when they reach the point where four states intersect – Colorado, New Mexico, Arizona, and Utah. At a specific location, travellers will be able to set foot on all four states at once. They will also find themselves in a geographic area rich with more than one hundred Anasazi (the Ancient Ones), archaeological ruins located within 100 miles of that four state intersection.

This important intersection was once the habitat of the pueblo (meaning village dwellers) peoples, so named by the invading Spanish in 1540. Further south is the historic dwelling place of the Hohokam, who

For over three centuries, the Puyé cave dwellings were home to about 1500 Pueblo Indians. Puyé is considered the ancestral home of Santa Clara Pueblo and other pueblos in New Mexico.

gave the world a special form of pottery as well as its first etching process, and still further south once lived the Mogollon whose population also spilled into what is now Mexico. Among other cultural contributions, the Mogollon domesticated the turkey.

To some extent the Pueblo Indians were already living a very satisfying lifestyle when the Spanish arrived. Each of the various bands and tribes lived within its respected area, and all were farmers to some extent. There was no feudal system and there were no slaves. While each family had its own designated piece of land for farming, in poor years those who had ample produce shared it with their neighbors if they had need. Whole tribes often banded together in farming, hunting, food gathering, irrigation, and care of the land. Their entire way of life was grounded on faith in the Creator to provide for the people, and because He faithfully did so, each of His gifts was received with supplication and thanksgiving.

> When the Spanish arrived, under the leadership of Captain Hernando de Alvarado, they did not take note of the many Pueblo cultural inventions. They came to deliver what they perceived to be a superior culture.

When the Spanish arrived, under the leadership of Captain Hernando de Alvarado, they did not take note of the many Pueblo cultural inventions; they came to deliver what they perceived to be a superior culture. They arrived under the strict orders of Governor Francisco Vázquez de Coronado to deliver their interpretation of civilization. The invaders were not intrigued that the Anasazi had built the first high rises in America – stone castles that were four and five stories high and often carved into the sides of tall cliffs. The Spanish invaders were not particularly aware that the Hohokam (the first irrigation farmers), had domesticated cotton and tobacco, harvested wild desert plants, and developed extensive trade relationships. The Spanish probably ignored the fact that the Mogollon were the first south-westerners to cultivate corn, make pottery, and build pit-houses in which to live.

The Spanish came for gold – which, by the way, did not exist, despite the power of the rumor that there were "Seven Cities of Cibola" (gold) in the American southwest. Close behind the economic imperialists were missionaries bent on delivering the "right" form of religion to the Pueblo people. Their mission would be to spread a utopian form of viewing the universe.

Between 1620 and 1680, Spanish priests seized Pueblo lands and set up missions. The priests were the governors of these missions so they felt free to establish strict rules for the Indigenous peoples to follow. Those who refused to yield to the rule of the priests were severely punished. Locals were forced to build three huge cathedrals in an area beginning an hour drive south of the City of Albuquerque, New Mexico, the ruins of which may be seen today. These massive cathedrals are known as Abó, Quarai, and Gran Quivira. Each of these magnificent edifices once contained an auditorium in which to hold religious services, living quarters for the priests, and pens for domesticated animals such as sheep, goats, burros, and cattle – all introduced by the Spanish. Pueblo slaves lived near the cathedrals and while they were being Christianized, for some reason they were allowed to construct and worship in kivas (traditional religious ceremonial rooms) while the construction of the cathedrals was going on. As slaves the Pueblo People were also expected to tend gardens, maintain buildings and grounds, tend livestock, and serve their masters in other ways. The priests' hope was that when the cathedral complexes were completed, the people would no longer see a need for the kiva. This plan did not materialize. In all three cases, today's explorers will find ruins of kivas located right beside the cathedral ruins.

In 1680, unable to put up with colonial oppression, the pueblo peoples revolted against Spanish rule. Their victory was short-lived. Twelve years later the Spanish again attacked and because of their superior military night, the Spanish prevailed. Thus the Pueblo Peoples were forced to yield to Spanish rule. While the corn growing agricultural milieu of the Pueblo People continued, the Spanish introduced a number of cultural items that today are very much a part of pueblo culture. Their list of contributions includes chilies, watermelons, a superior quality of onions, and the famous beehive oven.

To some extent the program of forced utopian ideals – both economic and religious was successful. Today many Spanish Catholic traditions are practiced by the Pueblo Peoples in their nineteen traditional-looking pueblos. They seem to have adjusted to the nuances of Spanish imperialism, both economically as well as religiously. Their traditional interpretations of the good life seem to have been altered, and their modified cultures continue to thrive.

For Further Reading

Dozier, Edward P. (1983). *The Pueblo Indians of North America.* Prospect Heights, IL: Waveland Press.

Friesen, John W. (1995). *You Can't Get There From Here: The Mystique of North American Plains Indians Culture & Philosophy.* Dubuque, IA: Kendall/Hunt.

Lavender, David. (1980). *The Southwest.* Albuquerque, NM: University of New Mexico Press.

Lister, Robert H., and Florence C. Lister. (1989). *Those Who Came Before.* Globe, AZ: Southwest Parks and Monuments Association.

Sando, Joe. (1976). *The Pueblo Indians.* San Francisco, CA: The Indian Historian Press.

Wormington, H.M. (1978). *Prehistoric Indians of the Southwest.* Fourteenth printing. Denver, CO: The Denver Musuem of Natural History.

Puritans in America: Utopia Was A Very Serious Pursuit

Much has been written about the very organized manner that the English Puritans adopted when they relocated to the United States in 1620. Quite frankly, they were very serious about everything – especially religious, moral, and societal reform.

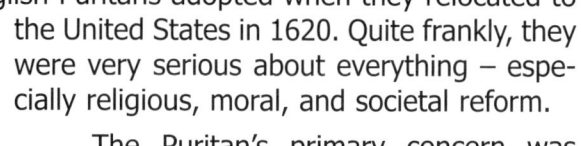

The Puritan's primary concern was that the 17th century Church of England had become the product of political struggles and liberal doctrines. The Puritans claimed that the English Reformation had not gone far enough in amending Roman Catholic doctrines and practices. They claimed that the emerging Church of England was still too

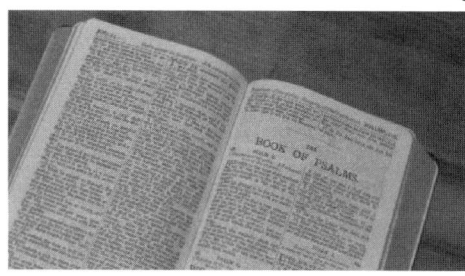

The Book of Psalms in the Holy Bible served as the hymnbook for the Puritans.

Catholic. Puritan reactionary philosophy, therefore, consisted of three fundamentals: (i) Biblical orthodoxy, (ii) an uncompromising anthropology – which implied belief in the total depravity of mankind, and (iii) the formation of an oligarchic, albeit theocratic form of governance.

In designing their rigid form of theocracy the Puritans seem to have ignored the advice of John Cotton, teacher of the Puritan Boston Church, who warned that people should "give mortal men no greater power than they are content they shall use – for use it they will." As it turned out, the first Puritan leaders in America were quite power hungry. For example, their theologians pushed the doctrine of original sin to the limit, citing as encouragement the words of the Psalmist about newborn babies; ". . . they go astray as soon as they be born, speaking lies (Psalm 58: 3b KJV). St. Paul nicely echoed this sentiment for the Puritans in 1 Corinthians 15:22 (KJV); "For as in Adam all die, even so in Christ shall all be made alive." As it turned out, the somewhat dictatorial Puritan theocratic leaders appointed overseers to assure themselves that the people were obeying all of their rules. Punishment for violations was swift and strict.

While they were still in England, the Puritans found themselves quite in harmony with other dissenting groups on the theme of criticizing the Church of England, but when they approached King James I about their concerns, he rejected all of them outright. Shortly thereafter, all Puritan-minded clergy were expelled from the Church of England and their followers were assigned the label, "nonconformists." Fortunately, the United States was looking for immigrants, and the Puritans were prepared to migrate there and establish a religious utopia. In fact, shortly after they arrived, they appointed a governor who tried to organize a mandatory public worship service for everyone to attend.

The first Puritans in America were the Pilgrims who landed at Plymouth Rock in 1620. Within a decade, many more English dissenters joined their ranks. Under the direction of such men as Richard Mather and John Cotton the Puritans organized a series of congregational churches with very strict rules for membership. After all, with the doctrine of predestination in hand there was a real danger of jeopardiz-

Fortunately, the United States was looking for immigrants, and the Puritans were prepared to migrate there and establish what then was perceived to be a religious utopia.

ing such a Divinely appointed position – if one had it at all. Individuals approved by God via predestination were expected constantly to be involved in doing good. Conversion meant complete separation from all worldly pleasures and a strict adherence to Biblical principles. If utopia was going to work, the Puritan leaders insisted, it meant that everyone was expected to toe the line. Great pains were taken to warn members, especially children, about the lurking lures of the world. Even the alphabet was taught to very young children in theological terms, for example, (A) "In Adam's fall, we sinned all." (B) Thy life to mend, God's book attend," (C) "The cat doth play, and after slay." Two significant contributions of Puritan culture to the American way of life were these – the promotion of literacy, and the establishment of the first public compulsory school system. Both concepts were founded on the notion that literate individuals, trained in theologically based schools, would better be able to read, understand, and obey the Scriptures. Remnants of the commitment to universal, equal education still remain in America.

As the nation grew increasingly secular, strict religious mandates gradually waned and in some sectors were even shelved completely. Despite the efforts of orators like Jonathan Edwards and George Whitfield, by 1800 Puritanism had lost its grip on America. It did leave behind the formation of a strong tension between fundamentalism and modernism, the debate of which continued to engulf American theology in the decades that followed. Politically, Puritanism set the stage for another American value – the complete separation of church and state.

The Puritan commitment to universal education should not easily be underestimated. After all, literate people are better able to elaborate the details of their utopian dreams!

For Further Reading

Bayles, Ernest E., and Bruce L. Hood. (1966). *Growth of American Educational Thought and Practice*. New York: Harper & Row.

Haefeli, Evan. (2004). Making Papists of Puritans: Accounting for New English Conversions in New France. *The Spiritual*

Conversion of the Americas. James Muldoon, editor. Gainesville, FL: University Press of Florida.

Mather, Cotton. (1969). *Liberty of Conscience. Issues in American Protestantism: A Documentary History From the Puritans to the Present.* Garden City, NY: Doubleday & Company.

Miller, Perry, editor. (1958). *The American Puritans: Their Prose and Poetry.* Garden City, NY: Doubleday and Company.

Miller, Perry, and Thomas H. Johnson. (1963). *The Puritans.* Volume 1. Garden City, NY: Harper & Row.

Montgomery, John Warwick. (1981). *The Shaping of America.* Minneapolis, MN: Bethany House Publishers.

Tichi, Cecelia. (1979). *New World, New Earth: Environmental Reform in American Literature from the Puritans Through Whitman.* New Haven, CT: Yale University Press.

Quakers: Sharing the Utopian Dream

Nonconformity to state religion ran high in 17th century England, and George Fox (1624-1691) was a leader for one such movement – the Society of Friends.

Fox left home at the age of nineteen and searched for several years to find personal meaning. At one significant point in his life he was the recipient of a personal vision based on St. John's Gospel (1:9 KJV), "The true Light, which lighteth every man that cometh into the world." Fox immediately translated this phrase to mean that every individual (male and female) had equal access to God and so there was no need for a priestly class. He also explained that if an individual lived a personally pious lifestyle, there was no need for creeds of dogma, ceremonies, or rituals. Following the inner light would lead individuals to living godly lives.

The First Quaker Meeting House west of the Alleghanies located in Mount Pleasant, Ohio.

Although George Fox is often credited as founder of the Society of Friends, there is evidence to suggest that people like James Nayler and Edward Burrough may have been strong proponents of the movement. Fox's followers were taught to worship in silence, and only those individuals would speak to a group who were moved by the Holy Spirit. Gradually the group came to be known as "Friends of Truth," and later, simply as "Friends." The term "Quaker" arose when Fox appeared before a judge because of his nonconformist beliefs. Fox told the judge to "tremble at the Word of the Lord," but the judge apparently refused to do so. Immediately Fox's phrase was translated to mean "one who quakes," and the name stuck. Over the next half century, some 3 000 Quakers spent time in English jails for their beliefs and many died in prison.

> Quaker philosophy is this: if utopia is to be realized, it must be shared with everyone regardless of race, sex, color, or creed.

One of the obstacles to the practice of the new found Quaker faith was the passing of the *Quaker Act* which mandated that everyone had to take an Oath of Allegiance to the Crown. As pacifists, the Quakers were hardly able to take the oath, arguing that God was in control of the universe, not the leaders of some political institution. What followed were charges of blasphemy against the Quakers. Small wonder that when the opportunity to migrate to America lent itself, it looked very promising to the would-be migrants.

In 1682, led by William Penn (1644-1718) a charismatic Quaker leader, a group of Quakers landed in America at what is today Long Island, New York. Penn had procured a tract of land on which to settle his followers, but when the community settled in, they quickly discovered that the neighboring Puritans in Massachusetts Bay Colony were not going to be kind. Persecution of Quakers began immediately. Their books were burned and their property was confiscated. Many Quakers were imprisoned, some were flogged, and some were even executed. Quaker leaders wrote to Governor Peter Stuyvesant, reminding him that religious freedom had been promised to them in the New World, and things gradually did improve. Essentially this happened because the Quakers left the area and moved to other locations.

Perhaps the most outstanding characteristic of Quaker philosophy has been their concern for others. Themselves victims of persecution so many times, Quakers have over time assisted many religious minorities in their quest to find locations for peaceful living. Groups such as Doukhobors, Hutterites, and Old Believers can testify to the fact that the Quakers often petitioned for fair treatment on their behalf. The Quakers also befriended the Aboriginal people in the New World, and in America no Indian wars were fought that included a single Quaker soldier. Quaker philosophy is this; if utopia is to be realized, it must be shared with everyone regardless of race, sex, color, or creed.

One of the first concerns Quakers voiced about inequality in New America was slavery. It is true that some of the Quakers who first came to America owned slaves, and the existing orientation at that time was that if a slave owner attended to the physical and spiritual needs of his slaves, the arrangement was perfectly acceptable. By 1775, Quakers were active in trying to abolish slavery, having finally applied their views on equality to the immediate situation. Later that year Virginia's governor announced that slaves in his state would be freed if they agreed to enlist in the fight against Great Britain.

Today there are more than 300 000 Quakers scattered throughout the world, nearly half of them living in the United States. They are highly respected for their work ethic, honesty, and high moral character. Easily their most notable characteristic is the way they continually speak out on behalf of suffering minorities all over the world.

If an idyllic lifestyle does emerge, the Quakers (Society of Friends) will certainly be concerned about sharing it with others.

For Further Reading

Barbour, Hugh, and J. William Frost. (1988). *The Quakers.* Santa Barbara, CA: Greenwood Press.

Howard H. Brinton, and Margaret Hope Bacon. (1965). *Friends for 350 Years: The History and Beliefs of the Society of Friends Since George Fox Started the Quaker Movement.* Wallingford, PA: Pendle Hill.

Ingle, H. Larry. (1994). *First Among Friends: George Fox and the Creation of Quakerism.* New York: Oxford University Press.

Kennedy, Thomas Cummings. (2001). *British Quakerism 1860-1920: The Transformation of a Religious Community.* New York: Oxford University Press.

Moore, Rosemary. (2000). *The Light In Their Consciences: Faith, Practices, and Personalities in Early British Quakerism. (1646-1666).* Philadelphia, PA: Pennsylvania State University Press.

Trueblood, D. Elton. (2002). *The People Called Quakers.* Richmond, IN: Friends United Press.

http://mb-soft.com/believe/txc/quakers.htm

http://www.quaker.org/

Route 66:
An All American Utopian Dream

"Get Your Kicks on Route 66," the song goes, but the road-weary Okies who traversed this famous highway during the 1930s, got anything but kicks out of the journey.

The Okies were people who in economic desperation left the dustbowl that Oklahoma had become in the 1930s and struck out for California. Photographs collected by museums and state libraries show the devastation that these brave individuals left behind, wind-blown dust covering everything in sight. Described in detail by novelist, John Steinbeck in *Grapes of Wrath,* Route 66 became the pathway to utopia. Sometimes caravans of old automobiles dotted the highway, all of them loaded with family members, personal belongings, and even the odd stick of furniture.

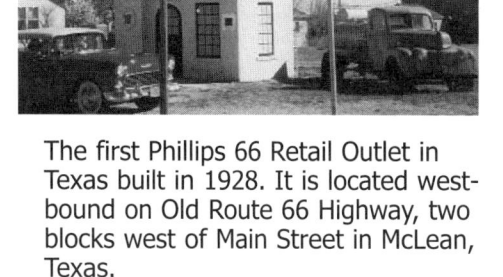

The first Phillips 66 Retail Outlet in Texas built in 1928. It is located westbound on Old Route 66 Highway, two blocks west of Main Street in McLean, Texas.

Michael Wallis describes the devastating conditions of his famous road in his 75th Anniversary Edition of *Route 66: The Mother Road.* Wallis notes that those who observed the

Okie migration could even gauge the economic status of these weary travellers by the number of mattresses strapped to the roofs of their cars. A car with three mattresses on the roof meant a "rich" family; two mattresses implied that a family with mediocre means owned them, and one mattress indicated abject poverty. Sometimes only a sense of humor about the pathetic conditions back home and the condition of the road that represented economic success, was all that kept people heading on to the southwest.

Route 66 became the pathway to utopia.

The all-American utopian dream that Route 66 represented, originated in the 1920s with the completion of Route 66 from Chicago to Los Angeles. Also known as America's Main Street, Route 66 was christened in 1926 during the reign of President Calvin Coolidge. This was perhaps the first major thoroughfare in the nation because it managed geographically to pull together the western two-thirds of the nation. Spanning some 2 400 miles, three time zones and eight states, Route 66 started at Grant Park in Chicago, Illinois, and wound its way in a southwesterly direction through Missouri, a tiny portion of southeast Kansas, Oklahoma, Texas, New Mexico, Arizona, and finally to Los Angeles, California.

For those interested in reliving an alluring chapter of America's past, a trip to what is left of the bits and pieces of the Mother Road is heartily recommended. In the heyday years of this revered highway, a multiplicity of small towns with a wide range of attractions greeted weary travellers when they arrived. There were flashing neon signs everywhere advertising motels, trading posts, truck stops, and restaurants serving up hamburgers, fried onions, sodas of various flavors, including coca-cola. Gasoline was available via old-fashioned gas pumps, often served up by uniformed gas jockeys. Each place of business gave its all in terms of trying to outdo other retail outlets, with many of them yielding to the temptation to develop unique attractions. Some them exist even today, albeit in somewhat damaged or worn condition. These include "66" Park Theatre in Missouri, the Marsh Rainbow Arch Bridge in Kansas, the world's largest teepee in Oklahoma, the leaning water tower in Texas, Barringer's Crater in Arizona, the Virginia Dare Winery in California, and many, many more weird and wonderful attractions of all kinds. Anyone travelling Route 66 today should make it a point to stop at the Midpoint Café located in Adrian, Arizona. This site marks the half-way point of the famous highway, and the staff of the restaurant will offer its customers good food, friendly service, and delicious homemade pies.

Each bend and rise in the winding ways of Route 66 once offered new sights and sounds and smells to travellers, many of them indicative of very inventive minds. Restaurants, service stations and adjoining buildings were designed in many different forms – caves, teepees, totem poles, and auto courts. One very special invention was the 10-stool hamburger stand complete with soda fountain and grill. Manufactured in Wichita, Kansas, these portable diners measured no more than 200 square feet in size and could easily be hauled on the back of a truck. If business in one location proved to be less than adequate, the "restaurant" would be loaded up and hauled to a new location further down the road. The sale price for one of these mobile eating establishments was about three thousand dollars and was paid for by the owner putting $1.40 into a special slot in the diner each day. Once a month a company employee would come around to collect the deposited funds.

Today the lure of this magical road still draws thousands of travellers to its surface, particularly those who remember stories about it from their childhood days. Younger generations are learning about the importance of the Mother Road to America's history with the release of the movie, *Cars*. It is important that this generation becomes aware of the determination exhibited by the brave and adventurous individuals and families who kept alive the dream that there are always better days ahead.

Perhaps just the pursuit of a utopian dream can represent the true essence of what it means to be an American – and human.

> *Perhaps just the pursuit of such a dream represents the true essence of what it means to be an American – and human.*

For Further Reading

Olsen, Russell A. (2004). *Route 66 Lost & Found: Ruins and Relics Revisited*. St. Paul, MN: MBI Publishing Company.

Wallis, Michael. (2001). *Route 66: The Mother Road.* New York: St. Martins' Griffin.

Webb, Walter Prescott. (1959). *The Great Plains.* Lincoln, NE: University of Nebraska Press.

Witzel, Michael Karl. (2003). *Route 66 Remembered.* St. Paul, MN: MBI Publishing Company.

Sikhs in Canada: A Perpetual Quest for Utopia

For a people who contribute generously to such charities as the Interfaith Food Bank, Steve Fonyo's Miles for Millions, The Mexican Earthquake Relief, the Ethiopian Relief Fund, and the Consciousness International Foundation, it is a sad commentary on Canada that the pacifist Sikhs still have to struggle with daily onslaughts of discrimination and racism.

The Five K's Kes Kirpan Kanga Kacha Kara

The Five Sacred Sikh symbols are commonly known as the Five K's because they all begin with the letter K.

Sikhs work hard, practice honesty, and make good neighbors, but apparently that is often not enough. Perhaps the adherents to this unique form of religion encounter prejudice simply because of their atypical form of attire; there can be no other reason.

The first Sikhs arrived in Canada in 1887 and in the decade that followed their numbers grew to include 2 600 souls. Originating as a sect in the Punjab in India, the Sikh movement developed as an anti-faction against the caste system, and promoted the idea that people are to be regarded as equal – regardless of race, class, sex, culture, or complexion.

The Sikh faith grew through the leadership of ten gurus (spiritual leaders), beginning with the ministry of Guru Nanak (1469-1539). Each of the ten Gurus added special insights and practices to the faith, with the tenth leader, Guru Gobind

Singh (1666-1708), announcing that after his death the people had no further need for such leadership. He declared that the people would now serve as Gurus. He left his followers with these principles of daily living: practice love, not hollow rituals; deeds alone are valued, not empty words; live honestly; physical renunciation is of no value; and, service is the only true form of worship. Most believers in a variety of world religions would undoubtedly agree that these are admirable principles.

Beliefs and practices initiated by the ten Sikh spiritual leaders included this list: equality of all people regardless of caste or sex; compilation of the Sikh scriptures (including some sacred Hindu and Islamic writings); special rites regarding birth, marriage, and death; building of the Golden Temple in Amritsar, Punjab; the practice of pacifism and forgiveness; and, establishment of the five "K's."

It is perhaps because of the practice of the five "K's" that Sikhs in North America encounter the most misunderstanding and prejudice. These practices are required of all baptized Sikhs. They include (i) *Kesh*, which means never cutting the hair as a symbol of simplicity, saintliness, and purity; (ii) *Kanga*, which is a wooden comb worn in the hair to indicate that even as old hair is combed out, new hair replaces it. So, in life, there is need for constant cleansing of one's spirit; (iii) *kara*, a steel bracelet, is worn on the wrist because it serves as a constant reminder not to use one's hands for sinful acts; (iv) *Kirpan*, is a small sword worn at the side to remind the wearer to curb the root of one's personal ego; and, (v) *Kacha*, which is white underwear worn by baptized Sikhs as a caution against committing sinful sexual acts. Once again, many believers of other world religions would probably agree that these are useful symbols.

The first Sikhs who travelled to North America were lured by the notion of freedom and the push of discrimination in India. Both Hindus and Muslims opposed the beliefs of Sikhism and gave no peace to Sikh followers. As a result of persecution, economic advancement in resource rich Punjab did not accrue to the Sikhs, so many left their homes. They travelled by ship to North America, many of them being forced to live on deck because they could not afford comfortable passage. Added to this discomfort, they also found that much less than a warm welcome awaited them.

Clifford Sifton, Canada's Minister of the Interior at the time was busily trying to populate the West. Under his leadership, between 1880 and 1891, more than one million immigrants arrived in Canada to make their homes in the west. Sifton, however, was a prejudiced individual. For example, he was strongly opposed to Asian immigration, and tried to stop immigrants arriving from any Asian countries. Discrimination lingered, however, even after Sifton's departure. In 1905, a shipload of Sikhs who arrived at the Vancouver Harbor was sent back to the Orient by a federal Order-in-Council. Another Order-in-Council in 1908 mandated that all immigrants arriving in Canada should have at least $200 with them. This was particularly difficult for the Sikhs whose annual individual wages in the Punjab averaged about $50 a year.

The first Sikhs who travelled to North America were lured by the notion of freedom.

The first Sikh immigrants who did make it to Canada obtained menial jobs in lumber camps, on railways and in sawmills, or as laborers on small farms. At first they were not allowed to vote or work as professionals, but this changed by special legislation in 1947. Later, in 1973 the Canadian government granted immigrant status to Sikhs who came to Canada as visitors with the hope they would eventually be allowed to remain in the country. Today, even though their members have involved themselves in a variety of successful Canadian engagements – business, the arts and literature, politics, banking, and sports, Sikhs still suffer enormous challenges and often face discrimination simply because "they look different." For example, there have been many disputes about the right of baptized Sikhs not to cut their hair if they join the army or the Royal Canadian Mounted Police. Authorities in those institutions seem to dislike the wearing of turbans. Donning the Sikh ceremonial sword, the *kirpan*, has also caused public stir even though there is not a single incident on record of any Sikh ever having used that item for any other than a symbolic religious purpose.

Despite these unfortunate historical and contemporary realities, Sikhs are proud citizens, perpetually in search of the right to live peacefully in what they perceive as the Canadian utopia.

For Further Reading:

Friesen, John W. (1993). *When Cultures Clash: Case Studies in Multiculturalism.* Second edition. Calgary, AB: Detselig Enterprises. Chapter ten.

Hopfe, Lewis M. (1994). *Religions of the World.* Sixth edition. Englewood Cliffs, NJ: Prentice-Hall. Chapter seven.

Koehn, Sharon D. (19912). Ethnic Emergence and Modernization: The Sikh Case. *Canadian Ethnic Studies, XXIII*(2), 95-116.

McLeod, W.H. (1976). *The Evolution of the Sikh Community.* Oxford, UK: Clarendon Press.

Minhas, Manmohan Singh (Moni). (1994). *The Sikh Canadians.* Edmonton, AB: Reidmore Books.

Singh, Gopal. (1990). *A History of the Sikh People: 1469-1988.* New Delhi, India: World Book Centre.

http://www.explorasian.org/history_sikhcdn.html

Utopia, Ohio: Utopia For Real!

Welcome to Ohio, the home state of the town Utopia, Ohio, located approximately one-hour drive south east of Cincinnati, Ohio on US 52.

Yes indeed, there really is a place literally named Utopia!

The community of Utopia in southeast Ohio, was founded by Josiah Warren in 1844 as one of Charles Fourier's "phalanxes" which the latter had visualized as an ideal form of communal living. Among other things, Fourier believed that the world was about to begin a period of 35 000 years of peace. When that occurred, everyone would be able to live in a phalanx type lifestyle. Each phalanx would be three square miles in size and have its own library, school, stables, and farmland. As a model phalanx, Ohio's Utopia was developed on 1 140 acres of land located close to the Ohio River. More will be said of Fourier's philosophy in the second section of this book.

The original inhabitants of this particular Ohio commune believed in Fourier's notion that in an ideal commune, all work and profit would be shared equally. The residents (about twelve families) built a thirty room brick dwelling as well as a series of smaller houses. Unfortunately, the experiment lasted only two years, primarily because of financial reasons. It did not take long and everyone left town; as a result only a remnant of the original settlement exists today.

Scarcely a year went by after the village was vacated, and a spiritualist, John Wattles purchased the commune. He settled one hundred followers there. Despite warnings from neighbors about flooding by the Ohio River, Wattles ordered that the thirty room brick building be dismantled, brick and brick, and moved to the water's edge. He also arranged to have an underground church built. On December 12, 1847, the Ohio River overflowed to the point that people had to be ferried to the main house by boat. The very next evening, however, Wattles sponsored a dance for now 165 residents when a massive flash flood quickly washed out the walls of the building and drowned most of the residents. Only fifteen individuals survived the flood.

Today some visitors to the location have claimed that the place is haunted. Several visitors have reported encountering ghosts at the site, and strange lights have been reported moving around or hear the river's edge. Even if untrue, reports like this serve very well to intensify the curiosity of tourists.

There are very few remains of Utopia's architectural past in onsite except Wattle's underground church and a few ruins of other buildings. Several underground chambers are also on site, but their original purpose is uncertain. Only a few individuals still live in Utopia, and a small store and gas station is its only business establishment. In 1975, a dredging operation brought up bricks from the original house, and the foundation is only visible when the Ohio River level is very

Each phalanx would be three square miles in size and have its own library, school, stables, and farmland.

Fourier's notion of an ideal commune was that all work and profit would be shared equally.

low. In 2003, the State of Ohio erected a historical marker to commemorate the interesting history of the town.

Even with the name, the town of Utopia seems to have fallen away.

For Further Reading

Holloway, Mark. (1966). *Heavens on Earth: Utopian Communities in America, 1680-1880*. New York: Dover Publications.

Pitzer, Donald E. (1997). The New Moral World of Robert Owen and New Harmony. *American Communal Utopias.* Donald E. Pitzer, ed. Chapel Hill, NC: The University of North Carolina Press, 88-134.

http://wwwroadsideamerica.com/story/11893

Western American Trek: Determined Interlopers

"Go West, young man, go West, and grow up with the country," is a statement attributed to American journalist, Horace Greeley (1811-1872). The intent of the statement reflected the American notion that if things did not work out in the eastern part of the country, one could always head west. The future of the country was perceived by many as being located anywhere west of the Mississippi River. Truly the conquest of the American West is one of the greatest adventure stories in the country's history.

Marion County, Kansas, is the crossroad of two famous western American trails, the Santa Fe Trail and Chisholm Trail.

By the 1830s, the wheels of heavily loaded wagons cut deep ruts in the dirt of the Great Plains on the east side of the Rocky Mountains. The great western trek was in full force. Only two years later, however, water travel came of age and boats like the Yellowstone ascended the Missouri River to Fort Pierre in what is now South Dakota. For the next half-century thousands of excited American settlers and adventurers travelled through Indian country in hopes of fulfilling their dreams.

The challenges faced by these western bound idealists were immense. Rivers, like the mighty Missouri, had to be forded, mountain trails had to be conquered, and wagons were constantly in need of repair. In addition, travellers were often attacked by Indian tribes who were annoyed by the incoming streams of interlopers and trespassers. When the California Gold Rush of 1949 reached its peak, population growth was so rapid that California was granted statehood without the necessity of first going through the territorial phase. Thoroughfares like the Oregon Trail became famous simply because of the sheer numbers that traversed it. Between 1841 and 1867, more than 350 000 people made the trek westward. Their numbers swelled from only a trickle in 1841 to a high of almost 50 000 in 1852. These brave souls endured rugged territory, annoying mosquitoes, strong winds and the heat of the burning sun for the reward of homesteading on fertile farming lands near rich forests, amid Oregon's mild climate.

"Go West, young man, go West, and grow up with the country."

Fort Benton, Montana, located near the north end of the Missouri grew rapidly because of trade with St. Louis at the other end of the Missouri River. Soon there were 10 000 people living in Fort Benton. Thousands of immigrants and miners marked this landing as the place to obtain supplies that were shipped north from St. Louis. In 1868, thirty-nine steamers unloaded 8,000 tons of freight and 10 000 passengers at Fort Benton. One steamboat returned to St. Louis with 1.5 million dollars worth of gold. Then trains came. The Union Pacific Railroad made a fortune outfitting settlers, and St. Louis expanded its parameters on fortunes made in the fur trade.

These brave souls endured rugged territory, annoying mosquitoes, strong winds and the heat of the burning sun . . .

The American Civil war temporarily halted westward expansion, but when the war ended, the westward trek resumed. Once again, the lifestyle of Native Americans was upset, and governments were not always just in their dealings with them. Often volunteer but untrained soldiers were solicited to stave off Indian raids and decades of American history were riddled with conflict and bloodshed. Eventually the American army sent Confederate soldiers into Indian territories to assist settlers, and for a while it looked as though the army had won – but only for a while. Sioux Chief Red Cloud's warriors were defeated by the army's new breech-loading rifles, but the Battle of the Little Big Horn of 1876 belonged to the Sioux and the Cheyenne. It was only with the unjust military fiasco of 1890 at Wounded Knee that journalists could announce the end of Indian resistance. The West was now officially open for business. For the incoming settlers, Utopian dreams were finally being fulfilled.

No discussion of America's treatment of Native Americans can omit reference to the Oklahoma Land Rush of 1889. Having convinced itself that the Indians were not making proper or full use of western agricultural lands, the government of the United States through the Department of the Interior yielded up some two million acres (8 000 square kilometres) of land for eager settlers. On April 22 of that year, an estimated 10 000 people lined up for their piece of paradise. At noon, they took off to the sound of an army bugle, heading west on horseback, in horse-drawn wagons, and even on foot. Soon only a cloud of dust remained at the starting line. Later it would be discovered that some settlers had come early and laid claim to some of the best land before the day of the land rush. Some estimate that as many as nine tenths of these settlers had arrived the day before, and never joined the "chariot race" on the approved day. In any event, even for these illegal interlopers, paradise had been gained, and Native Americans had again been shortchanged.

Utopia for many, it sems, is sometimes gained at the expense of others.

Utopia for many, it seems, is sometimes gained at the expense of other people.

For Further Reading

Brown, Dee. (1996). *History of the American West.* New York; Simon and Schuster.

Milner II, Clyde A., Carol A. O'Connor, and Martha A. Sandweiss. (1996). *The Oxford History of the American West.* New York: Oxford University Press; Reprint edition.

Utley, Robert M. (1984). *The Indian Frontier of the American West, 1846-1860.* Albuquerque, NM: University of New Mexico Press.

http://www.essortment.com/all/oklahomalandru_rccj.htm
http://www.library.cornell.edu/Reps/DOCS/landrush.htm

Part Two
Communal Utopias

...somewhat unusual exper-
...f them inspired by 17th
...hose North America as a
...ms of idyllic living. All of
...e exception of Hutterites,
...ippie haven in Tennesee.
...udy of each community
...pursuit of human visions.
...inventors will underscore
...lustrate possible implica-

Amana

Although the "Community of True Inspiration," as the members this group called themselves, folded

[handwritten annotations in margin:]
Amana, virtually, intact, informative, peasant, lath, forefront, secularization, breakaway, contrive, abstinence, temperance, wakeful, reprimand, expulsion, regimented, stipend, coffer, nuptial, institute

onslaught, toll, implement, dissolve, probation, excommunication, rung, banishment, lodge, aligning, waned

...kommen! to Amana colonies The Hand-
...ed Escape. Welcome to Amana Colonies,
...tional historic landmark made up of seven
...es located just off I-80 in Iowa.

...ld be shipped to
...were also sold to
...s, soap, lumber,
...es was specifical-
...cart between the
...ght. Instead, vis-
...bile, dine in style
...ops, or purchase
...p-to-date stores.
...lore, such as the
...d the traditional
...est of the seven
...needs including
...lights include the
...and Clock Shop,
...gh Amana Store,
...rs to the Amana
...ist annual num-

...Germany in the middle of the 19th century with two names at the forefront.

Each of the seven villages was specifically designed to be about an hour's ride by ox-cart between the vilages, but today there are no ox-carts in sight.

The first, was Christian Metz (1794-1867), and second was Barbara Heinemann (1795-1883). Heinemann served as spiritual leader (prophetess) of the Amana group after Metz died. She held her post until her death at the age of 88 in 1883. After she passed away a spirit of secularization set in and no spiritual successor was named. Two other individuals who influenced the origins of the theology of the Inspirationists were Eberhard Ludwig Gruber and Johann Friedrich Rock, but it was Christian Metz who led the group to America.

> *Communal living mandates living close to one's neighbors, an arrangement that requires a great deal of patience and cooperation.*

Primarily a breakaway group from the Lutheran Church, persecution motivated the Inspirationists to seek refuge in America. Originally Metz had a vision from God to settle his 350 followers in New York in 1842, but controversy about pushing local Indians off of their land, led Metz to contrive another vision that took the group to Iowa. Here, on 26 000 acres some of the best farmland in the country, the Amana people built their villages and developed a series of profitable industries. Best known, perhaps was the Amana kitchen appliance company, started in the 1930s by two Amana individuals and then overtaken by the Amana society. The company was sold to private ownership in 1950.

Communal living mandates living close to one's neighbors, an arrangement that requires a great deal of patience and cooperation. Naturally, communal living requires that an

Amana Barn Restaurant offers Amana food featuring German specialties.

Built in 1865, the *Amana Community Church* building in Homestead represents the religious practices and beliefs of the Amana Community of True Inspiration Church.

abundance of regulations be implemented for everyone to obey so that order can be maintained. Although most of Metz' rules were quite reasonable in nature, he did design some rather unique regulations. His list of "twenty-one rules for the examination of our daily lives," begins with "Obey without reasoning, God, and through God your superiors," and ends with these two: "Dinners, weddings, and feasts, avoid entirely; at the best there is sin," and "Constantly practice abstinence and temperance, so that you may be as wakeful after eating as before." In principle all day-to-day decisions that affected village life were made by a group of four or five older men in the community, and their rule was more or less absolute. Penalties for disobedience ranged from reprimand to public ridicule to permanent expulsion.

Heritage Designs Needlework and Quilting – a quilter's inspirational paradise.

Amana Woolen Mill, established in the 1850's in "main" Amana, is Iowa's only woolen mill. Weaving the woolens has long been an important part of Amana's heritage.

Daily activities were fairly regimented by a breakfast bell announcing the first daily meal at six-thirty in the morning with the meal served simultaneously in 15 dining halls. Kitchen duties were under the supervision of one of the older women in each respective village. Everyone downed their food as fast as possible, then thanks to God were said, and each individual went off to his or her place of work. Amana society members were granted a small stipend of cash for their labors, and beyond that their various needs were met from community coffers.

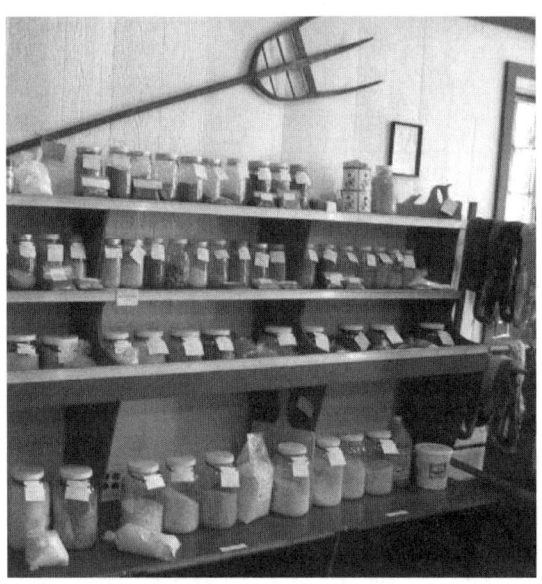

Metz established a formal ruling council made up of only males to preside over certain activities such as setting standards regarding marriage. This arrangement suggests that an unhealthy dose of sexism was inherent in community operations. The council set specific regulations about dating and courtship because Metz was concerned about lax behavior on the part of village youth. There were a few instances of young women getting pregnant before they married, so Metz mandated that premarital sex was forbidden and couples were required to obtain permission from the council before they could wed. If a couple was granted permission, they had to wait a year before their nuptials could be performed, and they were allowed to date only three times a week. Young men were not permitted to marry before the age of twenty-four.

Bulk natural food for sale at Henry's Village Market in Homestead.

An interesting arrangement was instituted about death at Amana, namely that burial sites were selected chronologically, regardless of family connections. When an individual passed on, he or she was simply buried next to the last burial site. After all, the Bible mandates that in heaven all believers will be regarded as equal (Matthew 22:30). Why not practice that belief on earth?

Everything was shared in Amana. Each individual was assigned a job to do and was expected to do it well. Village members ate their meals together, sent their children to the same single-sex schools, and attended the same village church. Children learned to perform the three "R's," and instrumental music was forbidden. Instruction was undertaken in English for five days of the week and German was taught on the sixth.

The onslaught of World War I took its toll on Amana. This influence was evident in the community in a myriad of ways. Clothing styles, for example, began to change to more modern apparel, and because of increased industrialization Amana mills were faced with the challenge of having to undergo extensive changes toward modernization. Required renovations were were very expensive so elaborate plans to make changes were drawn up. Before these could be implemented, however, one of the mills unexpectedly burned down. Then came the Great Depression that also negatively affected Amana sales, so the society fell into heavy debt. The solution was to reorganize as a joint stock company and abandon communalism, but keep the people together as a religious sect.

When the Amana Society as a commercial enterprise was dissolved in 1932, there were 1 365 members, down from a peak of 1 813 in 1881. Occasionally outsiders would seek membership in the Amana society, and they would be required to serve a period of probation before being admitted. On occasion individuals would be asked to leave the community if they deliberately and consistently violated the rules. The process to determine that an individual should be asked to leave was thorough, and proceeded step by step. At first the deviant would be reprimanded, first privately, and then publically. If there was no change in behavior, the council of elders would proceed to the next step. The last rung in the process was excommunication and perhaps banishment from the society. To make things fair, once a year everyone in the community was "called on the carpet" for spiritual examination, including elders. If a complaint against anyone was lodged it would have to be examined by the appropriate body of elders who would determine an appropriate action.

During the last years of Amana's operation, a trend toward modernization became evident. Young men now played baseball, and even card games, and young women adopted contemporary hairstyles and donned brightly colored clothing. The advent of the railroad brought new business acquaintances, visitors, and other influences to Amana. These

Everything was shared in Amana. Each individual was assigned a job to do and was expected to do it well.

developments assisted in aligning Amana philosophy with emerging American individualism. With dissolution, individuals began to purchase farms outside the villages and young people took day jobs in nearby communities. Gradually the religious teachings of German Separatism waned as the Amana people began to assimilate into mainstream America.

Today the Amana Society flourishes as a private enterprise with shareholders who are descendents of the original communalists. Although the American Amana commune officially lasted 89 years, the community recently celebrated its 150th anniversary, and its 300th anniversary as a religious organization.

The highlight of this organization's history and uniqueness can easily be captured by a visit to the site.

For Further Reading

Andelson, Jonathan G. (1997). The Community of True Inspiration from Germany to the Amana Colonies. *American Communal Utopias*. Donald E. Pitzer, ed. Chapel Hill, NC: The University of North Carolina Press, 181-203.

Claeys, Gregory, and Lyman Tower Sargent, editors. (1999). *The Utopian Reader.* New York: New York University Press.

Crum, Dorothy. (1998). *Life in Amana, 1867-1935: Reporters' Views of the Communal Way.* Iowa City, IA: Penfield Press.

Fogarty, Robert S. (1980). *Dictionary of American Communal and Utopian History.* Westport, CN: Greenwood Press.

Gutek, Gerald, and Patricia Gutek. (1998). *Visiting Utopian Communities: A Guide to Shakers, Moravians, and Others.* Columbia, SC: University of South Carolina Press.

Liffring-Zig, Joan. (1975). *The Amanas of Yesterday: A Religious Communal Society.* Iowa City, IA: Penfield Press.

Holloway, Mark. 1966). *Heavens on Earth: Utopian Communities in America, 1680-1880.* New York: Dover Publications.

Nordhoff, Charles. (1993). *American Utopias.* Stockbridge, MS: Berkshire House Publishers.

Shambaugh, Bertha M.H. (1988). *Amana: The Community of True Inspiration.* Ames, IA: State Historical Society of Iowa.

Yambura, Barbara with Eunice Willis Bodine. (1960). *A Change and a Parting: My Story of Amana.* Ames, IA: The Iowa State University Press.

http://www.nps.gov/history/nr/travel/amana/utopia.htm

Back-to-the-Landers

When World War II ended, Canadians and Americans found it necessary to regroup and redefine social values in preparation for a somewhat unpredictable future. The happy-go-lucky television shows of the 1950s did little to assist in the search for new social values, founded as they were on shallow, frivolous, unrealistic family structures. Family television shows portrayed every member of the group as very happy, very agreeable, and quite phony. In truth, none of this really happened; families in the 1950s struggled with the same challenges that families always had. They struggled, argued and fought, and in between, enjoyed some good times. Family life in the 1950s was not all peaches and cream!

McKenzie Beach Resort is the oldest year-round resort in Tofino, British Columbia.

Then came the 1960s. This was the decade in which North American youth questioned the renewed sense of capitalism that had emerged after the war with its underlying design to rebuild what the two nations – Canada and the United States – had lost during World War II. A myriad of social movements originated featuring government and college protests, religious realignments, civil rights campaigns, and the formation of alternative lifestyles. The back-to-the-landers movement constituted one particular reaction to the treadmill of conformist-type middle class living that had evolved, and it literally attracted thousands of North American youth. Individuals of this persuasion represented a wide range of lifestyles.

One particular group of back-to-the-landers simply decided to spend weekends in the country, occupying small plots of land on which they parked beat-up trailers or quickly constructed sheds. They spent most of the weekend working on the land mending fences, growing gardens, or tending ani-

Their experiments in building a better society sometimes included use of solar power, composting toilets, and using photovoltaic cells and retrofitted superinsulation.

mals they managed to raise in their spare time. Vacation time was spent entirely in the country.

A second kind of back-to-the-landers included those who spent their entire summers on the land and then moved back to the city for the winter where they usually found employment in service related occupations. Some of these folk were hoping to retire early so they could spend all of their time on the land. Some of the more ambitious families tried to remain on the land year-round and operate small businesses from their homes or in a nearby small town. Mainly they were content to do little more than eek out a living from the land, not prosper economically.

Back-to-the-Landers occupied this beach area during the 1960s.

Back-to-the-Landers built homes from available materials.

A third type of back-to-the-landers were more daring. They actually tried to make a living entirely in rural areas. Their goal was to be completely self-sufficent. They grew their own food, sewed their own clothes, raised a few cattle or sheep, burned wood for fuel, and built a lifestyle that virtually resembled that of the pioneers who lived a century before them. As time went on, however, these communities developed parallel social structures to those operating in urban centers. They published newsletters, organized community meetings, and raised protests against various dominant societal developments. Their experiments in building a better society sometimes included use of solar power, composting toilets, and using photovoltaic cells and retrofitted superinsulation.

There is little doubt about it; had this segment of society been more keenly listened to, significant benefits might have accrued that were only much later on taken up by the proponents of the "going green" campaign of the twenty-first century.

Perhaps the more intriguing social sectior of the back-to-the-landers movement of the 1960s were called hippies, so labelled because of their complete abandonment of all things social – sometimes including clothing. The hippie movement seems to have originated in protest against the American involvement in the Vietnam War, thus producing a new protest group called draft dodgers.

The Vietnam War seemed to drag on with no end in sight, and in the meantime hundreds of youth were called on to engage in military combat for no valid reason – at least according to the hippies. In reaction to this injustice, hundreds of American youth fled the country in search of alternative places to live. In Canada, British Columbia's west coast seemed to be a desirable resting place, and a large contingent of hippies migrated there to build ramshackle dwellings near the town of Tofino on Vancouver Island. To onlookers they resembled scruffy-looking, drug-using, astrology-oriented misfits who engaged in continual sex relations. They apparently lived on yogurt and sunflower seeds and sold candles and beads on town sidewalks to passers by. But the duration of their subculture was relatively short-lived. Within two decades virtually no sign remained of this subculture, most of the members having either moved back to the United States or joined the Canadian middle class of small shop owners.

Back to the land meant back to the good old days.

Urban-living people tried a modern homesteading life frequently in semi-wilderness environments. Consequently, as an example, raising sheep for wool (carding, dyeing and drying) was part of life.

For true Back-to-the-Landers, no scrap of material was discarded; as the last go-round in the life of a piece of fabric, Grandma carefully pieced it into a quilt.

Further inland, closer to the Canadian plains, hippie numbers were significantly smaller, probably because of the inclement weather on the plains. There were protests, to be sure, some of them targetting university life and in general accusing non-hippies of giving in to middle class conformity. A bank of computers was smashed at Sir George Williams University, and the toilets at Simon Fraser University were plugged in protest. In Calgary, Alberta, a group of hippies took over a local park until the family who had donated the park threatened the city with legal action unless the squatters were removed.

Then, as always, when the storm subsided and normalcy set in, the hippie movement disappeared, and the back-to-the-landers began to exhibit an almost enviable lifestyle. Increasing numbers of people began to consider that pursuit of the North American dream might not be worth it after all. Committing to a treadmill mentality just did not seem sensible. Many former hippie families had children who did not share their parents' rebellious orientations and even joined the ranks of the capitalist world. Others joined the New Age movement or promoted the greening of North America cause. Life in North America seemed to return to "normal," then shifted to the reality of financial cut-backs in the 1980s and 1990s.

Utopian forms of lifestyles, like all others, seem to have to cope with perpetual crises, forced changes, and internal challenges.

Utopian forms of lifestyles, like all others, seem to have to cope with perpetual crises, forced changes, and internal challenges.

For Further Reading

Coontz. Stephanie. (1992). *The Way We Never Were: American Families and the Nostalgia Trip.* New York: Basic Books.

Jacob, Jeffrey. (1997). *New Pioneers: The Back-to-the-Land Movement and the Search for a Sustainable Future.* University Park, PA: The Pennsylvania State University Press.

Miller, Timothy. (1999). *The 60s Communes: Hippies and Beyond.* Syracuse, NY: Syracuse University Press.

Scott, Andrew. (1997). *The Promise of Paradise: Utopian Communities in B.C.* Vancouver, BC: Whitecap Books.

Spencer, Metta. (1990). *Foundations of Modern Sociology.* Scarborough, ON: Prentice-Hall Canada.

http://www.knowledgerush.com/kr/encyclopedia/Back-to-the-landers/

http://cr.middlebury.edu/es/altenergylife/definition.htmbstract.html?res=9C01EFD81F3BE633A25750C2A9679C946596D6CF

Bethel

Elim. The house built in 1848 for Bethel's founder, Wilhelm Keil.

Fest Hall Restaurant, Bethel, MO is famous for home-cooked German and American meals and is still open today seven days a week.

Most utopian experiments initiated during the past two centuries seem to have been developed on the basis of someone's dream or vision.

The origin of Bethel Village in Missouri is a case in point, having been spawned by the dream of a very unusual individual named Wilhelm Keil (1812-1877). Dr. Wilhelm Keil, as he liked to call himself, was a charismatic self-styled doctor and immigrant preacher who claimed miraculous powers derived from a book written in blood. His explanation was that a mysterious woman in Germany known for her healing powers, had provided him with his book of magical cures only on condition that, having received information on the healing powers, he leave the country.

Keil managed to attract a group of dissidents who had been part of the Harmony Society of Pennsylvania (which will be described later), and formed a more lenient community, free from imposed celibacy and stringent regulations. Keil was born in Ehrfurth, Prussia, and in 1836, at the age of 24 he married Luise Ritter who remained his most faithful supporter.

> The commune's most profitable industry was the distillation of corn and rye whiskey, a product which they marketed for twenty-five cents a gallon.

That same year the couple migrated to the United States where Keil was converted to Christianity through the evangelistic efforts of William Nast, the "Father of German Methodism." Although Keil initially joined the Methodists as a probationary preacher, he was soon expelled for his outspoken views on the role of clergy. He believed that ministers should not accept salaries nor should they be granted ecclesiastical authority. Later he took it upon himself to condemn all religious denominations and became an independent preacher who emphasized a non-institutionalized form of simple, pietistic Christianity. His favorite books of the Bible were Daniel and Revelation, both much given to prophecy. Keil himself predicted the Second Coming of Christ several times but always found it necessary to revise his prophesies.

The *Colony School House* at Bethel, MO built in 1876.

Keil's preaching tours brought him into contact with former Harmonists and together with them and a few dozen followers, moved to Missouri in 1844 to organize a new Christian commune. Keil's adherents dutifully sold their properties and followed him to Bethel, Missouri. Two years later the community numbered 600. Keil eventually wrote up a constitution (which was never signed), and personally arranged tasks for everyone to perform. He appointed overseers to manage the affairs of the community, and it is said that he himself labored right alongside other colony workers. Agricultural in basis, the Bethel settlement also raised cattle and sheep. The managers also organized or built a tannery, distillery, gristmill, sawmill, woolen mill, general store and a post office. Within a very short time they were virtually self-sustaining.

Das Grosse Haus, Bethel, MO. Unmarried male members lived on the second floor. The first floor housed a tavern, which welcomed colonists and travellers alike.

Bethel-made plows became quite popular throughout the American Midwest, and gloves made in the colony won first prize at the world's fair in 1858. The commune's most profitable industry was the distillation of corn and rye whiskey, a product which they marketed for twenty-five cents a gallon.

Daily activities in Bethel were quite typical of the lifestyle in small towns across America, although tourists complained that the place was unkempt. Grunting pigs foraged everywhere, and no one gave much attention to personal appearance. Apparently, the Bethelites took life easy – a bit too easy according to visitors. Still, village life went on; couples got married and gave birth to children, and each family had their own house, garden plot, and barn in which to raise pigs and chickens. Keil advocated that village life should follow the principles of obedience, love, cleanliness, plain living, and economy. He used his bimonthly Sunday sermons in the colony church to encourage his followers to abide by these principles and to publically admonish transgressors. Keil rejected the Sacraments of Holy Baptism and the Eucharist, and preached sermons quite literally based on Biblical content.

Colony Bake Oven, Bethel, MO. The colony had several community bake ovens such as the reconstructed one in this photo. The women who baked the community's bread set up a schedule.

A village school was opened in 1876 to provide children with instruction in the English language. Several youth were encouraged to attend a nearby college in order to return home and provide leadership in essential areas. The school continued to offer classes until 1913.

In due course a special house, *Das Grosse Haus,* (The Big House) was built for William Keil. In addition to providing living quarters to Keil and his wife, the main floor of the house served as a hotel, restaurant, guesthouse, and boarding house. The second floor was occupied by unmarried male members. The house was (and is) equipped with four lightening rods, which Keil for some religious reason disallowed on members' homes. Keil frequently entertained guests at Bethel while remaining legal, religious, and social head of the community.

Music constituted a vital part of Bethel life, and even today the village band offers a series of public concerts including a fiddle camp, a summer youth concert, and a Christmas arts festival. The village also sponsors an annual wildflowers and fiber arts festival featuring spinning exhibits, sheep shearing contests, llama exhibitions, educational displays, and delicious feasts. During Keil's reign, a band of some thirty performers sometimes played to an audience of five thousand. Hymns, classical German music, dance tunes, and folk songs were part of the band's repertoire, and visitors came from miles around to hear them perform.

Band Stand, Bethel, MO. The home stage of the Bethel German Band, the oldest and still thriving community band west of the Mississippi.

In due course William Keil grew restless and decided to organize a branch colony in Aurora, Oregon. Some sources suggest that objections to his rule arose in Bethel and he felt it best to "get out of town." Others suggest that he was concerned with too many worldly visitors frequenting the town and he feared that their presence might have a negative impact on his children. In any event, in May 1855, Keil led a caravan of 25 wagons and 75 people some 2 000 miles across the plains along the famous Oregon Trail. Accompanying the caravan was a casket filled with alcohol containing the body of Keil's 19 year-old son, Willie, who longed to go to Oregon but died before the journey commenced. Keil had promised Willie that he would see the great northwest, and so the caravan carried his body along as fulfillment of the promise. What could have been hostile Indians along the way did not transpire because they were too much filled with wonderment about the strange casket the party had with them.

Daily activities in Bethel were quite typical of the lifestyle in small towns across America, although tourists complained that the place was unkempt.

When the Bethelites arrived in the northwest they settled at Willapa, Washington, where they buried Willie. Keil soon decided that he did not like the location and so began a new settlement at Aurora, Oregon, so named after his daughter. Half of Keil's flock followed him to Aurora, where he appointed deputies to help him maintain sole charge of both settlements. He also held all property in his own name although he allegedly governed with a board of trustees. Under Keil's direction a new town soon arose at Aurora including all of the amenities required at that period in history – a hotel, a church, and a variety of vocational and trade buildings. By 1872 the commune included 1 000 adherents and held title to 23 000 acres of land. The colony hotel and restaurant were famous throughout Oregon Territory, and the rich musical traditions of Bethel were also established in Aurora. The group who remained at Willapa very quickly dwindled in numbers and disappeared.

In 1872 Keil probably realized that the colony would not thrive without him so he subdivided the communal property by giving deeds to the male member of each family. Three of Keil's own children were still alive at the time, but none of them showed any interest in living in Aurora. Most of the young people their age had already left Aurora as soon as they were able to sustain themselves economically.

There was also tragedy in the Aurora Colony. Between November 22 December 14, 1862, four of Keil's children died of smallpox,

Old Aurora Colony Commercial Building.

Aurora Train Station.

The houses and buildings from the Aurora Colony, including the Old Aurora Colony Museum, represent one of the largest concentrations of structures built by German craftsmen in the Pacific Northwest.

A sketch of the *Frederick Keil House* by Clark Moor Will. The home of William Keil's son built about 1862 still survives.

The typical Aurora Colony village home has a Classical Revival Style, and was constructed about 1864.

This wagon was used in Aurora about the turn of the twentieth century, it is rumored to have been a delivery wagon for the hotel as early as the mid-1880s.

The Aurora colony lathe is the museum's most impressive tool. It was used to turn the spool pattern so common to Aurora bedposts and pillars. Aurora's furniture was not as "plain" in comparison to many other American communal groups.

brought into the settlement by a member of the group who had gone to help a neighbor striken with the disease.

William Keil died on December 30, 1877, and soon after both the Bethel and

Aurora colonies dissolved, Bethel in 1879 and Aurora in 1883. The small town of Bethel, Missouri, continues to function and the Aurora Museum which was organized in 1956 and dedicated in 1966 is a must visit. Visitors to both places will be delighted to find excellent published guides that will explain the history and major features of the colonies as they walk about the grounds.

Few communal experiments in North America can boast such an unusual history.

For Further Reading

Arndt, Karl J. (1997). George Rapp's Harmony Society. *America's Communal Utopias.* Donald E. Pitzer, ed. Chapel Hill, NC: The University of North Carolina Press, 57-87.

Gutek, Gerald, and Patricia Gutek. (1998). *Visiting Utopian Communities: A Guide to Shakers, Moravians, and Others.* Columbia, SC: University of South Carolina Press.

Holloway, Mark. (1966). *Heavens on Earth: Utopian Communities in America, 1680-1880.* New York: Dover Publications.

Nordhoff, Charles. (1993). *American Utopias.* Stockbridge, MS: Berkshire House Publishers.

Schroeder, Adolf E. (1990). *The Musical Life of Bethel German Colony, 1844-1879*. Bethel, MO: Historic Bethel German Colony.

Schroeder, Adolf E. (1990). *Bethel German Colony, 1844-1883*. Bethel, MO: Historic Bethel German Colony.

Schroeder, Adolf E. (1990). *Bethel German Colony, 1844-1879: Religious Beliefs and Practices.* Bethel, MO: Historic Bethel German Colony.

Snyder, Eugene Edmund. (1993). *Aurora, Their Last Utopia: Oregon's Christian Commune, 1856-1883.* Portland, OR: Binford & Mort Publishing.

Sutton, Robert P. (2003). *Communal Utopias and the American Experience: Religious Communities, 1732-2000.* Westport, CN: Praeger.

http://www.bethel.macaa.net/vp/upVau/welcome.html
http://en.wikipedia.org/wiki/Bethel,_Missouri

Bishop Hill

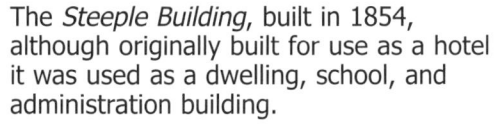

The *Steeple Building*, built in 1854, although originally built for use as a hotel it was used as a dwelling, school, and administration building.

The common room and dining room in the *Apartment House* built in 1855.

Located 157 miles south-west of Chicago is a restored 19th century immigrant settlement that looks much like a transplanted Swedish village. Elegantly constructed classic structures onsite that were built to accommodate a communal way of life seem out of place in a contemporary Midwest farming community. The commune only lasted fifteen years, but its testimony is well preserved as a state historic site. Sixteen of the original buildings have recently been restored.

Bishop Hill was founded in 1846 by a group of Swedish immigrants who followed Erik Jansson (1808-1850) to America. In 1830, at the age of twenty-two, Jansson fell from a horse and through the experience obtained a vision from God telling him to become a preacher. Jansson was a charismatic though uneducated farmer and travelling wheat salesman, but he had the ability to fire up his followers to live out their religious convictions. The separatists he attracted held meetings without clergy present, a move that was not approved by the Swedish Lutheran Church. State officials sent police to break up their meetings, but the group persisted. Clerical opposition soon led to Jansson and his adherents

The commune grew cotton and flax, Indian corn and broom-corn, and other crops suited to the soil and climate of the locale.

being ousted from the state church. Church officials called Jansson's beliefs heretical, but Jansson as it turned out, did not advocate doctrines that were much different than those of many fundamentalist religious groups in the United States at the time. To the Swedish clergy, however, Jansson's ideas were considered false and dangerous. Perhaps the fact that he called himself "the prophet endowed with all the perfections of God" justified some of the theological complaints against him.

Jansson proclaimed that individuals could actually become perfect by being transformed through God's Holy Spirit. He came upon this doctrine having often been tempted to be unfaithful to his wife. He claimed that as a result of their being sanctified by God's Spirit, individuals could forever be free from sin. Jansson declared that it was by being sanctified that he ceased being tempted. He also claimed that the Bible was the only true source of Christian beliefs, and all church dogma and traditions were to be avoided. In fact, he and his followers burned religious literature published by the Swedish state clergy, an act that did nothing to endear him to them. When Jansson came across the Constitution of the United States he was impressed with its guarantee of religious freedom and immediately decided that this was the country in which he wanted to build a New Jerusalem. A friend of his, Olof Olsson, travelled on ahead to America to find a location for the experiment, and was soon able to report that he had found the ideal place.

In the spring of 1846, some 1 500 individuals followed Jansson to Henry County in Illinois. They sold their goods to pay for passage and boarded a ship to New York, then travelled on to Chicago by steamer.

The *Colony School*, built in 1861 was used from 1861 to 1953 when it was closed.

The group walked the last one hundred miles to Bishop Hill, the site of their envisaged utopia. Here the plan was to manage a sizable farm and engage in a variety of related careers. The good news was that the travellers retained more than

$10 000 in their possession even after paying for their passage to America. With it they purchased 200 acres of choice farmland located in the heart of the Illinois Midwest. Not all of Jansson's followers moved to Bishop Hill, however, several hundreds of them having chosen to stay in New York when

The *Colony Store* built in 1853 was both store and post office for the Colony. Today it is bustling with tourists buying up an array of locally crafted goods.

The *Colony Church* built in 1848 is one of the oldest buildings in Bishop Hill. The basement and ground floor together have twenty rooms and each room was used as living space for a family.

their ship landed. Sadly many adherents lost their lives in a subsequent outbreak of cholera in September 1849.

Bishop Hill, named after the town in which Jansson was born, became prosperous within five years with a population of 800 souls. By 1859 the society owned ten thousand acres of land with a debt load of less than one hundred thousand dollars. To their credit, they also constructed an impressive town. In addition to farmers, the settlement included several carpenters, wheelwrights, and shoemakers, as well as a carriage builder, a miller, and a harness maker. In order to keep population numbers under control, Jansson insisted that celibacy be practiced and married couples refrain from having marital relations. He also assigned single men and women to live in separate dwellings. In 1848 he lifted the marriage ban

It is a fortunate day for the tourist who lands a quiet day at the broom making shop to enjoy a personal step by step craft demonstration from straw to a tightly-sewn broom you can proudly use in your home.

and shortly thereafter fifty-nine couples entered the blissful state of matrimony.

The largest building at Bishop Hill, named *Big Brick*, contains seventy-two family rooms with several dining rooms. According to Jansson's rules, all meals were to be eaten in silence, punctuated by prayers uttered by Jansson at the beginning and end of each meal. Each morning, after devotions, everyone set about their assigned tasks. The commune grew cotton and flax, Indian corn and broom-corn, and other crops suited to the soil and climate of the locale. Commune leaders arranged for the construction of a four-mile railroad extension to the nearest railway depot so they could ship sale goods easily. They were successful cattlemen and could boast a highly skilled labor force of men and women who could take on virtually any agriculturally related task. By 1862 the commune owned assets totaling $846 278.00, all of which had to be dissolved during the years following with the unexpected death of their leader.

Janson's death occurred this way. A dispute over a man's wife did Jansson in. Jansson tried to break up a marriage between his cousin Charlotta and a recent convert named John Root. The agreement was that after marriage, Root and Charlotta would remain in the colony. It turned out that this was not Root's intention. Shortly after the wedding Root left the colony with his wife and Jansson and a group of men followed and brought the new bride back. Root then surrounded the commune and threatened to burn the place down if Jansson did not give him back his wife. Eventually, Root was chased away and Charlotta remained in the commune. Later, however, Root shot Jansson in the head while he was attending to a matter in the local courthouse. Jansson's followers placed Jansson's corpse on the church altar hoping he would be resurrected as he had promised. Soon, however, for obvious reasons, his body had to be buried.

In 1850, after Jansson died, the people of Bishop Hill appointed a group of seven trustees to run their affairs. Among the trustees were Jonas Olsson and Olof Johnson, who became the primary leaders of the commune; they had been two of Jansson's closest confidants. For a time the colony continued to grow and flourish, even better than it had under Jansson's leadership. No one had to work particularly hard and when the day's chores were done, everyone enjoyed a fair measure of leisure time. Visitors commented on the kind and receptive spirit that prevailed in the settlement. In 1857, however, financial problems arose stemming from accusations of mismanagement against Olof Johnson. It happened that Johnson had privately made several large investments without colony approval, all of which ended in financial disaster. It soon became apparent that Bishop Hill was headed for economic ruin, and without trustworthy leadership to guide them the colonists voted to end the communal system. The lure of mainstream American life also drew many away from communalism and weakened the hold of leaders on their membership.

When Bishop Hill eventually dissolved many of its people were forced to move away. Some joined a nearby Shaker colony and others united with an Adventist movement. Still others followed noted American agnostic, Robert Ingersoll, in determining new direction for their lives.

Interest in restoring Bishop Hill dates back to 1875 although little effort was made to achieve that goal at that time. Finally, in 1962 the newly-formed Bishop Hill Society took steps to restore the site. The government of Sweden contributed to the effort and even issured a postage stamp to commemorate the life of the community.

In 2003 the State of Illinois declared Bishop Hill an historic site in order to preserve an intriguing part of America's past.

For Further Reading

Fogarty, Robert S., ed. (1980). *Dictionary of American Communal and Utopian History.* Westport, CN: Greenwood Press.

Gutek, Gerald, and Patricia Gutek. (1998). *Visiting Utopian Communities: A Guide to Shakers, Moravians, and Others.* Columbia, SC: University of South Carolina Press.

Nordhoff, Charles. (1993). *American Utopias.* Stockbridge, MS: Berkshire House Publishers.

Sutton, Robert P. (2003). *Communal Utopias and the American Experience: Religious Communities, 1732-2000.* Westport, CN: Praeger.

Wagner, Jon. (1997). Erik Jansson and the Bishop Hill Colony. *America's Communal Utopias.* Donald E. Pitzer, ed. Chapel Hill, NC: The University of North Carolina Press, 297-318.

http://www.bishophillartscouncil.com/

http://www.outfitters.com/illinois/henry/bishop_hill.html

Cannington Manor

"Wanted, young boys who are interested in learning how to farm; apply Cannington Manor, Saskatchewan."

The ad must have read something like that when Captain Edward Mitchell Pierce posted it as the drawing card to establishing the Cannington settlement in southeast Saskatchewan in 1882. Himself a British "gentleman and soldier," Pierce had been financially ruined by a bank failure in London, England, so the prospect of starting again in the great Canadian northwest greatly appealed to him. Although sometimes perceived as a commune, Cannington Manor was really a one-man show in terms of ownership even though everyone present pitched in to make the experiment a brief success. The theme of the experiment was Victorian, an unusual choice of lifestyle in the midst of the sparsely populated Canadian northwest.

A picture of what was once the main street of the village of Cannington Manor.

After arriving at his Canadian destination, Pierce settled his family in an available log house and set about forming his colony. In 1882 he offered to mentor young Englishmen of good birth and education in the profession of farming. Pierce believed that by attracting a few hundred young men each year he and his participants would be able to live a lifestyle similar to that of the English gentlefolk back home with only a few disadvantages. Pierce required a fee of somewhere between $500 and $1 000 for his supervisory services, but unfortunately his ads did not attract the protégés

The exterior of a Carrington house shows the simplicity of life for people who joined the group at Cannington Manor. This is the humble home of Cannington "bachelor" Arthur Le Mesurier, who settled permanently in the area.

he wanted. Instead a group of remittance men showed up who wanted to live the life of English gentlemen "in the colonies." These young men were bachelor sons of wealthy English families who, as it turned out, lived mainly on money sent to them by their families back home. For the most part they preferred play to work.

An air of romance was evident at Cannington Manor, as Pierce called it. The nearest railway line was nearly a dozen miles away so applicants really had to test their strength in moving farm produce for market by hand. Pierce's applicants came from several different communities including England and Scotland as well as from Ontario, Canada. However, few of them were prepared for the harsh challenges that waited them. Every candidate perceived the prospect of economic gain because Pierce had hinted that this was the land of milk and honey. Unfortunately, the dream was short-lived.

Much like the exterior of the houses, the house interiors were not ornate. Cannington Manor was the place where Edward Pierce proclaimed prospective settlers could "live like princes on the money required in England just for taxes."

A village did become a reality at Cannington Manor, and Pierce seems to have spent tuition monies well. The constructed structures included several quite impressive buildings such as a church and a community assembly building (which also operated as a school), as well as essential economic structures such as a grist-mill, blacksmith and wood-working shops, a hotel and post-office and a cooperative cheese factory. Pierce also founded the Moose Mountain Trading Company that was intended to serve as a vehicle for the assembly of commercial and service enterprises needed by the community. In 1883, the colony produced flour earned the community a gold medal at the World's Fair in Chicago.

Daily life at Cannington Manor emphasized a combination of work and play – but mostly play, it seems. James

Humphreys, a marine engineer from England, managed pork production at the settlement and arranged sales for the same in England. Two young men (Ernest and Billy Beckton), better known as the Beckton brothers were financed by their grandfather who had earned a fortune in textiles and quite willingly shared his wealth with his grandsons. The brothers used some of their inheritance to purchase 2 600 acres of land and build a private mansion – a palatial dwelling named "Didsbury." The house had twenty rooms, plus a bachelor wing with another five rooms. When the elder brother, Ernest married, he added a new wing with a billiard parlor to the Didsbury and it served as served as a sporting place for young bachelors. Here the occupants played billards, enjoyed drinks, read the newspapers, and cleaned guns for other guests. Their colony football team even won the 1891 Western Canadian rugby championship.

All the necessities of life were within arms reach.

The Beckton brothers frequently engaged in sports – cricket, hunting, football and tennis – which greatly appealed to the "drones" in the village, but there were other more cultural leisure activities as well. Choral music, poetry reading, painting and sketching, tea-time, and "scientific" discussions of politics and agriculture were also on the docket. Some residents engaged in such pastimes as theatrical productions, glee club, and literary activities. To add to the cultural repertoire of the colony, a foreman's house containing eighteen bunks for workers was built near the Didsbury, and foxhound kennels with thoroughbred dogs were nearby. An experienced jockey and head groom with highly respected credentials were retained.

Tea was served by local ladies in classic British style – on a tennis court with appropriate attire. Men were dressed in flannels and blazers, and women wore fancy summer frocks. A typical summer event was dining with friends or attending a private dance, card party, or midnight frolic. Discussions about politics and topics such as the South African War or the Klondike Gold Rush predominated. Eventually these activities dwindled when the Canadian Pacific Railroad built a spur line ten miles south, thus bypassing the settlement.

Pierce died unexpectedly in 1888, and without his leadership any sort of work ethic promptly disappeared. Most young male occupants in the community spent more time carousing and engaging in recreational activities. This reality, combined with lamentable local economic conditions – drought set in and grain prices deteriorated – severely threatened the existence of Cannington Manor, which soon virtually became a ghost town. Many local families had already relocated to the new village of Manor which appeared at the railroad spur line and only a few of Pierce's settlers remained onsite. In addition, the economic base of the colony was insufficient to finance all of the local leisure and cultural activities so Cannington Manor was doomed to fail. A few male occupants married local women and remained in the area while others returned to England.

At its peak the population of Cannington Manor had 200 occupants comprised of homesteaders, upperclass English families, and a group of young bachelors. When the end came, only a handful of residents remained.

All Saints Anglican Church built of local logs in June 1884.

Today tourists can visit Cannington Manor, walk the now near empty grounds, and marvel at the dream Pierce promoted – a Victorian high society in the midst of prairie brush. Several restored or newly built representative buildings may be viewed.

The Government of Saskatchewan through Tourism, Culture and Sport offers a series of one-day school-aimed educational programs at Cannington Manor entitled,

"Introduction to Cannington Manor, Daily Life at Cannington Manor, A Day at Cannington Manor," and "Life and Leisure at Cannington Manor."

Limited camping facilities are available.

For Further Reading

Douglas, R. Francis. (1989). *Images of the West: Changing Perceptions of the Prairies, 1690-1960.* Saskatoon, SK: Western Producer Prairie Books.

Owram, Doug. (1980). *Promise of Eden: The Canadian Expansionist Movement and the Idea of the Wes, 1856-1900.* Toronto, ON: University of Toronto Press.

Rasporich, A. W. (1977). *Utopian Ideals and Community Settlements in Western Canada: 1880-1914.The Canadian West.* Henry C. Klassen, ed. Calgary, AB: University of Calgary Press, 37-62.

http://www.gov.sk.ca/services/visitors/

http://www.virtualsk.com/current_issue/prairie_gentry.html-cyclopedia.com/index.cfm?PgNm=TCE&Params=A1ARTA0001351

"Wanted, young boys who are interested in learning how to farm apply Cannington Manor, Saskatchewan."

Doukhobors

DOUKHOBOR SHELTERS
УБЕЖИЩА ДУХОБОРЦЕВ

A NUMBER OF DOUKHOBOR FAMILIES ARRIVED FROM RUSSIA AT THE ONSET OF A BITTER WINTER IN 1899, IN WHAT IS NOW THE OOSPENIA DISTRICT. WITH LITTLE TIME TO BUILD HOUSES, SURVIVAL DEPENDED ON EMERGENCY SHELTER. MODIFIED DUGOUT CAVES (ZEMLANKIE), IN THE HILLSIDES OF THE NORTH SASKATCHEWAN RIVER VALLEY, AFFORDED SHELTER. AS HOUSES AND VILLAGES BEGAN TO BE CONSTRUCTED, THE DUGOUT SHELTERS WERE ABANDONED. ONE OF THE SIGNIFICANT SITES IN POPULATING THE SASKATCHEWAN PRAIRIES, THE 'CAVES' OFFER A GLIMPSE OF THE HARDSHIPS FACED BY EARLY SETTLERS.

Doukhobor Shelters, near Blaine Lake, Saskatchewan. Modified dugout caves provided shelter for Doukhobor people arriving from Russia in the winter of 1899.

Their original leader remains unnamed, but beliefs unique to the Doukhobors included communal living, rejection of clergy, pacifism to the point of being vegetarians, and the belief that each individual, regardless of age, sex, or color, has in them a Divine spark known as "Iskra."

It is quite challenging to trace the Doukhobor sojourn in Canada in so limited a space, since we have elsewhere published a full volume on the subject. It has been our privilege to have formed many long term friendships within the Doukhobor community so that we hold a fond appreciation for their ways. However, that is another story.

Doukhobors in Canada are probably among of the most misunderstood ethnic/religious communities in the nation's history. One of the reasons for this misunderstanding is because they once constituted the largest commune in Canada. At the peak of their economic success in British Columbia, the Doukhobor communal organization, The Christian Community of Universal Brotherhood (CCUB), consisted of some ten thousand people. Spread over three provinces, with amassed assets numbering in the millions of dollars. This was the case during a time when the country was involved in and supportive of two world wars, and the Doukhobors were a pacifist group. Many Canadians felt that the Doukhobors were not doing their part to help the war effort. Elements of American McCarthyism featuring a doctrine of intolerance for pacifist cultural and religious minorities, may also have spilled over into Canada, making life difficult for the Doukhobors.

The story begins in Russia where the Doukhobors originated in the 17th century. At that time the Russian Orthodox Church Archbishop Nikon introduced radical administrative and doctrinal changes in the church and many sects originated in protest. The Doukhobors were one such group. Their original leader remains unnamed, but beliefs unique to the Doukhobors included communal living, rejection of clergy, pacifism to the point of being vegetarians, and the belief that each individual, regardless of age, sex, or color, has in them a Divine spark known as *Iskra*. Not surprisingly, the Doukhobors were persecuted in their homeland and the possibility of Canadian immigration seemed like a gift from heaven. It did not help that in 1895, while still in Russia, the Doukhobors sponsored a public protest against Russian militarism by publically burning arms in bonfires all across southern Russia. This angered both the military and the state church, which combination produced a strong push for Doukhobor immigration to Canada. One Russian Archbishop, Ambrosius by name, called the new sect *Doukhobortsi,* meaning "those who wrestle against the Spirit of God." The Doukbobors adopted the name, arguing that they were wrestling "*in* the Spirit of God," not against it. The name stuck.

A traditional *Doukhobor Village* located near Grand Forks, British Columbia.

In Russia, the best-known Doukhobor leader was Peter Vasilievich Verigin, (also known as Peter the Lordly) who was preceded and trained by Lukeria Kalmakoff. Under Kalmakoff's reign from 1864 to 1886 the Doukhobors experienced a golden age of sorts. Kalmakoff presided over a prosperous economically, that was virtually ignored by the state church and government alike. When the Doukhobors sponsored the public Burning of Arms Ceremony, the insulted Russian military decided to enforce restrictions on them.

Enter Clifford Sifton, Canada's Minister of the Interior; as a politician seeking fame, Sifton intended to lure immigrants from abroad to help him populate the west. In 1899, after some negotiation and with the pleading of pacifist writer, Leo Tolstoy, 7 500 Doukhobors arrived in Canada by steamship, and settled in an area on the Saskatchewan-Manitoba border. It did not take them long to build fifty-seven communal villages in the area accompanied by the construction of a brick factory, a flour mill, and other economically-profitable industries. It was close to winter when the Doukhobors arrived, so it was impossible for them to plant crops on assigned lands. In a few short years, however, they had successfully harvested a variety of crops and collected 600 horses, 400 oxen, and 865 head of cattle. Everything was going well; the Doukhobors perceived that they had indeed found utopia.

A contemporary *Doukhobor Choir*.

Then a dreadful letter arrived from the office of the Canadian Interior cautioning the Doukhobors that if they wanted to keep their lands, they would individually have to swear allegiance to the British Crown. The new Minister of the Interior, Frank Oliver, was not keen on having pacifist groups enjoy the privilege of freedom from conscription. Thus the letter of warning Doukhobors to register their loyalty was originated. Naturally, the alarming news flew in the face of Doukhobor beliefs and a spirit of consternation developed in their settlements. In response to the threat, the community split three ways; one group of 236 families decided to take the Oath of Allegiance, thereby forming a new group called Independents.

A second group, consisting of some 1 000 individuals, and later known as the Sons of Freedom, staged a protest walk on Ottawa. The protest lasted several months and took participants many miles from home in cold fall weather. The protest ended when government officals seized Doukhobor possessions to pay for the cost of the protesters' train ride home.

A third group, composed of Orthodox Doukhobors, decided to abandon their homestead lands and migrate west, following their leader, Peter Verigin. The plan was to purchase privately held lands in British Columbia and avoid having to sign the dreaded Oath of Allegiance. A government appointed commission then made 258 880 acres of Doukhobor lands available to the public, located near the Saskatchewan-Manitoba border. In response, a land rush occurred, with hundreds of would-be settlers standing in line at the land registration office as many as twenty-four hours before it opened. At least twenty percent of Doukhobor lands had been broken to plant crops and proved a real boon to the new registrants. The Doukhobors received no compensation for what the government called "abandoned lands." A few Doukhobor families remained in Saskatchewan on special reserves the government allotted them. These reserves amounted to fifteen acres of land for every individual.

The ruins of a Doukhobor Prayer Home near Kamsack, Saskatchewan.

Meanwhile, under the direction of their leader, Peter the Lordly Verigin the community Doukhobors moved to British Columbia where they were able to purchase previously owned property. Here they were free from government interference – so they thought. Peter the Lordly proved to be a very capable leader, and the CCUB soon prospered. In 1912, thousands of orthodox Doukhobors moved to the British Columbia interior where they planted orchards, and built a brick factory, several sawmills, and a highly acclaimed jam factory. Now known as the Christian Community of Universal Brotherhood (CCUB), the Doukhobor colony consisted of ninety communal homes built on what eventually amounted to 21 648 acres of land.

Always concerned about the economic welfare of this people, in 1915, Verigin purchased 11 260 acres of farmland in southern Alberta, near Lundbreck, and settled 300 Doukhobors there. The plan was for them to raise grain and ship it from Alberta to the villages in the British Columbia. This arrangement would shorten the distance for providing needed grain from Saskatchewan farms. Now there were Doukhobors living in three provinces.

The ruins of a Doukhobor home near Langham, Saskatchewan.

In 1924, Peter the Lordly Verigin was killed in an explosion by a bomb while riding on a train and the Orthodox Doukhobors quickly sent to Russia for his son Peter Petrovich Verigin or Peter the Purger as he came to be named, to take his father's place. Peter the Purger took the title because he claimed he would "cleanse the dross" from the community – those who did not truly believe in the cause. He began an organization called the *Society of Named Doukhobors* in order to personalize membership in the CCUB, thereby enhancing the members' sense of loyalty.

Under Peter the Purger's leadership the CCUB underwent significant changes. He promoted the arts and established Russian language schools to ensure that Doukhobor youth would be well versed in cultural knowledge. He decentralized the community in order to increase productivity. This brought the success of production closer to each village and gave the people a stronger sense of ownership. Unfortunately, Verigin's successes were paralleled by his many irrational behaviors. These ranged from a fracas in Nelson, British Columbia, to his having to face a charge of perjury in Yorkton, Saskatchewan, where indeed he challenged a colleague with the same violation. This event led the Canadian government to attempt the secret deportation of Peter Petrovich to Russia. A Doukhobor lawyer, Peter G. Mararoff, successfully engaged in a series of daring actions to stave off the deportation order. Later, however, instead of being grateful, Verigin sued Makaroff on a related matter.

In 1938 the Canadian government for some reason decided to put an end to the CCUB, perhaps because of their success as a commune. Government action consisted of having two companies buy up demand notes at local banks and move quickly toward foreclosing on the CCUB. Thus the National Trust Company and the Sun Life Assurance Company took control of Doukhobor demand notes. It happened that the CCUB, with assets numbering in the millions, owed the sum of $319 276.00 in demand (temporary) loans to local banks. This amounted to a four percent debt load, but, unfortunately, the nature of the loans was such that they could be called in at any time. With government cooperation, the two companies suddenly announced that the CCUB had twenty-four hours to pay up the demand notes. Of course it was impossible for the CCUB to come up with that amount of money in so short a time, so they became the target of immediate foreclosure action.

The matter was taken to the Supreme Court of Canada, but that body sided with the foreclosure action. Quickly Doukhobor lands and properties were seized and sold off. The amount left after foreclosure was a mere $222 078.42, a small fraction of the real worth. Then, only in 1973 this money was finally made available to Doukhobor societies in the form of cultural grants. The CCUB was officially a thing of the past.

Peter the Lordly Verigin's home, and Headquarters of the Christian Community of Universal Brotherhood.

Peter Petrovich Verigin died of cancer on February 11, 1939, heartbroken and disillusioned. The CCUB tried to contact his son in Russia to take over leadership, but he was not to be found. As a result, Peter the Lordly's grandson, John J. Verigin was named honorary leader of a new organization called the Union of Spiritual Communities in Christ (USCC).

The philosophical foundation of the organization was that if the Doukhobors could not constitute a physical commune, they would at least remain so in a spiritual sense. John J. Verigin died in 2008, and his son John, was named his successor.

Of parallel interest to Doukhobor history is the Molokan story, for they consitute a sister protest group that also originated in 17th century Russia. Their name, "milk drinkers," derives from their practice of drinking milk on orthodox fast days. Molokans, Old Believers, and Doukhobors, are the only three 17th century Russian religious groups who have managed somewhat successfully to maintain their unique Christian identities. Like Doukhobors, the Molokans were persecuted for their beliefs, but found refuge by migrating to the United States. In 1900 there were 100 000 Molokans in Russia, with 2 500 of them having relocated to America just before the Russian Revolution, to avoid both war and economic depression.

Like Old Believers, the Molokans have zealously preserved many of their traditions including their traditional attire. Old Believers have clung to the liturgies of the Russian Orthodox Church, while Molokans and Doukhobors have framed new ones. Both Molokans and Old Believers place more emphasis on the value of the Holy Scriptures than the Doukhobors, and have adopted a more fundamentalist stance. Both groups reject the Sacraments, refuse to revere the cross, and sing without musical accompaniment.

Molokan theology is essentially very conservative; they unquestioningly accept the authority of the Holy Bible, and while they have a system of elders, unlike Doukhobors, do not place any authority in a single leader. Elders preach on Bible passages and lead congregations in prayer, but they do not add nor reinterpret established doctrines. Centuries ago, the Molokans did split into various camps, for example; at first

A Doukhobor Spinning Wheel.

there were two groups, the first of which followed a leader named Semen Uklein and continued to adhere their traditional concept of salvation. The second group followed another leader, Maksim Rudornetkin, who preached that the baptism of the Holy Spirit was essential to salvation. Since then, a series of Molokan sub-sects have developed, but many have left the fold to unite with Baptist and Evangelical Churches in America.

Today over 200 Molokans and related groups sponsor congregations locasted in countries around the world. There are 150 Molokan congregations in Russia and thirty in the United States, most of them residing along the American west coast. Russian language Bibles, songbooks, texts and language are used in all Molokan congregations worldwide.

For both Molokans and Doukhobors, it seems that persistence sometimes pays off.

For Further Reading:

Dunn, Ethel, and Stephen P. Dunn (1977). "Religion and Ethnicity: The Case of the American Molokans." *Ethnicity 4*:370-379.

Friesen, John W. (1983). *Schools With A Purpose.* Calgary, AB: Detselig Enterprises, chapter four.

Friesen, John W., and Michael M. Verigin. (1996). *The Community Doukhobors: A People in Transition.* Ottawa, ON: Borealis Press.

Janzen, William. (1990). Limits on Liberty: *The Experience of Mennonite, Hutterite, and Doukhobor Communities in Canada.* Toronto, ON: University of Toronto Press.

Tarasoff, Koozma. (2002). *Spirit Wrestlers: Doukhobor Pioneers' Strategies for Living.* Brooklyn, NY: Legas Publishing.

Tarasoff, Koozma. (1982). *Plakun Trava: The Doukhobors.* Grand Forks, BC: Mir Publication Society.

Tarasoff, Koozma, and Robert B. Klymasz, eds. (1995). *Spirit Wrestlers: Centennial Papers in Honour of Canada's Doukhobor Heritage.* Ottawa, ON: Canadian Museum of Civilization.

http://www.molokane.org/

http://molokane.org/molokan/Index.htm

Ephrata Cloister

Welcome to Ephrata Cloister, a radical 18th Century religious society best known for its original art and music, distinctive medieval Germanic architecture and prolific publishing centre.

Daily life in the Ephrata Cloister was not unlike that of a monestry. Devotees spent a lot of time in prayer and fasting, and were urged to engage in acts of charity, chastity, and obedience to colony regulations.

Although usually classified as a religious commune, this unusual group was really more mystical than religious, thereby often confusing observers.

Originating in Pennsylvania in 1732, the Ephrata Cloister was quite successful on several counts. Its strict order lent itself to accomplishments in several sectors including unique forms of original art and music, distinctive medieval Germanic architecture, calligraphy, and a prolific publishing centre. The Ephrata Cloister also managed one of the largest printing presses in America at the time, publishing some ninety books before 1794. On the negative side, however, were the many controversies surrounding the community. Essentially Ephrata's secrecy raised suspicions about its role in American society. Some critics believed that this was a secret Roman Catholic Order, while others accused the members of being spies for the French military. Ephrata's strict rules about chastity seemed contradictory while unmarried men and women occupied the same living quarters. Small wonder Ephrata was a convenient target for suspicion.

Grounded in both Lutheran and Reform traditions, the Ephrata Cloister operated for sixty-three years. Many of the medieval-type buildings erected by the colony exist today, and may be accessed by visitors for a nominal fee. At its peak, the membership was around 300 individuals, and a few daughter colonies were begun. One of them, called Snow Hill, lasted almost a century and folded in 1889. The Ephrata Cloister itself ceased formal operations in 1796, almost a century earlier, but a handful of celibate sisters remained on site until 1814. In 1941 the Pennsylvania Historical and Museum Commission assumed administration of the site and gradually restored nineteen of the original buildings. Restoration was completed in 1968.

A photo showing the pastoral view of Ephrata Cloister grounds.

The Meetinghouse (Saal) was the worship hall built in 1741. This building is where the congregation attended services that included scripture reading, biblical lessons, and music.

Ephrata Cloister was the brainchild of Conrad Beissel (1691-1768), a German immigrant who had served as an apprentice baker in his homeland. His interest in religion led him publically to condemn the lavish lifestyle of his Christian peers so he was subsequently excommunicated by the state church. A trip to North America put him into contact with a pietistic group known as "Women in the Wilderness," whose members believed that the way to salvation was through complete self-denial. When the membership of that group began to decline, Beissel took up with a group of conservative German Baptists known as "Dunkers." He also searched out the beliefs of Quakers, Brethren, and Mennonites and then formed his own version of German Baptist theology that advocated celibacy, living in "holy poverty," and keeping Saturday as the day of worship.

In 1732, Beissel published a book so forcefully condemning marriage that a number of unhappy local women left their husbands and came to Beissel looking for a place to live. In response, Beissel established a communal congregation near Philadelphia to acccomodate the women. Unprepared for so many new converts, Beissel did not have sufficient space to build a separate dormitory for women. As a result they were required to occupy a dormitory with single men while married adherents, known as "householders," lived in separate quarters. Naturally, this arrangement gave rise to ominous community rumors, but Beissel tried to assure everyone that nothing extraordinary was taking place. At one point Beissel and a woman were taken to court, accused of giving birth to an illegitimate child, but the case was thrown out of court.

A wooden water pump located outside the bakery.

Beissel's commune came to life during the years 1735 to 1746 when the community built eight major dormitories and meeting places, and their membership grew. Critics were dumbfounded that people would choose to live in such a strict environment, and Beissel seemed never to weary of inventing new doctrines, practices, and regulations. Ephrata Cloister never had a constitution so Beissel could make up new rules as he went along. He did just that. Like other pietist leaders of his time, he believed that Christ's Second Coming was near and twice he predicted an exact date for the event. Two comets that appeared in 1742 and 1743 were identified by Beissel as indicative of the Second Coming. Beissel also sponsored a lengthy pilgrimage for his followers, preaching as he went. Marching single file and dressed in pilgrim attire, the group was both praised and mocked by onlookers. The nature of the event did little to endear the group to the local community.

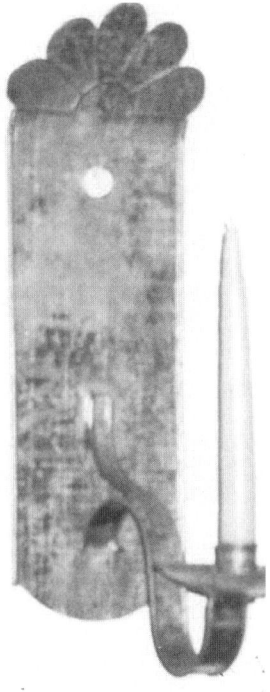

Beissel categorized the membership of Ephrata into two distinct levels. First in rank were celibate members who numbered around 100 in 1750 (the high point of the experiment). This group lived in the commune. Second, were about 200 married "householders," who lived off-site. Many of these families owned property, but oddly enough, Beissel never required them to turn over ownership to the cloister. Nevertheless, the householders contributed generously to its operation.

Daily life in the Ephrata Cloister was not unlike that of a monestry. Devotees spent a lot of time in prayer and fasting, and were urged to engage in acts of charity, chastity, and obedience to colony regulations. Beissel enforced strict rules about individual appearance; women were to cut their hair short and men were required to wear beards. Food was meager, consisting mainly of dry bread and porridge. At times the people of Ephrata also indulged in a meal of bread and a plate of pumpkin mush and barley. If they were more fortunate, they could also dine on cabbage, roots, greens, and cheese. Beissel seldom permitted his followers to eat meat. Sleep was limited, and like monks, the members rose at midnight to sing hymns and pray. They repeated this activity at five o'clock in the morning.

Wall mounted candleholder.

The buildings constructed at the Ephrata Cloister paralleled the rigidity of the community. Hallways were deliberately narrow (to represent the narrow way that leads to eternal life), beds were hard, and pillows were made of wood. All furnishings were required to be pristine in appearance so that even nail heads were polished brightly. Spiritual exercises reflected the rigor of physical surroundings. In fact, Beissel's teachings were so rigid and discipline was so severe that members virtually cringed when he chaired his weekly public examination of members' behaviors.

In 1745 Beissel gave up leadership of the settlement to Isaac Eckerlin, declaring that he would from that time on serve as an ordinary member. Unfortunately, Beissel was unable to contain himself from constantly criticizing Eckerlin's rule even though the commune gained increased profits from the way Eckerlin managed the mills. Eckerlin greatly expanded the financial base of the cloister by engaging in a number of other profitable enterprises. He purchased a sawmill and sold lumber. He expanded the colony orchard, constructed a paper mill, and opened a bookbinding shop. He opened a tannery and had workers cobble shoes and craft leather products. He also developed a pottery trade and introduced flax weaving. He restored buildings, constructed bridges, and acquired draft horses to pull plows. Even the energies of the celibate sisters were ignited, Eckerlin urging them to take up embroidery and basket weaving.

Old Ephrata Hospital, built in 1848, provided a full range of services including surgery and x-rays, among its 16-bed facility.

The Ephrata membership was impressed with Eckerlin's energy and ingenuity, so there was danger that he would become more spiritually powerful than Beissel. He was even able to confiscate Beissel's dwelling for himself, but this proved to be too much. Beissel was beside himself with envy, so he quickly expelled Eckerlin, and the cloister gradually resumed its former position of minimal financial status. By 1761, Beissel's health had deteriorated to the extent that his behavior was barely tolerated by the membership. He managed to live another seven years, constantly blaming himself for Ephrata's impending demise. When Beissel's next successor, Peter Miller, took over, there were only fifty members left, most of them quite on in years.

The handwriting was on the wall, and within a few years the Ephrata Cloister dissolved, an unusual and somewhat strange and relatively short-lived communal experiment in the ocean of similar endeavors.

Its austere spirit can easily be captured by a tour of existing buildings.

For Further Reading

Alderfer, E.G. (1995). *The Ephrata Commune: An Early American Counterculture.* Pittsburgh, PA: The University of Pittsburgh Press.

Durnbaugh, Donald F. (1997). Communitarian Societies in *Colonial America. America's Communal Utopias.* Donald E. Pitzer, ed. Chapel Hill, NC: The University of North Carolina Press, 14-36.

Gutek, Gerald, and Patricia Gutek. (1998). *Visiting Utopian Communities: A Guide to Shakers, Moravians, and Others.* Columbia, SC: University of South Carolina Press.

Holloway, Mark. (1966). *Heavens on Earth: Utopian Communities in America, 1680-1880.* New York: Dover Publications.

Pyle, Howard. (1889). *A Tale of the Ephrata Cloister.* Lancaster, PA: reprinted by the Aurand Press. Originally published by Harper's Magazine.

Rexroth, Kenneth. (1974). *Communalism: From its Origins to the Twentieth Century.* New York: The Seabury Press.

Sutton, Robert P. (2004). *Communal Utopias and the American Experience: Religious Communities, 1732-2000.* Westport, CN: Praeger.

http://www.ephratacloister.org/history.htm

The Farm

Visitors to *The Farm* are welcomed with a detailed map to guide them.

The Farm store purchases items in bulk to sell to the local community at discount prices. A wide variety of items is made available to The Farm community with a small area to have a cup of coffee and catch up on local news. The half finished dome over a gathering place is in the foreground.

There is little doubt about it; the 1960s were probably the most interesting decade in North America in the last half-century. This was the decade in which virtually every societal institution was under fire. North American youth protested against the way "things had always been done," including government practices, university operations, and religious functioning. For example, a religious movement known as the "Jesus People" invaded churches, took over services, and argued for less structure, less theology, and more touchy-feely contact. Some protest movements were quite violent in nature, while many groups of young people known as hippies simply sat around in city parks, sharing food and clothing while humming religious chants they borrowed from eastern countries.

A more serious and more formally organized form of hippie protest was rather inadvertently launched by Stephen Gaskin, then an instructor at San Francisco State College. In addition to his regular teaching duties, Gaskin began a series of Monday night lectures wherein he analyzed world religions and their emphases on compassion, personal character, self-reliance, and the interconnectedness of life. In his lectures Gaskin drew from Christianity, mysticism, and humanistic psychology. The response was overwhelming; apparently thousands of American youth were ready to respond to alternative ways of interpreting the essence of life. Soon Gaskin embarked on a coast-to-coast speaking tour lecturing in hospitable churches and on college campuses. He was followed by a caravan of brightly-painted busloads of hippie followers, eager to learn more.

Artwork on the granary is reminiscent of days when *The Farm* was established.

This home is reminiscent of the 1960s flower power days at *The Farm.*

After four months of travelling, the weary sojourners decided that their idyllic perceptions of life needed roots. They pooled their money and sent out a search party to identify a locale of paradise. The searchers decided on a location in the state of Tennessee where land was inexpensive and the rugged rural landscape very appealing. Before long hundreds of truth-seeking youth parked sixty-three ancient buses on a one thousand acre plot of ground that became known as The Farm. Here Gaskin continued his teachings, particularly condemning two person marriage as selfish and confining. He

FARMSOY – Premium Organic; Soygurt; Organic Cultured Soy; Plain Unsweetened; Dairy Free.

recommended a four-person unit to replace marriage between couples. After a short time the traditional model of marriage of two individuals was reinstated because the four-person arrangement caused too much jealousy. Gaskin also concluded that marriage would work best if the male's traditional primal drive to dominate was replaced by female aggressiveness in the marriage relationship.

The Farm survived this and other crises, and even thrived. Committed to vegetarianism, pacifism, and simple living, Farm dwellers advocated inner peace as the foundation for world peace. They were serious about their objectives. In 1974, The Farm formed a disaster relief organization named Plenty aimed at assisting communities hit by tornadoes, drought, and the like. They also experimented with ecologically sound technology such as passive solar construction and electric automobiles. By 1977 there were 1 000 people living on The Farm which had thus far received some 14 000 visitors. Satellite farms were started in a dozen different states, but soon faltered. None of the satellite farms exist today.

Living quarters at The Farm were quite complex involving both married couples and singles. The spirit of freedom was maintained however; toilets had no doors and showers were without curtains. Only draperies separated bedrooms. Women were encouraged to have as many children as possible since the ability to have children was regarded as a holy gift. Scientific forms of birth control were forbidden and women were urged to use the "cooperative method" based on the female menstrual cycle.

Though many Farm dwellers found it necessary to obtain work off-site, there were a number of industries that were quite successful. The Midwife School, for example, brought many young women to The Farm to have their children. The Farm motto was, "If you cannot afford to keep your child, we will raise it for you. You can have it back anytime you want." By the mid-1980s twelve midwives were admitting women to have their babies at The Farm as an option to confining themselves in local hospitals. The midwives also began instructing outsiders in the art. Income was generated through the Book Publishing Company, which produced books on vegetarianism, midwifery, natural birth control, and how to install solar electronics, photovoltaic panels and windmills. A series of farm foods were marketed including the produce of a soy yogurt factory. In 1990 farm workers added a senior citizens' complex and a visitor's centre called the Ecovillage Training Center from which some revenue was generated.

Eventually, The Farm collapsed from its own weight. Population growth had become too rapid to keep pace with meeting human needs. Some households had as many as thirty dwellers and dissatisfaction with living space intensified. At one point Gaskin was asked to resign from leadership and he did so, though remaining a strong supporter of Farm enterprises. During the 1990s Gaskin again resumed his speaking tours and enrollment began to decline.

Today, some 125 people live on The Farm, and a local privately-owned store brings in bulk food products for sale. Individual family homes are proudly constructed of recycled or reclaimed materials and owners pay rent for the privilege of living on The Farm. The soy factory is virtually shut down, manufacturing little more than the local market can absorb. A school operated completely by solar power educates children of Farm dwellers. A major concern is the financial wellbeing of the community.

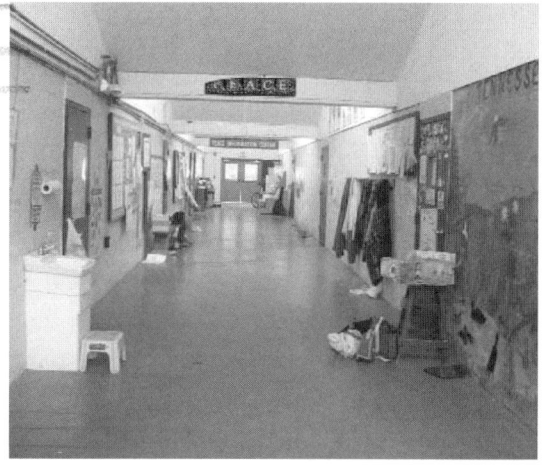

The school's interior corridor shows signs of bustling activity. The Farm School provides alternative education for school age students.

Utopian forms of lifestyles, like all others, seem to have to cope with perpetual crises, forced changes, and internal challenges. The Farm is an example of changing with the times.

> *Eventually, The Farm collapsed from its own weight. Population growth had become too rapid to keep pace with their ability to meet human needs.*

Visitors are welcome at The Farm, and their Welcome Centre is open April 1st to October 31st. Visitors are asked to e-mail or call ahead. The telephone number is (931) 964-3574.

For Further Reading

Fike, Rupert, ed. (1998). *Voices From the Farm: Adventures in Community Living.* Summertown, TN: Book Publishing Company.

Jacob, Jeffrey. (1997). *New Pioneers: The Back-to-the-Land Movement and the Search for a Sustainable Future.* University Park, PA: The Pennsylvania State University Press.

Miller, Timothy. (1999). *The 60s Communes: Hippies and Beyond.* Syracuse, NY: Syracuse University Press.

Spencer, Metta. (1990). *Foundations of Modern Sociology.* Scarborough, ON: Prentice-hall Canada.

Sutton, Robert P. (2004). *Communal Utopias and the American Experience: Secular Communities, 1732-2000.* Westport, CN: Praeger.

http://www.thefarm.org/
http://www.thefarm.org/midwives/index.html
http://www.thefarmcommunity.com/thefarmschool/
http://www.thefarm.org/general/visit.html

Fourier's Phalanxes

Francois Marie Charles Fourier (1772-1837), was a French philosopher and idealist who dreamed up the concept of phalanx – a unit of communal living that would characterize the society of the future, a society of absolute peace and harmony. Fourier believed that eventually human passion for free competition, greed, and power would vanish and instead people would pursue peaceful living and mutual enjoyment. In case you're wondering, it appears not to have happened yet.

The European society in which Fourier found himself was undergoing a number of significant social and economic changes. The birth of the Industrial Revolution, societal distrust of government, and the emergence of romanticism raised serious questions about the quality of life in Europe. The state church did not escape criticism, and was charged with blocking human reason and the granting of universal equal rights. The restless mood gave rise to utopian socialism promoted by men who saw a better future for the continent through the advancement of reason. These thinkers often created specific recommendations, and Charles Fourier was one of them.

Welcome to Ripon Historical Society, Ripon, Wisconsin.

Fourier was born in Besancon, France, the son of a wealthy cloth merchant who eventually lost his fortune. Propelled by the French Revolution, storming Parisian troops broke into Fourier's father's place of business and destroyed all of his stock. Greatly affected by this development, Charles Fourier was for a time involved in the French counter-revolution, and served in the Army of the Rhine. Aside from that, he lived most of his life in Lyons and Paris, doing odd jobs, working as a travelling salesman, preaching his idea of peace and harmony, and looking for a patron to finance his dreams. He drew up a list of 4 000 potential patrons, and advertised in a

> Although many such models eventually sprang up in America, Fourier himself never lived in one. In fact, he never left France, and died in Paris even before the first phalanx was created.

newspaper that he would be home 24/7 if any of them cared to visit him and perhaps finance his venture. No one came forth with any money. Fourier loved to put words into print, and write he did. Some critics suggest that most of his ideas did not make any sense, and it is a wonder that he gained any followers at all. But he did attract followers.

In 1803, Fourier published his notion of a new society in an article entitled, "Universal Harmony." This was followed by the publication of dozens of articles, pamphlets, and books, but few people adopted Fourier's ideas until two decades later. Eventually a Fourier society was formed and charged with the publication of a journal. In 1836 Fourier dreamed up the concept of a unique model for peaceful communal living called a phalanx. Although many such models eventually sprang up in America, Fourier himself never lived in one. In fact, he never left France, and died in Paris even before the first phalanx was created.

Inspired by Fourier's disciple, Albert Brisbane, between 1843 and 1858 some forty phalanxes were built in a dozen American states, most of them short-lived. Realistically, the close living quarters that comprised a phalanx caused tensions, conflicts, and disagreements, which led to their quick demise. Disputes arose over such issues as compulsory religious services, communal dining, consumption of alcohol, and differential wages. Even when phalanxes were modestly successful there was always the temptation for some individuals to sell their shares, take the money, and individually buy land elsewhere.

In Ripon, at the corner of North Street and Warren Street, you can find the "Long House," a 400-foot building.

Twelve of the American phalanxes did not survive their first year of operation. A saying that came into being was; "a phalanx will fail when the first mortgage payment comes due." Despite this pessimistic outlook, several phalanxes lasted three years; the Wisconsin Phalanx lasted six years, Brook Farm in Massachusetts lasted six years, and only one, the

North American Phalanx in New Jersey, lasted more than a decade By 1860, the phalanx movement was dead. In the meanwhile, however, Fourier's ideas were followed up. Albert Brisbane, for example, wrote a book, *Social Destiny of Man*, which attracted the attention of Horace Greeley, editor of the *New Yorker*. Greeley was so impressed that he offered Brisbane a regular column in his paper. This gave an increasing and lingering attention to Fourier's philosophy in the United States.

According to Fourier, when properly organized, a phalanx would follow a strict design that he originated. Fourier argued that God had created an orderly world and society should do no less with its organization. Each phalanx was to contain 1 620 members who would live on three square miles of territory. Their home was to be a six-story building with a long body, two wings, and an inner courtyard. The membership of a phalanx would be subdivided into groups of seven people, five groups would form a series, and each series would be involved in a specific aspect of the settlement's enterprises such as gardening, education, field work, and so on. Individuals would belong to several series, perhaps as many as thirty or forty, and thus round out their social and physical skills. You get the idea.

The Long House housed tenements, an amusement or lecture hall, and a dining room where all ate at a common table. Tenants' board was provided at cost.

Fourier envisaged that a phalanx would be set up like a joint stock company with a central office that would charge members for rent, board, and other expenses. Not everyone would be required to become a stockholder. Profits were to be shared with the highest earning group, namely laborers, being paid the highest amount. Next in the ladder of recipients were actual stockholders, then writers and artists. A phalanx was not intended to operate exactly like a commune, but in practice there was little difference.

Naturally, Fourier also had some very unique ideas about family life. He felt that nuclear families often got too wrapped up in their own orbits that they neglected the social needs of the outside community. This meant that the family as it existed in his time, was actually the lowest form of social living. Fourier preferred that one third of his phalanx members be celibate and the remainder married couples with only one or two children per family.

To some extent, Fourier was also a realistic thinker. He did not envisage that his scheme would become relevant for at least 30 000 years at which time people would have wearied of revolution, stratification, and inequality. Fourier's alternative of peace and harmony would then be implemented in several stages. When fully realized, the new society would consist of 2 985 984 phalanxes, enough to contain the entire world population. There would be one universal language, and Constantinople would be the capital city.

This building housed the Ripon Phalanx communal bakery.

Of course none of this ever really happened, but it certainly makes for interesting reading – and musing; what if...

The most publicized version of a Fourier phalanx was Brook Farm in Massachusetts, which was established in 1841 by the Rev. George Ripley, a Unitarian minister. Ripley and a dozen friends who were influenced by Boston's Transcendental Club, managed to purchase 200 acres of land and design a miniature society that attracted the attention of such thinkers and writers as Ralph Waldo Emerson, Margaret Fuller, Nathaniel Hawthorne, and Robert Owen.

In 1844, Brook Farm and its 120 members adopted the administrative structure advocated by Charles Fourier. Their phalanx became a joint stock company with some members contributing labor and others donating money. Although often assigned very difficult tasks, women fared well in the phalanx, following Fourier's philosophy of equality for both sexes. The women shared such responsibilities as food preparation, housekeeping and childcare, but they also helped in the fields and joined in evening corn huskings. As a reward, a wide range of cultural activities were available to them, often hosted by nationally known writers, musicians, and reformers.

Unfortunately, too often the membership of Brook Farm was so much engaged in cultural and recreational activities that their work began to suffer. Thus, in reality, Brook Farm never became financially self-sustaining.

In 1845 the members of Brook Farm decided to apply the finer details of Fourier's recipe for peace and harmony, so a series of newly created departments was designed – agriculture, domestics, labor, and mechanical arts. Their futuristic dream of success was never fully realized because the phalanx burned down that same year and the membership never recovered. The following year the land and few remaining buildings were sold at a loss and the company disbanded. Nevertheless, the power of Brook Farm was such that for three generations after its demise, descendants of the original membership continued to meet at an annual summer camp and reminisce about the heritage of the good ole days.

Ceresco Park. Ceresco, part of present day Ripon, Wisconsin was founded as a utopian community in 1843.

The North American Phalanx began in 1843 at Red Rock, New Jersey, and attracted ninety individuals who immediately settled in, planted crops, and developed shops and mills. Unlike Brook Farm they were very careful about whom to admit to the settlement, and their care paid off. Everyone they admitted was committed to work so the end result was that the efficient colony operation much resembled that of a Hutterite community. Work and play were carefully governed, and all went well until a fire broke out in 1854 and destroyed most of the property. Disillusioned, the membership voted to disband the community, while a small number of adherents led by Victor Considerant, leader of the French Fourierists, moved to the Dallas area in Texas to start again. The name of their new colony was to be the Victor Considerant Colony. Here a small group of Americans and 300 Frenchmen struggled with drought, rattlesnakes, and internal dissension – and lost. Within a short time their new community also dissolved.

The Wisconsin Phalanx was located in Ripon, the original home of the Republican Party of America. Started in 1844 by twenty hard-working individuals, the colony soon owned a series of very successful industries; a gristmill, blacksmith shop, water dam, schoolhouse, and henhouse were among their holdings. This group was very careful about admitting new members; only sixty percent of those who applied were admitted, and new members had to serve a four-month probationary period. Within a short time a total of 259 individuals made up the membership of the phalanx, with an annual turnover of twelve percent. Interestingly, though the colony tried to implement Fourier's ideas, women were not granted the right to vote in direct contradiction to Fourier's thinking. Five years after the phalanx began, and at the height of their success, the membership grew tired of living like shareholders instead of being individual owners. Then, much to the surprise of onlookers, the group suddenly voted to disband. Property was divided up and each individual received his or her just share. They were probably the only phalanx to end with a profit. By 1850 the Wisconsin Phalanx was no more, just a short six years after they followed their dream.

Today several historical sites reminiscent of previously operating phalanxes can be located in various American states.

For Further Reading

Claeys, Gregory, and Lyman Tower Sargent, eds. (1999). *The Utopian Reader.* New York: New York University Press.

Fourier, Charles. (1999). Selections Describing the Phalanstery. *The Utopian Reader.* Gregory Claeys and Lyman Tower Sargent, eds. New York: New York University Press, 192-199.

Freibert. Lucy M. (1993). Creative Women of Brook Farm. *Women in Spiritual and Communitarian Societies in the United States.* Wendy E. Chmielewski, Louis J. Kern, and Marilyn Klee-Hartzwell, eds. Syracuse, NY: Syracuse University Press, 75-88.

Guarneri, Carl J. (1997). Brook Farm and the Fourierist Phalanxes: Immediatism, Gradualism, and American Utopian Socialism. *American Communal Utopias.* Donald E. Pitzer, ed. Chapel Hill, NC: The University of North Carolina Press, 88-134.

Holloway, Mark. (1966). *Heavens on Earth: Utopian Communities in America, 1680-1880*. New York: Dover Publications.

Jones, Gareth Stedman, and Ian Patterson, eds. (1996). *Fourier: The Theory of the Four Movements.* Cambridge Texts in the History of Political Thought. Cambridge, UK: Cambridge University Press.

Rexroth, Kenneth. (1974). *Communalism: From its Origins to the Twentieth Century.* New York: Seabury Press.

Riasanovsky, Nicholas V. (1969). *The Teachings of Charles Fourier.* Berkeley, CA: University of California Press.

http://www.vcu.edu/engweb/transcendentalism/ideas/brhistory.html

http://www.trivia-library.com/a/attempted-utopias-society-fourier-phalanx-movement-part-2.htm

http://www.historyguide.org/intellect/lecture21a.html

http://www.ripongame.com/press.htm

Harmonists

Undoubtedly, the Harmonists were one of the most ambitious urban developers in 19th century America. Led by a Separatist preacher named George Rapp (1757-1847), these Lutheran Separatists fled Germany to seek refuge in the United States. Once in America their leader planned an idyllic way of life for his followers that efficiently blended work and play.

Johann George Rapp, or "Father Rapp" as he preferred to be called, was born into a Lutheran family in Württemburg, Germany. As he grew older, he studied the Bible and became disillusioned with the theology and practices of the state church. Rapp accused the clergy of neglecting the Scriptures and breaking down the barriers between politics and religion. In response to these charges, state officials threw Rapp in prison for two days and threatened with exile if he did not refrain from preaching. Rapp, however, continued his reactionary activities. One day he even disrupted a local church service in protest. This time he was fined for his disrespectful behavior, but the incident did nothing to change his mind about condemning the state church for its weak position on worldly influences.

It was 1791 when peasant-born, self-styled preacher George Rapp began to hold Separatist church services that surprisingly attracted hundreds of adherents. He managed to gather funds from his followers and supporters, and then, leaving his congregation in the hands of Frederick Reichert, he

Harmony. First home of Harmony Society, founded 1804, by George Rapp and German followers. In 1814 moved to New Harmony, Indiana and settled at Economy in present Ambridge, Beaver County, in 1825.

Original log home in Old Harmony. The famed communal Harmony Society began with the building of nine log cabins.

For over 150 years, the *Harmony Inn* has been a favorite stop for travellers across the globe.

and his son, John set off for America to find a place for his new congregation to locate.

Rapp and his son travelled to Pennsylvania where they purchased 4 500 acres of land located about 26 miles north of Pittsburgh. There they planned to build a communal settlement for Rapp's followers back in Germany. Rapp sent word to his congregation that life in frontier America would be challenging, and only the brave-hearted should seek to immigrate. Immediately 839 people expressed interest in Rapp's plan, but when the time came only 300 set sail for Baltimore. Eighty of them travelled on to Pennsylvania to clear land and build the first of Rapp's three towns.

On February 15, 1805, the Village of Harmony was born, bolstered with a constitution drawn up by George Rapp. The agreement read that all property would be held in common, but registered in Rapp's name and that of three other trustees. The constitution stipulated that anyone who signed it and later chose to leave the commune would forfeit ownership of all worldly goods. The newly built commune functioned well; within a year, the members of the Harmony Society had built some fifty log houses and cleared 150 acres of land on which to plant crops. Frederick Reichert was appointed as Rapp's right hand man because he had kept the group together in Germany while Rapp arranged matters in the United States. Reichert established seven departments in the village and appointed a manager for each one. Under Reichert's leadership, Harmony became an efficient organization, operating a sawmill, a flourmill, a series of vineyards, and other industries. Rapp claimed that he would only look after the spiritual needs of his people, but as it turned out, every colony action, religious or otherwise, required his signature.

Harmony Clock. A basic clock with only one time-keeping hand, with the dial between the hour markers being divided into two equal parts making the clock readable to the nearest thirty minutes.

A replica Christmas table decoration beside an authentic calendar for December 1897. The family living in this Harmony household was undoubtedly anticipating the New Year, 1898.

In 1807 a religious revival broke out in Harmony, and Rapp, equal to the challenge, amended his spiritual outlook. He now decreed that all marriages would be dissolved and celibacy would be practiced by his followers. He ruled that the extra energy couples would derive as a result would be directed towards hard work and more community service. Women would now be able to devote an extra nine months of service to the cause because they would no longer be getting pregnant. Not everyone agreed with or followed Rapp's dictates because between the years 1803 and 1813, 262 births were recorded in the Harmony Society. From 1814 to 1824, there were 69 recorded births. When Rapp got really serious about his celibacy rule, he punished those who indulged in sexual pleasure. Rapp's own son, John, for example, was castrated for his deviance. It has been alleged that John died as a result of complications from the operation. Later, to fill the void Rapp adopted Frederick Reichert Rapp as his son.

By 1813, a spirit of restlessness became evident in Harmony. Life in Rapp's utopia was not quite as idyllic as it had been advertised. Life was too tedious and the people had grown weary. Daily activities consisted of little more than hard work, religious services, and obedience to rules. Rapp sensed this, and quickly moved a new plan into gear. He drew attention to the fact that while Harmony had greatly prospered in a relatively short time, the town desperately needed access to a river in order to ship goods to customers. As it was, the closest river was 12 miles away. Besides, Rapp mused privately, a new project would keep his followers busy. After all, the idle mind is the devil's workshop.

On May 15, 1815, a Mennonite capitalist named Abraham Ziegler purchased the entire town of Harmony and 7 000 acres of land for $100 000. Rapp estimated that the village gained about $8 000 profit on the venture. Now the Harmonists set out for a 30 000 acre site on the Wabash River

Modern Main Street, New Harmony, Indiana.

A New Harmony house built by the Owen brothers in 1830.

in Posey County, Indiana, where they named their next utopia, New Harmony. Rapp sent 100 individuals ahead to prepare housing for the congregation, and within a year the Harmonists moved and the village of Harmony was turned over to Ziegler. New Harmony now had 700 residents including 130 newly arrived German immigrant members. In order to emphasize that the central focus of the settlement was religious, the first building erected in New Harmony was the church, an outstanding landmark for the community. A few years later a bolt of lightning struck the building, but George Rapp refused to have lightning rods put on the roof. He told his people to trust God to take care of the church. His own house was an exception – it had lighterning rods on the roof because there was nothing more that Rapp feared than lightning – except perhaps steam engines.

Thanks to their access to the Wabash River, the Harmonists were able to ship more than $12 000 worth of goods down river each year. The community grew wealthy and the village treasurer was thus able to announce that financing was available for the building of 180 additional, comfortable homes, a schoolhouse, a library, a store, a bank, a post office, a tavern, and other facilities. Rapp was very concerned about educating colony children in music, language arts, and vocational trades. He felt that such a curriculum would enable them to take on needed community vocations when they became adults.

These hard working German immigrants known for their planning, order, and cleanliness moved to the Indiana Territory and carved New Harmony out of the wilderness.

By the 1820s the Harmonists had amassed a library of 360 volumes, a rare sized collection for those days. A special home was designed for George Rapp, measuring sixty by sixty feet square, with shuttered windows in high surrounding walls. Whenever Rapp wanted to see how his project was faring, he would open the shutters and literally spy on his people. Individual needs were obtained from community stores, but requests for supplies always had to be approved with the personal signature of George Rapp. In addition, Rapp held nightly confession sessions for those who had "sinned" during the day.

In order to emphasize that the central focus of the settlement was religious, the first building erected in New Harmony was the church, an outstanding landmark for the community.

New Harmony continued to grow by attracting German immigrants as well as African American slaves who were purchased from their owners by Rapp who then turned them free to live in his settlement. Not everyone was pleased with the influx of new members and conflicts often arose. Eventually, so many outsiders requested to join New Harmony that Rapp had to turn them away. By Rapp's order, many potential members were turned away by the adoption of more stringent rules.

One day Rapp burned the Book of Debts, a record that indicated how much each member had contributed to the society when they joined. He did this so it would be more difficult for them to lay claim to property if they chose to leave.

By 1824, New Harmony was one of the largest towns in Indiana, and its commercial reputation stretched to include twenty-two states and ten foreign countries. Rapp was even able to offer a loan to the state of Indiana with an interest rate of six percent.

Every utopia, it seems, has to cope with unexpected challenges, and in time New Harmony was no exception. In time a disease known as ague, a form of malaria, invaded the settlement and 120 people caught the disease and died. Rapp grew worried. In addition, the village began to feel the pressure of increased commercialism across the country, and competitive prices drove the managers of New Harmony to consider alternative marketing practices. Neighboring businesses were worried that they could not compete with the New Harmony mill. In addition, Rapp's village controlled the only landing place on the Wabash River for miles around and the Harmonists charged for the privilege of using it. Neighboring businessmen complained that this was a sheer case of monopoly. In addition to these troubles, Rapp discovered that Indiana soil was not as productive for growing grapes as that back in Pennsylvania. When things deteriorated even further, Rapp grew very concerned. He suddenly discovered that neighboring businessmen had convinced Indiana state officials to seize the Harmonists' mill to stop the monopoly. For George Rapp, that did it! It was time to move, so Rapp announced that God was calling the Harmonists back to Pennsylvania.

Enter Robert Owen.

"If we can not reconcile all opinions, let us endeavor to unite all hearts." Robert Owen.

In 1824 a Welsh-born industrialist, Robert Owen (1771-1858), bought the town of New Harmony and its adjoining parcel of 20 000 acres of land, for $150 000. Owen planned to attract would-be utopians from all over the world to the New Harmony location. His plan was to model a settlement that would develop a society representing an "ignorant, selfish system," and change it to an enlightened one, thereby "removing all causes for contest between individuals."

Owen had the reputation of being an ambitious but kind man who had been very fair to his employees in Europe. For New Harmony he envisaged that about 1 000 people would make their homes there and attain happiness by concentrating on environmentalism, gradualism, rationalism, communalism, and millenarianism. Owen also managed to lure a few intellectuals to his utopia who arrived in a ship that Owen called a "Boatload of Knowledge." Unfortunately Owen had no administrative plan in mind for his project; no one knew which jobs he or she would be assigned or if they had the necessary training to undertake that job. There was also no consistent religious or philosophical foundation for the planned community that could keep it together in times of crisis. Owen was also quite careless about whom he allowed to live in his village. Many who came had no particular trade skills. For example, there was no one to run the flour mill that Rapp had built which, at the peak of New Harmony's production, turned out sixty barrels of flour a day! There was also no one to handle the sawmill, the blacksmith shop, the kilns, nor the tannery.

Three years after Owen purchased New Harmony, the project was in financial ruins, so Robert Owen left the community and never returned. Owen's son, Robert, tried to restore order but divisions rose up among the members. Soon parcels of New Harmony lands were sold to resident individuals as well as to speculators. Despite this turn of events, New Harmony continued as a typical American town as it has to this day. Visitors can walk the

Harmony Society Church was constructed 1828-1831 with bricks made by Society members. It is believed that the church building was designed by Frederick Rapp.

streets of New Harmony, marvel at its architectural wonders, and muse about the commune's glory days.

In the meantime, still in 1824, George Rapp was busy designing his third utopian town at Ambridge, Pennsylvania. It would be called Economy, or "Divine Economy," signaling the new order that would arrive with the millennium. As usual, an advance party went on ahead to clear brush and build temporary homes. Again the commune prospered after a short time, marketing manufactured goods in nearby Pittsburgh. They even garnered awards for their high-quality silks at fairs in Boston, Philadelphia, and New York. Things were good, and Rapp could look out of the window of his luxurious home with a satisfied grin and stare at a beautiful statue of a shapely young miss named, "Miss Harmony," allegedly placed in the garden to signify the village motto of "Peace and Harmony." Then, in 1826, George Rapp fell in love.

Old Economy. Third and last home, 1825-1905, of the Harmony Society. It was here the society gained worldwide recognition for its religious devotion and economic prosperity.

The woman in question, Hildegard Mutschler, had been raised in Harmony and was well acquainted with its workings. For some reason, the villagers did not approve of the relationship and when Hildegard left Rapp to elope with one Jacob Klein, Rapp's adopted son, Frederick turned against his father. Rapp even sought to and managed to track down Hildegard and her husband and convince them to return to Economy.

Another problem at Economy was that Rapp had prophesied Christ's return to earth on September 24, 1829, and when this did not occur, the people grew critical of him. Further problems arose; Bernhard Müller, another would-be leader who had earlier joined the commune with fifty followers, managed to encourage a group of 176 people to move away from Economy. With that threat, the gradual decline of Economy became predictable. In order to maintain control of the organization, Rapp gave Müller the sum of $105 000 in three installments if he and his followers would leave within three months. They did so, and started a colony of their own at Philipsburg, Pennsylvania, just ten miles away, but it was unsuccessful from the start and soon dissolved. Some of Müller's followers later joined with William Keil to found a commune at Bethel, Missouri.

When George Rapp died on August 7, 1847, his son Frederick and two other managers took over the financial affairs of Economy. The commune continued to invest money, gained from the sale of their industries, but now they were no longer a productive society. They sold the factories and the distillery, and used the money to invest in oil drilling, coal mines, and railroads. They had some success in this, but by the 1870s the membership was ailing, the younger members having drifted away. Thus, by 1874, only 110 adults and twenty adopted children remained at Economy, and three decades later only two of the original members remained when the Harmonist Society was legally dissolved. When dissolution happened, the Commonwealth of Pennsylvania laid claim to one half of the Economy property because it had never been registered as a religious society.

There is no doubt about it. By all counts, the Harmonists were one of the most successful communalists in American history.

Feast Hall. Six times a year, all the Harmonists gathered in the 100 x 50 foot hall on the second floor to celebrate their anniversaries, hold their love feasts, and celebrate The Last Supper.

George Rapp Garden held the open pavilion with a female statue surrounded by well-manicured lawns and flowerbeds.

For Further Reading

Arndt, Karl J. R. (1997). George Rapp's Harmony Society. *American Communal Utopias.* Donald E. Pitzer, ed. Chapel Hill, NC: The University of North Carolina Press, 57-87.

Calverton, Victor Francis. (1969). *Where Angels Dared to Tread: Socialist & Communist Utopians Societies in the United States*. Freeport, NY: Books for Libraries Press.

Holloway, Mark. (1966). *Heavens on Earth: Utopian Communities in America, 1680-1880.* New York: Dover Publications.

Nordhoff, Charles. (1993). *American Utopias.* Stockbridge, MS: Berkshire House Publishers.

Sutton, Robert P. (2003). *Communal Utopias and the American Experience: Religious Communities, 1732-2000.* Westport, CN: Praeger.

Webber, Everett. (1959). *Escape to Utopia: The Communal Movement in America.* New York: Hastings House Publishers.

Wilson, William E. (1984). *The Angel and the Serpent.* Bloomington, IL: Indiana University Press.

http://www.nexusgrid.net/harmony-harmonists.htm

http://explorepahistory.com/hmarker.php?markerId=91

Hutterites

Laypeople, not clergy, seem to have dreamed up most of the designs for idyllic religious living in the past three centuries, and the Hutterian Brethren are no exception. Jacob Hutter (year of birth unknown), their original leader, was a hatter by trade, and was mentioned in church history books only in 1529 when he emerged as a lay leader in an Anabaptist congregation among the Tyrolese Anabaptists in Austerlitz, Austria. Hutter lived only a very short time, and in 1536 he was burned at the stake for his "heretical views."

Wolf Creek Hutterite Colony, near Olivet, South Dakota.

Anabaptists were a protest group known for their belief in the strict separation of church and state, rejection of the Sacraments, infant baptism, and taking an oath. Hutter's followers also became pacifists, refused to participate in the military, and exercised the most severe forms of church discipline via excommunication, and use of the ban. Hutter went even further and attacked the Anabaptists for disregarding the Biblical injunction that Christians should have all things in common (Acts 2:44). Hence the Hutterites became a communal group.

Hutter's reactionary ideas quickly attracted a following even though he urged his converts to abandon individualism and literally share their goods with one another. By 1530 Hutter's followers had split from the main body of Anabaptists and formed independent communes or bruderhof as they came to be known. The new organization also formally adopted the name, Hutterites or Hutterian Brethren. Persecution drove the pacifist communalists to various European countries including Moravia and Hungary. Although their numbers grew steadily, even numbering into the thousands, by 1631 events such as the Turkish War and the Thirty Years' War reduced their numbers to less than one thousand.

Always much committed to literacy, the Hutterites began the first kindergarten in Europe, concerned that their children should have ready access to the Holy Scriptures. At a time when most Europeans were illiterate, every Hutterite child could read. Hutterite preachers also committed many sermons and historical events to written form, but invasions by the Roman Catholic Society of Jesus in 1759 greatly reduced the holdings of Hutterite libraries. Fortunately, many of their works later showed up in European state archives.

An unexpected form of salvation for Hutterites occurred in 1770 when Catherine the Great invited them and other protestant groups to migrate to Russia and become farmers. These groups were offered religious freedom, the privilege of operating their own schools, military exemption, tax exemption for three years, and the right to practice their own form of local self government. The Hutterites agreed to become farmers, respect the Russian state government, and not try to make converts. Soon the first group of fifty-six Hutterites arrived in Russia, and was settled on Crown land. They were followed by other Hutterites eager to become Russian farmers, but the honeymoon did not last.

Hutterite made handicrafts – quillow and slippers.

Catherine the Great died in 1796 and Russia began to militarize in an attempt to become a world power. Certain privileges granted to the incoming groups a century earlier were revoked. Male youth were required to engage in military service and Russian became the official state language. Many young men of Anabaptist background – Mennonites and Hutterites – were rounded up during the night and if they refused to serve in the military, were either placed in concentration camps or were never heard from again. Once again, the Hutterites decided it was time to relocate.

Enter Clifton Sifton, Canada's Minister of the Interior.

Clifford Sifton wanted to populate the west, and he was not too worried about the details in accomplishing his goal. If a group wanted to immigrate to Canada and agreed to several specific conditions, they were quite welcome to Canada. The Hutterites were very pleased with the requirements posed by Sifton as follows; the Hutterites were expected to farm the land assigned to them, respect the federal government, and be prepared to pay taxes. They could manage their own schools, speak their own language, and engage in alternative service instead of enlisting in the military.

A German Bible and Fox's Book of Martyrs – basic Hutterite reading material.

During the 1870s, 18 000 Hutterites and Mennonites migrated to North America. The Hutterites chose South Dakota as their new home while the Mennonites went to Manitoba, Kansas, and Minnesota. In 1918 the first Hutterite colony was established in Alberta, Canada, due to problems stemming from forced military conscription in the United States. Several young Hutterite men were incarcerated at Alcatraz Prison for refusing to enter the military, and at least two of them died there. That was enough for some Hutterite leaders to begin to look to Canada as a place of refuge.

Meanwhile, back in Russia. When the Russian government realized that the exodus of Hutterites and Mennonites meant they were losing 45 000 of their best farmers, they tried to negotiate with them to remain in the country. The government placated some of the pacifists by offering them a form of alternative military service. As a result, many Mennonites and two Hutterite families chose to remain in Russia.

Today, life in some 700-plus Hutterite colonies in North America follows a daily and/or weekly routine that would appear to outsiders as tedious. There are generally no newspapers, radios, or television sets on a Hutterite colony, so other forms of leisure like singing and playing games turn out to be the mainstay of entertainment. Each baptized individual on a colony is assigned a task with limited rotation. Older women run the kindergarten and younger women take care of cooking and laundry. Men do outside chores and sit on the various councils and committees that run the colony. Their major responsibilities are agriculturally related, including working in the fields, operating tractors and other farm machinery, or serving as blacksmiths, carpenters, or teachers. The colony preacher holds his position for life and he will continue preaching as long as health permits. Preachers, like all other colony positions, are elected – with only baptized males being allowed to cast ballots.

Unbaptised young people (particularly males) are informally allowed a measure of behavioral freedom such as playing musical instruments or playing pool in a downtown location. Once they wish to be married, however, they must enroll in a catechism class and be baptized. Their potential marriage partner must be a baptized Hutterite approved by the colony board. Baptized Hutterites are expected to toe the line in obeying all colony regulations.

Growing old on a Hutterite colony is a relaxing and pleasurable experience. When individuals reach the age of 55 they are often released from doing heavy chores, but they can volunteer to work part time or engage in work related hobbies. Older people are treated with respect and are often sought out for advice or to share reminiscences about traditional Hutterite practices or colony history. Hutterites do not usually utilize the benefits of government social welfare programs though they do tend to frequent hospitals more than they used to. Sickly and elderly individuals are cared for on colony grounds and live with their respective families; there are no senior citizen homes on Hutterite colonies.

To be different is often to have to suffer unjust criticism. This is certainly true in the Hutterite case. Hutterites have frequently been the target of criticism for their way of life, often originating with groups and individuals who know little about their commitment to communalism and traditional Christian values. Some anti-Hutterites are even afraid that because of their high birth rate Hutterites will eventually outnumber other ethnic groups and become a threat to mainline society. Today the Hutterite birth rate is actually decreasing rapidly. In 1950, the birth rate stood at 45.9 per 1000, but decreased to 43.0 per 1000 in 1970. By 1990, it further plummeted to 35.2 per 1000 and the trend continues.

Critics of the Hutterian way of life are sometimes annoyed that they are exempt from military service, forgetting that when the Hutterites entered Canada, the Canadian government made that arrangement with them. Besides, Hutterites contribute generously to such war-related efforts as the work of the Red Cross and the Mennonite Central Committee.

There was a time in Alberta when Hutterites were not allowed to purchase additional farmland, even though their numbers were growing. In 1942, the Alberta Social Credit Party government passed the Communal Properties Act, which had to be repealed when the Alberta Conservative Party government passed a Bill of Rights. Related to this concern is the unfounded public fear that Hutterites do not pay sufficient income taxes. In Canada, however, colony incomes are divided among individuals who pay income tax as though they personally earned a portion of colony income. In fact, all colony income accrues to a communally owned treasury. In Alberta, Hutterite colonies also pay for the total cost of the operation of government-approved English language schools that use the provincially mandated curriculum.

Always much committed to literacy, the Hutterites began the first kindergarten in Europe, concerned that their children should have ready access to the Holy Scriptures.

There have been legal conflicts in the Hutterite community, many times involving with members who have left the colony. The courts have tended to side with the colonies in their efforts to discourage departures by enforcing agreements made at the time of baptism that all goods and lands remain colony property if members should choose to leave the community.

Finally, criticism has sometimes reached an all time point of ridiculous when rumored accounts prevail that due to fears about inbreeding, Hutterites advertise in local newspapers for outsiders to visit colonies and impregnate young

Hutterite women. To date no one has been able to prove that this is actually the case. Unfortunately, the ads do exist, but they have undoubtedly been placed to discredit the Hutterites. Anyone acquainted with the sexual mores of Hutterites would know that they consider the violation of sexual rules as one of the most offensive sins one can commit. In fact, when unbaptized Hutterites who have left the colony return to it, they are subjected to HIV tests! Sexual purity is one of the highest expectations of a Hutterite Christian.

It should be noted that there are three major branches of Hutterite communities – Dariusleut, Lehrerleut, and Schmiedeleut. The Schmiedeleut live in Manitoba, North and South Dakota, and Minnesota, and the Dariousleut and Lehrerleut live in Alberta, Saskatchewan, Manitoba, Montana, and Washington. There is one Hutterite colony in British Columbia. Today there 45 000 American Hutterites living in 460 colonies, and there are 28 020 Hutterites in Canada living in 309 colonies. The origin of the names of the three groups is as follows. The Dariusleut (Leute means people in German) derived their name from a leader named Darius. The Lehrerleut (teacher people) greatly emphasized the teaching/learning process, and the Schmiedeleut (blacksmith people) specialized in that trade.

To their chagrin, Hutterites have never been actively engaged in evangelizing outsiders, though their interpretation of the Scriptures does mandate such activity. Oddly enough, during the 1950s a Hutterite colony was developed in Owa, Japan, but it was a group of about twenty-four Japanese individuals who sought out the Hutterites to obtain information. Interestingly enough, some North American Hutterites are currently involved in a mission work in Nigeria, Africa. The mission is called Palm Grove, and though progress has been difficult, some 300 Nigerians now live in the community. Hutterite missionaries are involved in teaching the Nigerians to be self-supporting amidst severe economic and spiritual challenges.

In 2010, the Hutterites celebrated 480 years of communal living. Why have Hutterite communes lasted so long when other such communities have failed? The answer is not complicated. Hutterites practice a very mainline form of

Christianity. They hold quite orthodox theological views and have not fallen prey to any personally derived or perverse doctrines promoted by some self-styled prophet. Jacob Hutter is not regarded as either a hero or prophet hero; he was just an ordinary man who has served God in his own way in his time. For the most part the Hutterites continue to live a traditional agricultural way of life in the style that all North Americans once lived – with the exception of communalism. They work hard, practice good ethics, welcome their neighbors into their homes, pay taxes, worship God and obey His commands according to the Bible.

Oh yes, they also welcome visitors to their colonies.

For Further Reading

Esau, Alvin J. (2004). *The Courts and the Colonies: The Litigation of Hutterite Church Disputes.* Vancouver, BC: UBC Press.

Flint, David. (1975). *The Hutterites: A Study in Prejudice.* Toronto, ON: Oxford University Press.

Friesen, John W. (1977). *People, Culture and Learning.* Calgary, AB: Detselig Enterprises, chapters ten and twelve.

Hofer, John. (2004). *The History of the Hutterites.* Revised edition. Altona, MB: Friesens Corporation.

Hofer, Joshua. (1980). *Japanese Hutterites: A Visit to Owa Community.* Elie, MB: James Valley Book Centre.

Hofer, Samuel. (1998). *The Hutterites: Life and Images of a Communal People.* Saskatoon, SK: Hofer Publishers

Hostetler, John A. (1974). *Hutterite Society.* Baltimore, MD: The Johns Hopkins University Press.

Hostetler, John A., and Gertrude Enders Huntingdon. (1971). *The Hutterites of North America.* New York: Holt, Rinehart, and Winston.

Peter, Karl A. (1987). *The Dynamics of Hutterite Society: An Analytical Approach.* Edmonton, AB: University of Alberta Press.

Stahl, Lisa Marie. (2007). *My Hutterite Life.* Helena, MT: Farcountry Press Books.

http://www.hutterites.org/HutteriteHistory/index.htm
http://www.hutterites.org/

Icarians

The Icarians were a 19th century communal group founded on a platform of rational democracy. The organization had a fragile religious base, substituting economic pursuits as their underlying philosophy. Following their relatively short existence, one could also describe the Icarians as "wandering minstrels of communalism." Their various journeys took them to Lousiana, Illinois, Texas, Iowa, and California. Their founder, Etienne Cabet (1788-1856), was born in France and died in St. Louis, Missouri. The name Icaria, is derived from Greek mythology and implies "soaring high in adventurous flight."

The Icarian story began in France with the writings of Etienne Cabet, often described as a philosophical, idealistic, hot-headed politician. Still, he influenced the formation of a rather unique commune that reached its peak population of 500 in Nauvoo, Illinois in 1855, just seven years after it began. Cabet initiated plans for his idyllic dream by reading about previous utopian models in three languages – English, French, and German. He was significantly influenced by the work of another utopian dreamer, Robert Owen, and came to the conclusion that communal living in a spirit of fraternity and equality would bring out the best in people. Cabet reasoned that through communal living individuals would sacrifice their personal interests for the common good and learn to exchange selfish personal gain with a religious sense of sharing. Cabet projected that by expanding the limits of

The Nauvoo Icarian Community was established in 1849. "The Nauvoo Community survived until about 1860 – longer than any other secular communal society in Illinois."

human reasoning to build a new social order, mankind could soar to new heights. His book containing these ideas was entitled, *Voyage of de Lord William Carisdall en Icaria* (Travels and Adventures of Lord William Carisall in Icaria). The book became a best seller and was published in five editions.

A third-generation resident of the original Icarian community, Mary Baxter Logan has lived in Nauvoo, Illinois for over eighty years. She reminisces about her ten cents per hour job imprinting the government stamp on the box tops of grapes going for sale.

Mary Baxter Logan recounts that "by 1880 Nauvoo had at least 600 acres of grapes right in city limits of Nauvoo."

Cabet's writings quickly gained an audience on both sides of the ocean. However, French national leaders saw him as a threat so he was exiled from both France and Belgium. A trip to England saw him criticized by the church, state police, and the courts. He was viewed as a dangerous man because he questioned the status quo of capitalism and promoted what many saw as a viable alternative. Cabet also chastised the French government as well as the king, which was considered a very dangerous thing to do. His decision to move to the United States was therefore a very perceptive move.

When Cabet arrived in America few people warmed to his ideas, but his 500 followers in France were eager to help him develop his envisaged utopia in the new world. His converts arrived in a series of ships, Cabet travelling on one of the last ones. At the age of 60, he left his wife and family in France and set out on a new adventure in the United States. When he finally reached American soil he discovered that his followers who had gone before were crammed into two large houses, living in very unhealthy conditions. Quickly he resolved to do something about it.

Cabet's ideal commune was to be established in Texas, just north of the present city of Dallas. In 1847, with the help of Robert Owen, Cabet purchased 3 000 acres of homestead land along the Trinity River. The following year an advance party of sixty-nine stalwarts set out to occupy the land. The plan was that the commune would feature a strong administrative arrangement that would ensure every member having specific tasks to perform without remuneration. Departments with elected chairpersons would be established for education, health, leisure, finance, provisions, clothing, lodging, and publicity. So far, so good; then problems arose because Cabet also believed that all individuals are imbued with a strong work ethic, and this did not always work out. In the Icarian case, as long as donations from France kept coming in, the Icarians fared quite well. When these dried up and the land failed to produce enough food and salable products, the Icarians suffered.

Quite bluntly, the Icarian settlement in Texas was a disaster. The men who first travelled there suffered a great deal – their ill-equipped wagons broke down and they encountered unexpected swamps, and deserted prairies. When the temperature soared to 100 degrees Fahrenheit, and malaria struck, several men died; moreover, their physician went insane

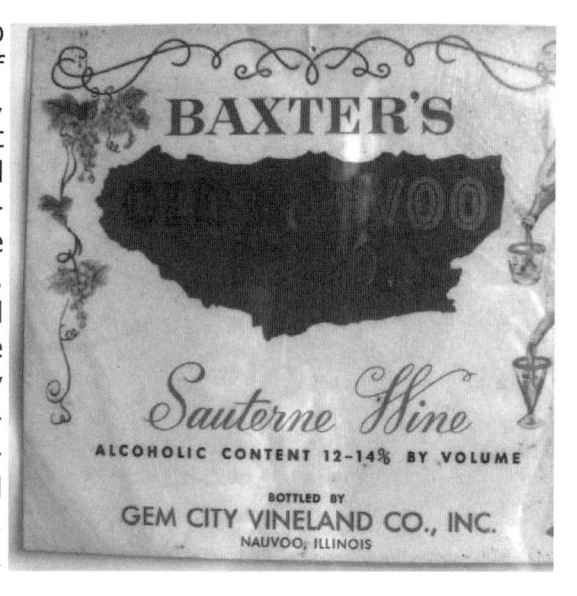

Baxter's Old Nauvoo Brand Sauterne Wine bottled by Gem City Vineland Co. Inc. Nauvoo, Illinois. Mary Baxter Logan explains that her "great grandfather started the winery in 1857."

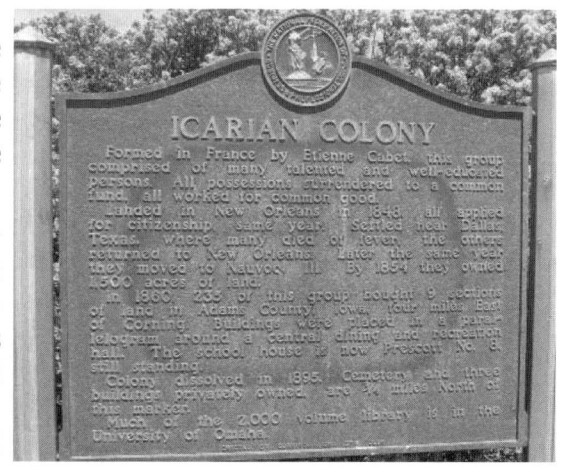

Icarian Colony formed in France by Etienne Cabet landed in New Orleans . . . to Dallas . . . to New Orleans . . . to Nauvoo . . . to Adams County, Iowa.

and wandered off. By the end of the summer of 1848, the party tried to make their way back to Shreveport, Louisiana, but it was a 250 mile trip under no better conditions than before. Cabet was quickly appraised of the situation and immediately determined to find an alternative place for his community to settle. A committee he appointed soon reported that the town of Nauvoo, Illinois had been abandoned by a group of Mormons and dozens of their vacated homes were ready for immediate occupancy. The Icarians were overjoyed.

A large company of 142 men, seventy-four women, and sixty-four children soon made their way to Nauvoo, travelling up the Mississippi River to their destination. Negotiations with agents who represented the departed Mormons gave Cabet access to an abundance of vacated homes, 2 000 acres of farmland, and the Mormon temple square. Within a very short time, the town of Nauvoo was up and running with stores and shops and mills and other businesses, all developed and operated by the Icarians. Then a tornado nearly destroyed the Mormon temple that Cabet had planned to use as a school. Under Icarian commitment, however, the temple square was soon rebuilt, although it never quite had the splendor of the Mormon temple. For the next century the new building served various purposes – school, dance hall, theatre, apartment house, and visitor's centre. The community motto was, "From each according to his talent; to each according to his needs."

French Icarian Colony Village four miles east of Corning in Adams County, Iowa.

Nauvoo was now a bustling economically successful centre of 500 Icarians. Their lifestyle was probably better than that of any 19th century commune in America. Their library contained 4,000 books, they published a weekly newspaper, and their industries were thriving.

Oddly, sometimes when things seem to go very well, trouble starts. This occurred when Cabet found it necessary to return to France to defend himself against charges of fraud in connection with the Texas fiasco. He remained in France for a year and successfully cleared himself of all charges. When he returned to Nauvoo, however, it was a different commune. Despite the settlement's economic success, in his absence Cabet's power had waned. Part of the difficulty came from Cabet's sudden concern that the morality of the colony was dissipating. He issued a series of strict rules that were not welcomed by the membership. Cabet was upset that smoking and drinking had become rampant and women were "obstinate and ignorant." Like the men, the women were smoking openly and wearing inappropriate clothing not made by colony seamstresses. Cabet originated forty-eight new articles of behavior and though the elected assembly adopted them, an insurrection quickly developed. One opposing group even burned Cabet in effigy.

In 1853, a group of Icarians left Nauvoo to form a commune at Corning, Iowa, but this did not deter Cabet. Instead he asked for a four-year term for his position as leader rather than only one year. To his suprises, his motion was defeated. He quickly dropped his request for a four-year term and was forgiven and restored to a one-year appointment. The following year, however, a new board that did not favor Cabet's leadership was elected, and Cabet refused to acknowledge it. In the end he was expelled from Nauvoo so he moved to St. Louis with 180 of his followers where he died on November 8, 1856. Without Cabet's leadership, the St. Louis group managed to survive for a short time by establishing a commune on thirty-nine acres at Cheltenham just outside of St. Louis. They operated a series of successful shops as cartwrights, blacksmiths, cobblers, and tailors, but their mortgage was too large to handle. Soon a split occurred and the colony was left with only a handful of residents. The commune was gone.

French Icarian Colony Village, Iowa. The Refectory (communal dining hall) included the kitchen, a sewing room, and a 2 000+ volume library.

By 1858, the Nauvoo Icarians suffered an economic depression and their creditors grew restless. Dissension arose among the members and most workers refused to fulfill their responsibilities. Soon the Icarian organization broke up, and those who remained began a very successful cultivation of grapes. Emile Baxter and his family, who had joined the Nauvoo Icarians in 1854, started a winery that won many medals for taste and quality. It has been reported that the oldest recorded concord grape vineyard in Illinois was planted by the Baxters in 1851 and is located in Nauvoo State Park. Today Baxter's Winery is operated by Baxter's great-grandson and is considered the oldest winery in Illinois.

In the meantime the Corning Icarians were facing a new set of challenges. Although they had purchased 3,100 acres of fertile settlement lands for only $1.25 an acre, they had assumed a large mortgage. They managed to make payments on time because they sold produce to Union Army agents who needed them for their troops. By 1870 they had 400 acres in corn and wheat and 400 acres in pasture and timber. They also owned a supply of horses and cattle. In no time, the Corning Icarian lifestyle resembled that of Nuavoo, very efficiently combining work and play.

New members were constantly joining the Corning commune, many of them coming with new ideas about how things should be run. In 1870 a contingent of young men joined the colony and tried to bring operations back into line with Cabet's more militant stance. In 1877 a split occurred and a group calling themselves Young Icarians relocated to a new settlement very close by. They claimed half the land and dragged

French Icarian Colony Village, Iowa, 1992 rededication of the French Icarian Cemetery, in memory of French Icanians buried there.

several buildings to the new site. Four years later, twenty-six young families from this group moved to California where they bought a ranch of 885 acres near Cloverdale, and planted grapes. This colony was economically very successful and operated with all assets in the name of the settlement. Members could own private property and would receive premiums or dividends from the colony's profits. Then, as though without warning, five years later the commune ended as quickly as it had begun – probably because of their prosperity. Admission requirements were stringent and attracted few. New members were supposed to be fully acquainted with Cabet's writings and be fluent in French. With this on their radar screen, many members felt they could do better individually and struck out on their own.

A marker dedicated to their brief sojourn as a commune is located near Cloverdale, California.

Finally, back in Corning, Iowa, the group remaining on the original property, shrank to only thirty-four people by 1886. Four years later, only seventeen people remained, most of them elderly. The commune was officially dissolved by mutually agreed, legal action on October 22, 1895.

Thus ended fifty years of some of the most interesting, yet conflict-ridden communal history in America.

Cabet projected that by expanding the limits of human reasoning to build a new social order, mankind could soar to new heights.

For Further Reading

Calverton, Victor Francis. (1969). *Where Angels Dared to Tread: Socialist & Communist Utopians Societies in the United States.* Freeport, NY: Books for Libraries Press.

Holloway, Mark. (1966). *Heavens on Earth: Utopian Communities in America,* 1680-1880. New York: Dover Publications.

Nordhoff, Charles. (1993). *American Utopias.* Stockbridge, MS: Berkshire House Publishers.

Sutton, Robert P. (1997). An American Elsyium: The Icarian Communities. *American Communal Utopias.* Donald E. Pitzer, ed. Chapel Hill, NC: The University of North Carolina Press, 279-296.

Synder, Lillian. (1996). *The Search for Brotherhood, Peace & Justice: The Story of Icaria.* Deep River, IA: Brennan Printing.

Webber, Everett. (1959). *Escape to Utopia: The Communal Movement in America.* New York: Hastings House Publishers.

http://nihs.info/history.html

http://www.beautifulnauvoo.com/

Koreshan Unity

Founder's House, built in 1896, is listed on the National Register of Historic Places.

Oh, oh, another special vision, right? That is correct; in 1869, a New York physician named Cyrus Teed (1839-1908) invented a new religion because he received a special vision informing him that he was the Messiah. He immediately tried to attract followers to the new movement that would specialize in communalism and celibacy (nothing new there), and its founding philosophy would be known as cellular cosmogony. This meant that the earth should be perceived as hollow with the sun and all life forms existing within the earth. The outer shell of the earth was perceived as concave rather than convex, and the central sun was always half dark and half light, resulting in day and night.

Theoretically, it should have been difficult for Teed to find adherents to this new kind of faith, but somehow he managed to do so. In 1880 he founded his first commune in Moravia, New York, but hostility toward the experiment motivated him to relocate to New York City.

Teed's philosophical journey was nothing less than spectacular. To begin with, he quit school at the age of eleven and went to work on the Erie Canal. Later, at the age of twenty, he began studying medicine with his uncle. During the Civil War he joined the Union Army, then finished a degree in medicine in 1859. That same year he married Delia Rowe and the next year they had a son, Douglas. Delia died in 1885. Soon after, Teed moved into a New York apartment with four women and began a preaching tour using Chicago as a base. His Baptist parents had always encouraged him to enter the ministry because of his gift of oratory, so in a sense, he followed their advice. In fact, in 1886 his remarkable speaking abilities even got him elected as president of the National Association for Mental Health.

While practicing medicine Teed became interested in the pseudoscience of alchemy and eventually claimed that he had been successful in transforming matter into energy and then reduced the energy into another kind of matter. He stated that this success proved that he had discovered the "philosopher's stone" for which so many had searched before. With this discovery he claimed to be able to transform lead into gold. From this point Teed went on to find himself mentally transported from earthly things to a spiritual realm, from his brain to his extremities. It was then that he encountered a beautiful woman who appeared in a vision, challenging him to undertake the role of Messiah. At that point Teed began to call himself Koresh, the biblical translation of his Christian name. His religion became known as Koreshanity. There is evidence that Teed drew some of his ideas about communalism from the Harmonists and the Oneida community. For a short time he was also admitted to membership in the North Family of Shakers at Lebanon, New York.

A canoeist enjoying a quiet afternoon paddling down nearby Estero River.

In 1888 Teed formed the Koreshan Unity Community that grew to 123 members in five years. As new converts (mostly women) joined the organization, Teed tried to establish branch communes in San Francisco, Denver, Baltimore, and Boston. When these branches failed, the converts moved to Chicago to practice celibacy, renounce alcohol, tobacco, and gambling, and yield up their possessions to Teed. Teed also started a number of organizations such as the Guiding

Star Publishing House, the Assembly of the Covenant Church Triumphant, and the College of Life which later became the Koreshan University.

The Conrad Schlender Cottage, built in 1903, is included in the National Register of Historic Places.

Teed's followers were stratified into three groups – celibates, who were regarded as being the highest order – investigatives, who only donated money, and – maritals who were married but had sexual relations only for procreation. Teed himself had a son, so he made it clear that those who remained celibate all of their adult lives were the closest to achieving higher mental and natural states. In due time the Chicago dwelling was overcrowded so Teed began to look for another location. The Chicago group was also facing a myriad of hostilities and lawsuits from newspapers and angry husbands whose wives had joined Teed's movement. Fortunately, another vision arrived just in time, this one about moving to Florida.

The land Teed found at Estero, Florida was too pricey for the pocketbook of his commune, but fortunately, Gustave Damkohler, a mourning widower offered to donate 320 acres for the commune. Damkohler claimed to have been the recipient of celestial vibrations similar to those that Teed had experienced. Teed arrived in Florida on January 1, 1894 with four female companions. Over the next six weeks the party negotiated for land with Damkohler, who retained twenty acres of the property for himself. Shortly thereafter, Teed returned to Chicago to arrange for his protégés to move to Florida.

Teed's concept of the New Jerusalem to be built at Estero was a star-shaped colony with streets 400 feet wide. Quickly he dispatched an advance party of twenty-four to Florida. The men quickly built a series of buildings including a huge home for Teed. They literally built an entire village out of Florida swampland, dredging the Estero River and digging drainage ditches. Soon a sawmill, post office, school, and dormitory comprised major facilities for the settlement, but it was not until 1903 that Teed invited the members still living in

Chicago to join the Florida contingent. Soon seventy-five additional members arrived, bringing the total number of residents to 200, a far cry from the six million members that Teed had predicted would join his commune. An array of newly constructed facilities were added to the commune, including a bakery that produced 600 loaves of bread a day, and a machine shop that ran entirely by steam. Other profit-making industries included a blacksmith shop, art hall, boat works, water taxi, plant nursery, printing press, cement-making shop, and barns and sheds to store goods and machinery. The communal library contained a diverse collection of books about astronomy, history, philosophy, and agronomy. The commune also published a newspaper, the *American Eagle,* and a magazine, the *Flaming Sword*. By 1906 the commune had built thirty-five buildings and had charge over 7 000 acres.

Teed operated a fairly despotic but philosophically liberal empire, however, as time went on many freedom-loving individuals left the colony. Some dissidents sued Teed to get their properties back, while others accused him of mandating celibacy for everyone except himself. Teed was adamant that children be taught the three "R's" plus music history, and geography, and he even went so far as to start a political party, the Progressive Liberty Party, whose members ran in 1906 county elections. One candidate was so convinced of the merit of his platform that he got into a fist-fight with a candidate from another party.

Koreshan Settlement *large machine shop* built in 1904.

Ezra J. Stewart, a Shaker visitor to Estero, after his visit observed that he had experienced a wonderful atmosphere at the Teed commune. He especially made note of the love relationship that existed between Teed and his compatriots. Stewart painted a somewhat idyllic scenario of life at Estero, describing the peaceful dormitories, sunken gardens, artistic footbridges, and flowering vines.

There is evidence that Teed drew some of his ideas about communalism from the Harmonists and the Oneida community. For a short time he was also admitted to membership in the North Family of Shakers at Lebanon, New York.

That kind of praise should have brought in new members! Stewart also met sixty-year-old beautiful, refined, and gracious Anne G. Ordway, whom Teed had renamed Victoria Gratia. She was Teed's right-hand associate and was eventually supposed to reign over the 144,000 sons of God who would later emerge. Still with us? Teed also predicted that he would eventually be martyred at which time Victoria would be exalted to divine motherhood and imperial pre-eminence. Victoria would then serve as divine natural head of all the orders of church and state. Teed claimed that he was immortal, and after being assassinated he would be resurrected. On October 13, 1906, at Fort Myers, a group conflict arose because enemies of Teed's commune tried to disenfranchise the Koreshan Unity. Teed tried to stop the scuffle that ensued but was struck down by the town marshal. Teed's injuries were such that two years later, on December 22, 1908, he died from them. Three days later, still watching over his remains, his followers waited anxiously for him to be resurrected, but it never happened. Finally county officials insisted that Teed's body be buried and his followers reluctantly agreed. His tombstone at Estero Island read, "Cyrus, Shepherd Stone of Israel." In 1921, a hurricane blew the tomb into the Gulf of Mexico, and some followers interpreted this event to suggest that Teed was now free of his mortal state and would indeed be resurrected in another form.

No leader of the Koreshan Unity emerged after Teed died, and a number of lawsuits about property ownership ensued. Many Koreshans scattered to other communities, but some simply wanted to remain in the village and retain individual property. A few residents continued to live on the site during the 1940s when a resident, Laurence W. Bubbert, was appointed to donate some of the land to the State of Florida. In 1961 the State of Florida named the colony the Koreshan State Historic Site that today comprises seventy-three buildings.

The last Koreshan dweller, Hedwig Michel, died in 1982, but the Korshan Unity lived on when Jo Bigelow was elected that year as the seventh president of the Koreshan Unity. The weekly *American Eagle* is still being published, but the last issue of the *Flaming Star* was printed in October, 1948.

As the experience of the Koreshan Unity suggests, some American utopias lived through interesting times.

For Further Reading

Division of Recreation and Parks (nd). *Koreshan State Historic Site.* Estero, FL: Florida Department of Environmental Protection.

Fogarty, Robert S., ed. (1980). *Dictionary of American Communal and Utopian History.* Westport, CN: Greenwood Press.

Gutek, Gerald, and Patricia Gutek. (1998). *Visiting Utopian Communities: A Guide to Shakers, Moravians, and Others.* Columbia, SC: University of South Carolina Press.

Landing, James E. (1997). Cyrus Reed Teed and the Koreshan Unity. *American Communal Utopias.* Donald E. Pitzer, ed. Chapel Hill, NC: The University of North Carolina Press, 375-395

Sutton, Robert P. (2004). *Communal Utopias and the American Experience: Secular Communities, 1732-2000.* Westport, CN: Praeger.

http://www.floridastateparks.org/
http://mwweb.org/koreshan/blog/
http://koreshan.mwweb.org/teed.htm

Oneida

The unusual Oneida community of New York is easily one of the most analyzed historical communes. Other than scholars devoted to studying so-called idyllic societies, however, few people are aware that the Oneida Silverware Company grew out of a somewhat unusual communal settlement that used to make animal traps!

Oneida Community Mansion House.

It all began with John Humphrey Noyes (1811-1886), a theologically trained but unordained, self-styled minister. Noyes became enamored of the idea to build a special kind of religious commune influenced by the preaching of the Reverend Charles Finney, a lawyer turned evangelist. Finney, who assisted in the founding of Oberlin College in Ohio, later chastised Noyes for promoting a community of free love. Although both men believed that a form of perfection or sinlessness could be attained by spiritually attuned Christians, Finney insisted that celibacy was the means by which to achieve and maintain that state. Noyes, on the other hand, believed that a sinless state was possible because he had attained it. His proof was that after the experience he was personally incapable of experiencing any feelings of guilt or despair. Because of this rather unique theological interpretation Noyes felt he was God's agent on earth, called to a special mission. Finney preached just the opposite, arguing that perfection was possible only through special human effort. He was so charismatic in his appeals that many students in his classes at Oberlin took vows of chastity. Some of then even went so far as to deliberately put themselves into situations of temptation just to prove that their "perfect" state would prevent them from yielding to its wiles.

Noyes' position was not one of free love per se, that is engaging in love (sex) and then leaving one's partner. Rather, his interpretation was that love stood apart from the sex act, and when the latter was entertained, it would be under very stringent and controlled conditions. The organization and operation of the commune he initiated clearly demonstrated this philosophy.

But let us go back to the beginning.

Born in Brattleboro, Vermont, in 1826, at the age of 15, Noyes entered Dartmouth College. This was the period of the religious "Great Awakening," in America and Charles Finney figured prominently in that movement. Noyes was so influenced by Finney's preaching that he later enrolled in Andover Seminary in preparation for the ministry. He often found himself in disagreement with his professors, and though his father cautioned him to toe the line lest he never receive a ministerial assignment, the younger Noyes demurred. He later transferred to Yale Theological Seminary because he believed that its teachings were more in keeping with his ideas. When Yale officials heard about Noyes' doctrine of free love, however, they withdrew his license to preach. During this time, Noyes' chosen girlfriend, Abigail Merwin left him to marry another man. Then, in 1838 Noyes married Harriet Holton, whom he clearly regarded as less desirable than Abigail. He did this simply to show his critics that he did not believe in celibacy in the same way that Charles Finney and the Shakers did. Noyes' letter of proposal to Harriet was business-like and indicated that if they did marry he would define what that meant later on. Apparently that was agreeable to Harriet.

Oneida Community Mansion House.

By 1845 Noyes had gained enough of a following that he and his assistants could form a commune of celibate perfectionists in Putney, Vermont. Harriet's dowry fund was used as collateral to buy a printing press as an assist to keep the membership informed. Through his publications Noyes condemned marriage because he feared that women, like land or other forms of chattel, could be considered property. His plan of "complex marriage" was designed to leave the sexual fate of both partners in the hands of an outside party. According to his interpretation, all adults in his commune should consider themselves married to everyone else. He required that everyone should love others equally. All communal members should share everything – sex as well as economics. This was a difficult perspective for some members to adopt since they had to unlearn many previous attitudes and behaviors.

Oneida Miniature Silver Tea Set.

Noyes argued that exclusive couples involved in an orthodox form of marriage could develop an attitude of privacy and selfishness. In Noyes' commune, if a couple wanted to cohabit, the arrangement was made by mutual consent and negotiated by a third party. Noyes seemed to have ignored his own advice in relation to a Mrs. Mary Cragin who, together with her husband George, spent a great deal of time with Noyes and his wife. Noyes favored Mrs. Cragin as a participant in many activities, and the two of them reportedly spent a great deal of time together at Willow Place in Brooklyn, New York.

In 1848, Noyes' group moved to Oneida, New York, where they purchased a rundown house and forty acres of land. At first the company suffered hardships, having to camp in two log houses and live off the avails of a sawmill and a blacksmith shop. As soon as the commune had reached some measure of economic stability, several non-communal satellite communities were established at Wallingford, Connecticut; Newark, New Jersey; Cambridge, Vermont; and Manlius, New York. By now Noyes' followers numbered over 200 members. A fundamental plank in Noyes' plan was that individuals of both sexes would be treated as equals. In practice, however, Noyes elevated several women above the rest; they were known as "mothers" or "aunts," namely his wife, his favorite lover, and his two sisters. Critics have pointed out that Oneida women generally had to concede to an explicit male superiority and hide any talents they had that might threaten the patriarchal basis of the community. Further proof of this inequality was that the age of twelve, girls experienced an abrupt end to their schooling, while males were allowed to continue their studies towards college. Eventually five community men earned degrees in medicine, two in engineering, and one in law.

The initial economic focus of Noyes' endeavors at Oneida was agriculture. The community grew crops and sold their produce, and also ran a sawmill and a blacksmith shop. Then a community innovator, Sewell Newhouse, invented steel animal traps, first making them by hand, and later manufacturing so many of them to the point that the business became a major enterprise. By the late 1880s the Oneida community was manufacturing close to 300 000 traps a year. They also showed their ingenuity in other ways. They invented the first lazy Susan, a mechanized mop wringer, a potato peeler, and a washing machine. Two decades after their establishment, Oneida boasted 300 people with an accumulated wealth of half a million dollars. Most of the members lived in a huge mansion some 93 000 square feet in area, containing thirty-five apartments, eight guest rooms, and a large dining room. Management of economic affairs was in the hands of twenty-one standing committees and forty-eight administrative departments.

Noyes argued that exclusive couples involved in an orthodox form of marriage could develop an attitude of privacy and selfishness.

Daily life at Oneida included yielding to a number of Noyes' regulations pertaining to good health. These included celibacy and vegetarianism, and restraint in terms of using tobacco or drinking alcohol. The people of Oneida ate only two meals a day accompanied by either coffee or tea. Noyes also invented a ceremony called "mutual criticism" that resembled a kind of confession whereby members could point out inappropriate behaviors or inadequacies on the part of their peers at regular meetings. The idea was that mutual criticism would serve as a form of therapy while at the same time reducing backbiting. Before these meetings began, no doubt some members may have been a bit nervous about what might be said about their behavior. Mutual criticism was apparently designed to be a means of helping members maintain a clear conscience, and this was also supposed to assist in the process of maintaining good health. Noyes himself was exempt from the ritual because he felt that the group should not criticize their leader.

The rules and arrangements created by Noyes appeared to work, because the community continued to prosper. At this point Noyes decided it was time to enlarge the Oneida population by having children.

It must be noted that from time to time children were born at celibate Oneida, even though Noyes strongly discouraged having children. As an addendum, he reminded his people that until Oneida was on a strong financial base, they would be better off without adding numbers through birth. When things got better, Noyes' plan was to add numbers through birth, but only through selective breeding. To this end fifty-three women and twenty-eight men were chosen to take part in the experiment. Only those males and females deemed to be physically and intellectually worthy were allowed to participate. Matching-making of procreating couples was carefully arranged by members of a special committee that also screened prospective candidates. During the last decade of Oneida's existence, fifty-eight children were born through these liaisons. Later it became evident that Noyes himself had fathered nine children, and his son, Theodore, fathered eight. Child raising, however, was a communal affair, many children growing up cared for by several individuals rather than by a couple.

Life at Oneida consisted of much more than hard work pertaining to agriculture and manufacturing. There were times of leisure, during which members were expected to take part in religious discussions, Bible study, and individual contemplation. Evenings were devoted to the study of Scripture reading, writing, debating, singing, and prayer. Hebrew, Greek, and Latin were taught on Sundays as part of chapel meetings that were open to the public. Mutual criticism sessions were also held on Sunday evenings. Though contact with the outside world was considerable, visitors seldom chose to apply for membership though their numbers were high. For example, on July 4, 1863, more than 1 500 people visited Oneida.

Despite this high rate of interaction, there is no record of an unusually large dropout rate at Oneida.

As Noyes grew older he decided to pick a successor, his son, Theodore, a physician and an avowed agnostic who did not agree with much of Oneidan philosophy. Twice, in 1873 and in 1878 Theodore left Oneida to seek his fortune elsewhere. Naturally, there was criticism of the elder Noyes' choice in Theodore, but he remained adamant. For a while Theodore took the leadership role at Oneida, but his father felt compelled to take it back when he disagreed with Theodore's decisions. Theodore and his wife regarded themselves as an exclusive couple who preferred not to live at Oneida. Theodore warned the people to abandon communalism and group marriage or the organization would not last. Gradually the elder Noyes also came to this realization, and Theodore continued to serve as president until Oneida was reorganized to become a joint stock company.

As the end of the commune neared, the Oneida Holding Company issued 24 000 stock shares valued at twenty-five dollars each. Each adult received 4.25 shares for each year they had lived in the community. Later, in keeping with changes in the market, and under the leadership of Pierrepont Burt Noyes, another son of John Humphrey's, Oneida also shifted its primary manufacturing focus from animal traps to tableware. It was a very successful move. Today, Oneida heirs still manage a company that retails excellent silverware, and boasts stock that is worth millions.

The Oneida commune came to an end when company shares were divided among the members. Some individuals sold their shares and left town to participate in new beginnings. For others, this proved to be extremely difficult since they had no experience in handling household budgets or money in any form. Another challenge for members was to organize as families of some sort, since some group-born children were unable to identify their biological fathers. In the end, most children went with their mothers with their new husbands who suddenly found themselves serving in the role of stepfather. Shortly after August 28, 1879, as many as thirty-seven couples were joined in traditional marriage, and twelve young women with children remained single.

John Humphrey Noyes himself, as it turned out, had to flee to Canada to escape charges of statutory rape. It had been the practice that when young teenaged girls reached womanhood they would experience their entrance into womanhood with their "first husband," being Noyes himself. This event was part of Noyes' initiation process called "Ascending Fellowship." Some of these girls were very young when they were suddenly removed from the children's house and initiated into adulthood. Medical examinations by Dr. Van de Walker in 1877 confirmed that of a group of forty-two women, ranging in age from ten to eighteen years, twenty-three had been "first husbanded" by Noyes.

On June 22, 1879 in the dark of night and to escape prosecution, John Humphrey Noyes fled 200 miles north into Canada. He died in Niagara Falls, Ontario, on April 16, 1886, surrounded by small company of followers. He was buried at Oneida with a tombstone that bears only his name and life dates, 1811-1886.

In 1987 the New York State Board of Regents declared the Oneida Mansion an historic landmark. Today it features a museum, a restaurant and dining room, overnight lodging, residential apartments, and banquet and meeting facilities.

Visitors to the mansion will undoubtedly be very impressed with what is left of this highly unusual commune.

For Further Reading

Carden, Maren Lockwood. (1998). *Oneida: Utopian Community to Modern Corporation.* Syracuse, NY: Syracuse University Press.

Claeys, Gregory, and Lyman Tower Sargent, editors. (1999). *The Utopian Reader.* New York: New York University Press.

Foster, Lawrence. (1997). Free Love and Community: John Humphrey Noyes and the Oneida Perfectionists. *American Communal Utopias.* Donald E. Pitzer, ed. Chapel Hill, NC: The University of North Carolina Press,253-278.

Garden, Maren Lockwood. (1998). *Oneida: Utopian Community to Modern Corporation.* Syracuse, NY: Syracuse University Press.

Gutek, Gerald, and Patricia Gutek. (1998). *Visiting Utopian Communities: A Guide to Shakers, Moravians, and Others.* Columbia, SC: University of South Carolina Press.

Holbrook, Stewart H. (1957). *Dreamers of the American Dream.* Garden City, NY: Doubleday & Company.

Holloway, Mark. (1966). *Heavens on Earth: Utopian Communities in America, 1680-1880.* New York: Dover Publications.

Kephart, William M., and William W. Zellner. (1994). *Extraordinary Groups: An Examination of Unconventional Life-Styles.* Fifth edition. New York: St. Martin's Press.

Klee-Hartzell, Marlyn. (1993). Family Love, True Womanhood, Motherhood, and the Socialization of Girls in the Oneida Community, 1848-1880. *Women in Spiritual and Communitarian Societies in the United States.* Wendy E. Chmielewski, Louis J. Kern, and Marilyn Klee-Hartzwell, eds. Syracuse, NY: Syracuse University Press, 182-200.

Nordhoff, Charles. (1993). *American Utopias*. Stockbridge, MS: Berkshire House Publishers.

Robertson, Constance Noyes. (1972). *Oneida Community: The Breakup, 1876-1881.* Syracuse, NY: Syracuse University Press.

Sutton, Robert P. (2003). *Communal Utopias and the American Experience: Religious Communities, 1732-2000.* Westport, CN: Praeger.

Webber, Everett. (1959). *Escape to Utopia: The Communal Movement in America.* New York: Hastings House Publishers.

http://www.1902encyclopedia.com/O/ONE/oneida-community.html

http://www.believersweb.net/view.cfm?ID=632

http://www.nyhistory.com/central/oneida.htm

Shakers

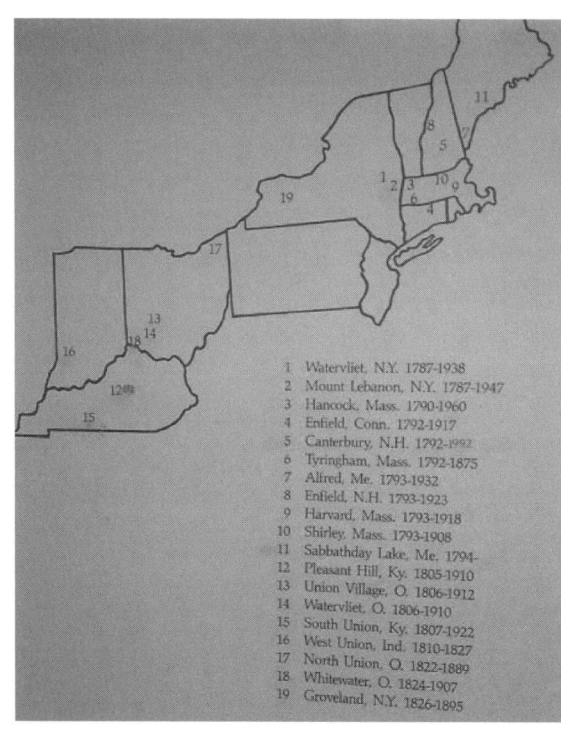

Canterbury Shaker Village, NH founded in the 1780s and formally established in 1792. *The Schoolhouse* was one of 100 buildings on the 4 000 acre site.

Map showing locations of 19 Shaker Communities/Villages in the United States.

1. Watervliet, N.Y. 1787-1938
2. Mount Lebanon, N.Y. 1787-1947
3. Hancock, Mass. 1790-1960
4. Enfield, Conn. 1792-1917
5. Canterbury, N.H. 1792-1992
6. Tyringham, Mass. 1792-1875
7. Alfred, Me. 1793-1932
8. Enfield, N.H. 1793-1923
9. Harvard, Mass. 1793-1918
10. Shirley, Mass. 1793-1908
11. Sabbathday Lake, Me. 1794-
12. Pleasant Hill, Ky. 1805-1910
13. Union Village, O. 1806-1912
14. Watervliet, O. 1806-1910
15. South Union, Ky. 1807-1922
16. West Union, Ind. 1810-1827
17. North Union, O. 1822-1889
18. Whitewater, O. 1824-1907
19. Groveland, N.Y. 1826-1895

The first group of Shakers arrived in the United States in 1774, making it the oldest (there are still a few Shakers in America), and at one time the largest communal society in the country.

Founded by Ann Lee (1736-1784) a blacksmith's daughter, the Shakers were persecuted for their beliefs in England, their land of origin. After some planning, eight of Lee's thirty adherents followed her to the New World where they grew to over 6 000 members located in nineteen communities. The Shakers originated from within the Quaker movement, but their label originated in derision; they were the "Shaking Quakers," because of their ecstatic and violent bodily agitation during worship. In 1772, Ann Lee was imprisoned in England for her unorthodox religious views, such as claiming that through a series of visions she had been designated as the female incarnation of Jesus Christ. Her imprisonment led to her plans to leave England.

On January 5, 1762, at the age of twenty-six, to please her parents Ann Lee married Abraham Standarin. Both Ann and Abraham signed the marriage register with an "X" since both were illiterate. In due time Ann gave birth to four children, each of whom passed away shortly after birth. In 1766, when her last child died Ann decided that marriage was an evil institution and thereafter she renounced both her husband and the institution of marriage, and devoted herself to celibacy. She also concluded that communal living was more in keeping with the Christian faith than individual ownership of property. When Ann Lee took control of the Shaker movement and instituted new practices, criticism by outsiders targetted what they saw as Shaker fanaticism. The Shakers were also accused of blasphemy, and heresy, and regarded with suspicion. Those who despised the Shakers even made an attempt to stone Ann Lee and her followers, but the attack was defused, just in time.

The small group of Shakers who migrated to America arrived in New York City on August 6, 1774, and immediately set to work to find employment. Several of them went up river to clear land and erect a building just outside Albany, then called Niskayuna. By 1776, the year that marked the beginning of the American Revolution, the little band of believers had a firm grip on settlement life. Because they were communalists and pacifists, it was necessary for the Shakers to keep

Canterbury Shaker Village, NH. This intact first-generation *Dwelling House* was the heart of the Shaker home and social life at this village.

Canterbury Shaker Village Horse Barn was constructed in 1819 to house trustees horses and to accommodate the horses that brought visitors to the village to conduct business with the Shakers.

Canterbury NH. "Put our hands to work and give your hearts to God."
– Mother Ann Lee, founder of Shakers.

The oval box is a Shaker icon. These oval boxes neatly stored necessary, but otherwise unsightly items, around the house and workshop. Constructed from one continuous strip of wood, the oval box is simple to make yet functional.

a low profile while the country was at war. However, when the surrounding public learned of their unique beliefs and practices, hundreds of curious folk travelled from New York and Massachusetts to observe these peculiar people.

The United Society of Believers in Christ's Second Coming (their official name) grew out of the inspiration of Jane and James Wardley, with "Mother" Ann Lee eventually taking Jane's place to fill out the feminine side of the equation. The objective of the Shakers was to reform the Quaker movement whom they accused of becoming too formal, an approach that had apparently weakened their Christian witness. When their planned reformation found no root, the Shakers broke away to form a separate identity.

Ann Lee's theology grew out of her visions in which God told her that salvation was possible only through the guidance of both parents, Jesus Christ being the male side of the equation. It was up to Ann to reveal and manifest the female role in salvation. Thus Christ's Second Coming was believed to have occurred through Ann's incarnation. As an addendum belief, one of Ann's visions showed that Adam and Eve were chased out of the Garden of Eden for having sexual relations. After that, Ann went on a campaign to extoll celibacy and emphasize the evil of sexual relations. Ann's husband followed her to America, but when she made it clear to him that she wanted nothing to do with marriage, he left her. Divorce in

18th century America was very difficult and it is doubtful that either Ann or her husband even pursued it.

Although considered a bit offbeat in their beliefs compared to orthodox Christian theology, the Shakers soon found disciples in America during the revival period of the late 18th century. The group was very brave in continuing in their patterned beliefs because they were often physically attacked by mobs, dragged from their beds and whipped, then driven out of town. This form of negative treatment is sometimes cited as a contributing factor to Ann's early death. Lee died in 1784 at the age of only forty-eight, though she had prophesied that she would live 1 000 years. After her death her successors tried desperately to maintain the order at the expense of giving up efforts to evangelize outsiders.

The first major Shaker breakthrough occurred in 1780 during the Revolutionary War. Religious revival was in the air. During that time various Shaker missionaries were rumored to have traveled 1 000 miles on foot to evangelize the lost. The result was that five new Shaker colonies were established in Indiana, Kentucky, and Ohio. Shaker membership peaked in 1830 with a membership of 6 000 and remained there for the next quarter century. It was

PLEASANT HILL

Mother Ann Lee and small band of converts came from England to New York, 1774. She was founder of Shakerism in America. Shakerism introduced in Mercer County by Elisha Thomas, Samuel and Henry Banta. After attending a Revival at Concord, Bourbon Co., Ky., Aug. 15, 1805, they were converted by missionaries to acceptance of the doctrine of United Society of Believers in Christ's Second Appearance.
1806 - Believers located at Shawnee Run on Thomas' farm near each other for religious worship and protection. Dec. 3, first family covenant signed by 44 converts, agreeing to mutual support and common-property ownership.
1808 - First meeting house built. Name "Shaker" came from vigorous worship practice. The Shakers were devout, orderly and followed celibacy; excelled in architecture, farming and inventions. At its height there were 500 members, 5,000 acres of land with 25 miles of rock fence.
1910 - Last 12 members deeded land to private citizen; he to care for them during life.
1923 - Sister Mary Settle, last Shaker in Mercer County, died.
1961 - Present restoration was begun.

At Pleasant Hill, Kentucky on December 3, 1806, forty-four converts signed a contract "agreeing to mutual support and common-property ownership." Shakers "excelled in architecture, farming and

Pleasant Hill was one of the large western Shaker settlements.

difficult for the movement to grow by natural means because the group had renounced procreation. This meant that growth could occur almost entirely by attracting converts. Bringing in and adopting orphans from England also helped. A school was built for the orphans, as well as for children of couples who joined the Shakers. The children lived in a separate house, separated by sex, and supervised by adults who were not their parents.

Shaker candleholder on a signature Shaker peg rail situated roughly shoulder height on the wall. These peg rails stored many things, including bonnets, hats, candles, and even chairs.

Shaker style furniture was straight-lined and practical. These beds are evidence of that practicality as one bed was stored under the other when not in use.

Despite these efforts to increase membership, by 1845, Shaker membership began to decline.

The basic economy of Shaker communes was agricultural and included such jobs as looking after cattle and sheep, cleaning barns, and working in related shops.

The communes also manufactured furniture, brooms, and baskets, and grew, packaged, and sold seeds. Colonies were strategically located near waterways to make the transportation of goods more feasible. Music, as a form of leisure and worship played a big part in Shaker life, and on Sundays when members would gather for worship they would also engage in various forms of dance. With men seated on one side of the room and women on the other, the two groups would rise and dance toward one another long enough until the dance grew frenzied and members eventually fell exhausted on the floor. The dance was intended to help individuals burn off any extra sexual energy that their work responsibilities might have missed. The Shaker label originates from this practice. Sometimes a congregation might indulge in gestures known as "motionings" while singing. They might skip, run and leap towards one another, but always without touching. In 1811, the Shakers invented the "quick dance," in which everyone skipped around in a circle to show their spiritual zeal.

"Put your hands to work." A Shaker woodshed typically full, organized and prepared.

Daily life in a Shaker commune was austere and followed strict rules laid down by Mother Ann. Rules appeared in written form after 1821, and deviance was not tolerated. Elders and eldresses took the initiative in addressing inappropriate behavior with excommunication being the final step in the process. When it came time to replace elders and eldresses, the rank and file had no say in the matter.

Ann Lee's motto, "Put your hands to work and give your hearts to God," became the watchword of the community. She directed every aspect of community life. Wake-up time was 4:30 a.m. in the summer and 5:00 a.m. in winter – men first, and then women, making sure that the men were outside first. When everyone was out of bed and prayers had been said, beds were stripped for airing and bedcovers were folded over the backs of chairs. Next it was time for breakfast, with little time allowed for conversation, and then only before meals, not during. Meals were eaten in silence.

The objective of the Shakers was to reform the Quaker movement whom they accused of becoming too formal, an approach that had apparently weakened their Christian witness.

Group units of men and woman known as "families" lived in separate sections of Shaker dormitories, where they were under the supervision of an elder and an eldress. Family members were not allowed to visit in each other's homes, and they received assignments according to families. Stringent rules also applied to the workplace where there was little opportunity to cross the boundaries of sex. If a man needed something from the women's shop he would first ask his supervisor to speak to the women's supervisor about obtaining the needed item. Shaker men and women were allowed to visit in one another's rooms from time to time, but only under supervision and no form of physical contact was allowed. Men sat on one side of the room and women sat on the other while they visited. Members were allowed to visit non-Shaker neighbors only if they thought there might be a chance that the outsiders would join the Shaker movement. When loneliness burgeoned to the full, there were instances of women literally begging neighborhood men to take them away from the austere Shaker lifestyle.

The Shaker interpretation for the demise of the movement was that their membership gradually gave into the lures and temptations of the world. Some disillusioned members who left the community organized literary campaigns to belittle the reputation of the Shakers. Soon the reality was that the Shaker membership not only decreased in numbers, there were also no new converts forthcoming. In the decade of the 1830s, a kind of last-ditch effort was made to restore Shaker spirituality through revivals that took place in some colonies. During the winter of 1837-38, for example, female residents in the New York commune at Watervliet, suddenly began receiving visions with messages from God. The excitement soon spread to other communities where similar events occurred. Shaker elders were convinced that this awakening would bring in new members, but this did not happen. A few years later, the spark was gone and decline set it.

The 1820 *Meeting House* at Pleasant Hill, Kentucky, was the Shakers' place of worship.

Obviously, the practice of celibacy made it necessary, yet difficult, for the Shakers to recruit new members, but there were economic factors that also contributed to the failure of their movement. When first arriving in America and as the organization flourished, the Shakers purchased land that was available to them without paying attention to its fertility. As American agricultural productivity generally increased, the Shakers were not able to keep up with the competition. In addition, they did not keep up with industrial changes that were occurring in the country. Their dedication to more traditional methods severely hindered them from keeping up with their neighbors. As a charitable organization, they had also been quite generous with the needy, so that when additional capital was needed to modernize their operations, it was not available.

Pleasant Hill, KY. The *Dining Hall* still serves meals today with breads fresh from the oven and vegetables grown on site and/or locally.

By the 1850s, the handwriting was on the wall; Shaker numbers were rapidly declining. Frederick Evans, who served as an elder during the 1870s noted that the Shakers had grown "fat and lazy," and though he tried to revive the old Shakerism, it was to no avail. The adoption of British orphans had been initiated to increase the Shaker membership, but that strategy also failed. Between 1840 and 1870, the Shakers lost forty percent of their membership, and the trend continued. Of 197 children raised at the Mount Lebanon Commune between 1861 and 1900, only one joined the Shakers.

It took several decades to dismantle the Shaker colonies, so that by 1963 only three remained – one in Hancock, Massachusetts, one in Canterbury, New Hampshire, and one in New Gloucester, Maine. By 1989 there were two tiny Shaker homes in Maine and New Hampshire with only a handful of members.

Today visitors can access a number of former Shaker communes and sites such as the Sabbathday Lake Shaker Village in New Gloucester, Maine, which is the only remaining active Shaker village. It was named a national historic landmark in 1974. Here four members, two of them males in their

> Ann Lee's motto, "Put our hands to work and give your hearts to God," became the watchword of the community.

40s, pray for more converts, hoping to keep the lifestyle of the three "C's" alive – celibacy, confession of sin, and communalism. Although they receive as many as seventy inquiries about possible membership every year, there is little hope that active Shakerism will survive in America. From time to time novices have joined the movement, but none of them have lasted more than a year.

Other available Shaker sites include Pleasant Hill and South Union in Kentucky; Shaker Historical Museum in Ohio; Mount Lebanon Shaker Village and Shaker Museum and Library in New York, and Hancock Shaker Village in Massachusetts. The Golden Lamb Inn in Lebanon, Ohio, built by Shakers, is the oldest inn in Ohio and still operates as a tourist attraction.

For Further Reading

Andrews, Edward Deming. (1963). *The People Called Shakers*. New York: Dover Publications.

Brewer, Pricilla. (1986). *Shaker Communities, Shaker Lives*. Hanover, NH: University Press of New England.

Brewer, Pricilla. (1997). The Shakers of Mother Lee. *American Communal Utopias*. Donald E. Pitzer, ed. Chapel Hill, NC: The University of North Carolina Press, 57-87.

Carpenter, Delburn. (1975). *The Radical Pietists: Celibate Communal Societies Established in the United States Before 1820*. New York: AMS Press

Foster, Lawrence. (1991). *Women, Family, and Utopia: Communal Experiences of the Shakers, the Oneida Community, and the Mormons*. Syracuse, NY: Syracuse University Press.

French, David, and Elena French. (1975). *Working Communally: Patterns and Possibilities*. New York: Russell Sage Foundation.

Gordon, Berverly. (1993). Women's Work and Presentation of Self in the Community Context in the Victoran Era. Women in Spiritual and Communitariam Societies in the United States. Wendy E. Chmielewski, Louis J. Kern, and Marilyn Klee-Hartzwell, eds. Syracuse, NY: Syracuse University Press, 89-103.

Mac-Hir Hutton, Daniel. (1987). *Old Shakertown and the Shakers*. Harrodsburg, KY: Harrodsburg Herald Press.

Newman, Cathy. (1989). *The Shakers' Brief Eternity*. National Geographic, 176(3), 302-325.

Nordhoff, Charles. (1993). *American Utopias*. Stockbridge, MS: Berkshire House Publishers.

Richter, Peyton E. (1971). Community of Celibates: The Shakers. *Utopias: Social Ideals and Communal Experiments*. Peyton E. Richter, ed. Boston, MA: Holbrook Press, 87-89.

http://www.shaker.lib.me.us/about.html

http://www.shaker.lib.me.us/about.html

http://www.boston.com/news/globe/magazine/articles/2006/07/23/the_last_ones_standing/?page=full

Silkville

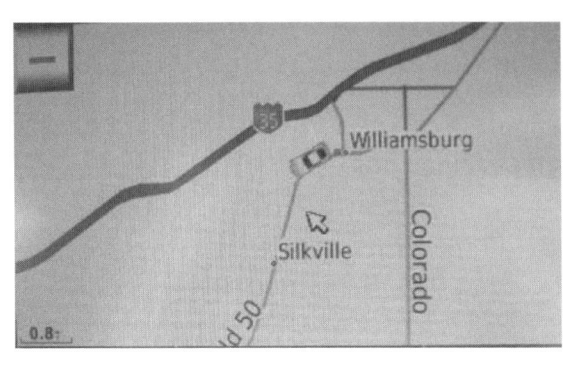

Our GPS showing the location of Silkville, Kansas, just off I-35 on Old 50, south of Williamsburg.

A number of historical communal experiments were begun through collaboration, particularly in the case of such communities as Amana, Brook Farm, the Harmonists, Oneida, and the Shakers. The origin of Silkville, Kansas, was no exception, and although it never developed into the self-sustaining commune that its originator envisaged; its history is unique in that respect.

In 1869, having recently arrived in America, Ernest de Boissiere (1811-1894), a French aristocrat, decided to develop a Fourierist commune. Having collaborated with Charles Fourier and two partners, Albert Brisbane, and Elijah Grant, de Boissiere purchased 3 500 acres of land from a defunct Fourier colony known as the Kansas Educational Association of the Methodist Episcopal Church. Both Brisbane and Grant contributed start-up funds with plans to build a farm devoted to manufacturing silk.

De Boissiere was middle aged when he arrived in the United States, quite wealthy from income garnered in forestry and fisheries. Banished from France by Napoleon III because of his political ideas, de Boissiere studied the climate of Kansas and believed it to be similar enough to that of France so that a successful silk farm could be developed. Within a few years his dream became a reality and he made plans to expand the operation. In 1873 de Boissiere issued a prospectus to potential socialists to join his experiment, but the campaign had little success.

A large stone building housed silkworms.

Funding for de Boissiere's colony was not really a problem, but it would still take a few years before the project realized

By the year 1872, looms housed in a large stone building, had a capacity of making 224 yards of silk ribbon a day.

The commune once known as Silkville is now a working ranch called *Silkville Ranch*.

any profit. De Boissiere's vision was that Silkville (sometimes known as the Kansas Cooperative Farm) would become a self-sustaining industrial community where workers would share income. De Boissiere informed his workers that they would have to provide for themselves financially until the colony became self-supporting. Initially each worker had to contribute a $100 deposit and pay room rent for two months in advance.

To get things started de Boissiere imported forty expert silk workers from France who worked in Kansas with untrained local workers to build a three-story building, known as "The Chateau," which was large enough to accommodate 100 people at a common meal. The elaborate sixty-room mansion also included a library of 2 500 books, making it the largest collection in the state of Kansas. In total the value of the various buildings erected at Silkville amounted to more than $100 000.

De Boissiere's workers soon placed 150 acres under cultivation to grow crops. They also planted seventy acres of mulberry trees (to feed the silkworms), and built a silk factory, a winery, and a schoolhouse. Silkworms were imported from France and Japan, and before long colony looms were turning out over 200 yards of finished materials in a single day. The Kansas Legislature provided funds to promote de Boissiere's silk in forty-six Kansas counties and as a result its popularity was greatly enhanced. Continuing his experimental efforts, de Boissiere soon discovered that the leaves of the Kansas Osage Orange, often called hedge trees, provided better food for silkworms than those of Mulberry trees.

In order to gain a wider market, de Boissiere successfully displayed his silk products at local fairs and sponsored excursions to local towns so people could travel to Silkville to see how silk was made. Media reports of such events were very positive. Motivated by his local success, in 1876 de Boissiere exhibited silk at the Philadelphia Centennial Exposition where it was ranked equal to the silk produced in France, Italy, and Japan. De Boissere's silk also won a prize at the Paris World Exposition in 1886.

Despite these very positive indicators, in 1881, a little more than a decade after the idea blossomed, Silkville came to an abrupt end. There were at least three reasons for this

This shows the interior of one of the stone buildings, which housed looms and silkworms.

The Silkville Commune's three-story and sixty-room manor house before the fire of April 29, 1916.

happening. First, competition from the cheaper labor of foreign countries forced a shift towards the dairy industry, which was also initially successful. De Boissiere's workers found they could obtain higher wages in that sector, so instead of waiting for profits to be derived from shares, they abandoned the colony. Some female workers also left to marry local American farmers. A second reason for failure was that homestead lands were opening up in the west, and the prospect of owning land was particularly appealing to de Boissiere's workers. Third, competition from abroad was increasing because of the rapid rate of industrialization in European countries.

Despite his best efforts to make the Silkville factory profitable, de Boissiere found that silk could be imported from China cheaper than his workers could manufacture it. Soon after that, production ceased and de Boissiere began to manufacture silk only on an experimental basis. To supplement the farm's income de Boissere starting raising livestock as well producing cheese and butter products. It was not enough. In 1886, Silkville farm operations ceased altogether as de Boissiere had returned to France. He came back to Kansas in 1892 to dispose of the property, then went back to France where he died two years later.

After being partially destroyed by the fire of 1916, this is the Ranch House as it is today.

The successive history of Silkville – the town that never really came to be, is as interesting as its origin. After the manufacture of silk waned and de Boissere tried to dispose of his property, he came to the conclusion that it should be willed to charity. The property included 3 100 acres of farmland, nine stone buildings, an apple orchard, and mulberry and walnut groves. De Boissere's huge home was nearly completely destroyed by fire in 1916. Later, one-third of the house was restored.

When the news was broadcast that de Boissiere's property was being made available to charities, many representatives of charitable organizations visited him, hoping to obtain the land. In the end, de Boissere donated the land to the Odd Fellow's Grand Lodge of Kansas who wanted to turn the property into an orphans' home. On June 7, 1894, the Odd Fellows Orphans' Home was dedicated, but some board members were opposed to the idea of managing an orphan's home.

As it happened, the orphans' home was never implemented because of conflict within the ranks of the Odd Fellows organization. Apparently, failure to formally operate the orphanage nullified the original agreement, and after a

Motivated by his local success, in 1876 de Boissiere exhibited silk at the Philadelphia Centennial exposition where it was ranked equal to the silk produced in France, Italy, and Japan. De Boissier's silk also won a prize at the Paris Exposition in 1886.

Despite his best efforts to make the Silkville factory profitable, de Boissiere found that silk could be imported from China cheaper than his workers could manufacture it.

long legal battle, the courts decided that the land should be awarded to de Boissere's sister, Madame Corrine Martinelli, who lived in France. A spate of clever legal maneuvers such as a lawyer's personal visit to Madame Marintelli in France resulted in the latter signing over the property to the legal firm of Troutman and Stone in Topeka, Kansas. These lawyers then sold the farm to a new owner. At least two families have owned it since.

The ghost town of Silkville is located in Franklin Country, Kansas, on a gravel road approximately three miles south of Williamsburg. Although quite difficult to locate, the visit is definitely worthwhile. There are at least four remaining buildings of interest, plus the possible encounter with ghosts of better days.

When we visited Silkville in the spring of 2009, we were fortunate enough to be able to explore the buildings, thanks to the kind-hearted hosting of the resident family.

For Further Reading

Blackmar, Frank W. ed. (1912). Kansas, *A Cyclopedia of State History,* Vol. 2. Chicago, IL: Standard Publishing Co., 694-696.

Carpenter, Garrett R. (December, 1954) *Silkville: A Kansas Attempt in the History of Fourierist Utopias, 1869-1892,* Emporia State Research Studies, 3(2).

Fogarty, Robert S., ed. (1980). *Dictionary of American Communal and Utopian History.* Westport, CN: Greenwood Press.

Guarneri, Carl J. (1997). Brook Farm, and the Fourierist Phalanxes: Immediatism, Gradualism, and American Utopian Socialism. *American Communal Utopias. Donald* E. Pitzer, ed. Chapel Hill, NC: The University of North Carolina Press, 159-180.

Hinds, William Alfred. (1975). *American Communities and Cooperative Colonies.* Blain, PA: Porcupine Press.

Kent, Alexander. (July, 1901). Cooperative Communities in the United States. *Bulletin of the Department of Labor, 35*: 563-64.

http://skyways.lib.ks.us/history/silkville.html
http://www.kshs.org/portraits/silkville.htm
http://www.old.depot.museum/virtual/silkville/

Trappists

The Trappist Monks of New Melleray Abbey, Peosta, Iowa.

Making *Trappist Caskets* is a work of the monks at New Melleray Abbey.

Communal monks? Yes, although few people would think that a monastry could be classified as a commune. In fact, the New Melleray Monastic Order in Peosta, Iowa, is a fullfledged commune.

About thirty-six monks live at New Melleray, which is located about fifteen miles from Dubuque, Iowa. These monks, however, do not brew Trappist Beer, which is famous the world over; these monks make coffins and urns! For the record, there still are six Trappist breweries located in different parts of the world, and Trappist monks are on the record for having established their unique breweries as early as 1685. The Trappists, like many other religious groups, originally brewed beer as a means of making money to fund their good works, such as feeding the poor as well as affording the monasteries a way of maintaining self-sufficiency.

Meanwhile, back to the beginning of our story.

The Trappist order originated in the Cistercian Monastery of La Trappe in France. Various Cistercian congregations had been in existence for many years, beginning in 1098, but by 1664 the Abbot of La Trappe felt that the Cistercians were becoming too liberal. He introduced strict new rules in the abbey, a break came, and a new order was born. Since then Cistercian monks have been divided into two orders, one of which (Trappists), is attached to the Abbey of La Grande in Normandy. Both orders have consistently held to the concept that monasteries should be self-supporting. At present there are 100 Trappist houses of men worldwide, and 60 female Trappist houses.

The philosophy of the Monks at New Melleray Abbey is to labor quietly with their hands in support of their life of simplicity.

The daily routine for the Monks at New Melleray Abbey is active from *rising* at 3:15 a.m. to *compline and rest* at 7:30 p.m.

The New Melleray Abbey was built in 1849 after Bishop Matthias invited a group of Trappists to settle in the area. At first only six monks arrived to build temporary living quarters, and when they were completed sixteen more monks came to join them. One thousand acres of rolling prairie land was purchased to provide an agricultural base for the monastery, and one cow and one calf were purchased for $14.00 to begin their venture into raising livestock. Main crops were alfalfa, corn, soybeans, potatoes, and oats. After some years when agricultural products lost their value, the monks turned their attention to other sources of income. It was then that the New Melleray monks began to manufacture coffins and wooden urns. The quality of their finely-turned wooden products is such that the coffins have even won national awards. Fortuitously, New Melleray land is rich with a rich variety of woods – black walnut, red oak, white oak, ash, maple and pine trees abound. New Melleray has ownership of the second largest privately owned forest in Iowa. The monks plant a tree every time someone is buried in a Trappist coffin.

The foundation of the New Melleray commune is to live together for the purpose of spiritual study and prayer – which is a constant process at this unusual commune. Monks attend seven church services every day, abstain from eating meat, and emphasize the dignity of work. As the monks' newsletter states, "This is the most effective way we can love and serve our brothers and sisters here and now." The day begins at 3:30 a.m., followed by breakfast an hour later. The morning is spent in prayer, reading of Scripture, and celebration of the Eucharist. Two hours of work follow, then more praying and studying, then Vespers at 5:00 p.m., followed by supper, with bedtime at 7:30 p.m. On our visit to New Melleray we were graciously invited to Vespers and felt privileged to attend.

New Melleray Abbey, founded in 1849 by Cistercian monks from Mt. Melleray Abbey in Ireland.

The New Melleray Monastic Center is always interested in having new members join them. Applicants must first pass through several stages of testing including a two-year term as an associate. The third floor section of the Guest House is set aside for associates, with a special dining room attached. Associates are booked into individual rooms to provide them with the opportunity to appreciate silence and contemplative solace. There is no cost to joining the program, and associates rise, pray, work, eat, and retire in the same pattern set by the monks. At least a dozen associates are now in training at New Melleray.

The day begins at 3:30 a.m., followed by breakfast an hour later. The morning is spent in prayer, reading of Scripture, and celebration of the Eucharist. Two hours of work follows, then more praying and studying, then Vespers at 5:00 p.m., followed by supper, with bedtime at 7:30 p.m.

Visitors are warmly greeted at the New Melleray Monastery, and weekend retreats may be booked through the central office. A small bookstore offers Bibles and other literature for sale.

New Melleray is an impressive and obviously very efficient commune, and a quiet pleasure to visit.

For Further Reading

Monastery Seasons. 48(2), 4 pp.

New Melleray Abbey. E-mail: monks@newmelleray.org

http://www.smithsonianmag.com/people-places/Making-_Ends_Meet.html?c=y&page=1

http://www.celticcousins.net/irishiniowa/newmelleray.htm

Underground Railroad

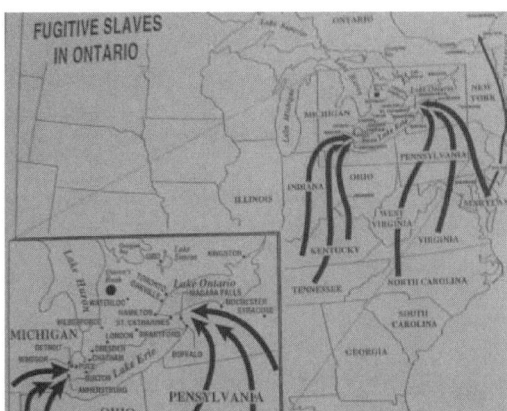

A replica of an Underground Railroad wagon that was used to transport former slaves on their way to Canada to find refuge and begin a new life.

Fugitive slaves used several routes to Ontario, Canada.

One of the most unfortunate, yet redemptive chapters in American history occurred in the half century before President Abraham Lincoln announced that slaves were to be freed.

The conditions that African American slaves had to endure at the hands of their masters, were very unfair and often cruel. As a result, many slaves tried to escape and some were successful. It has been estimated that between 1810 and 1850 the Underground Railroad effectively moved more than 100 000 slaves away from the south. Estimates are that between 40 000 to 60 000 former slaves made it to Canada, a relatively small number in comparison to the millions of African Americans who suffered through the ugly phenomenon of slavery. The majority of escaping slaves relocated to American states where slavery had been abolished.

Essentially the Underground Railroad was a vast organization of individuals of various backgrounds, who helped fugitive slaves move northward. The concept originated as early as the latter part of the 18th century. The record shows that in 1786, President George Washington complained about the loss of his slaves who had been aided in their escape by the Quaker organization. During the next several decades the cause grew until around 1830 it became known as the Underground Railroad. The organization provided travelling money, lodging and food, clothing, and "conductors" who would arrange depots where slaves would be safe. Members of the Underground Railroad invented a special language to help

Dawn Settlement, Dresden, Ontario. The church to the left of the photo, and Hanson House to the right. Henson house is significant for its association with Reverend Josiah Henson and as an example of mid 19th century vernacular domestic architecture.

One of the most famous "train conductors" on the Underground Railroad was Harriet Tubman (1820-1913), who personally guided more than 300 African Americans to freedom in Canada.

refugees avoid authorities. The word "hell" meant south, and "heaven" was a code word for north. The state of Ohio, the midpoint of the trip, was viewed as the gateway to freedom.

One of the most famous "train conductors" on the Underground Railroad was Harriet Tubman (1820-1913), who personally guided more than 300 African Americans to freedom in Canada. Tubman escaped from a plantation in Maryland at the age of 25, leaving behind her husband, parents, and siblings. She travelled safely to St. Catharines, Ontario, and from there guided slaves to Canada in nineteen trips over eight years.

It was not easy to run away from slavery. The first step was to get away from the plantation in which one was enslaved. Many slaves simply ran away, hoping to find a connection to the Underground Railroad. Sometimes a conductor would show up, disguised as a slave, and lead the slave to a safe house. "Trains" that carried slaves to safety often charged fares, money for this service being raised by various charities. Most slaves did not have ready access to money. Vigilant societies often provided funds and prepared letters of recommendation for escapees to find jobs.

During the 1800s, the Underground Railroad flourished, literally carrying thousands of courageous people, both conductors and slaves, who would have been severely punished, had they been caught for "taking the trip." Initiated by Quakers, the railroad carried out its assignment from station to station with wagonloads of passengers cramped into hidden compartments. "Stations" were barns, cellars, church belfries, and any underground cave that could double as a temporary "motel." Penalties for aiding runaway slaves in the United States increased with the passing of the federal Fugitive Slave Law of 1850. The law was passed to appease southern proslavery states that threatened to leave the union. Punishment for conductors who helped fleeing slaves consisted of fines of $2,000 or more, plus six months in jail. There is no evidence that the law discouraged anyone from continuing to assist slaves. Informal punishments of those who helped the slaves inflicted by proslavery individuals and organizations often consisted of barn burnings or being threatened by a mob.

Reverend and Mrs. Josiah Henson greet visitors to the Henson House.

A *smoke house* used to dry or smoke cured meats. This smoke house was made out of the trunk of a sycomore tree.

Stories of bravery and hardship dominated the route of the Underground Railroad. For example, in 1825, tavern owners Joshua and Rebecca Woodard of Ohio assisted a group of slaves who were passing through the area. When one of the babies started to cry, Rebecca persuaded the mother to leave her child behind lest the group get caught by the authorities. The mother did so, and the Woodards raised the child to adulthood. One slave, Henry Brown, had himself boxed and shipped from Richmond, Virginia, to Philadelphia, where he was unpacked by members of the Underground Railroad.

John Brown (1800-1859), probably the best-known supporter of the Underground Railroad, helped slaves in all of his various homes in Ohio, never tiring of assisting runaways. One of his sons recalled how his father used to wake him up in the middle of the night and tell him to scoot over in bed to make room for another escaping fugitive. A polarizing figure, John Brown was a devout Calvinist and militant abolitionist. In 1855 he endured his final stand when he arrived heavily armed at Harper's Ferry in Kansas. He was captured in a raid that followed, and on December 2, 1859, he was hung in Charleston, Virginia. It was an event that shook the nation and led inexorably to the American Civil War.

A number of historic sites commemorating John Brown's work are spread across the nation; for example, John Brown's Cave and Historical Village in Nebraska City, Nebraska. The site consists of twenty buildings, including an underground cave (known as John Brown's cave), and a newly built indoor exhibit containing ten early day shops, interiors, a brick street, and wooden sidewalks. It is documented that John Brown visited the site at least five times.

The story of the African American immigration to Canada via the Underground Railroad occurred in Nova Scotia in 1776, following the signing of the Declaration of Independence. Migrations to Upper Canada (later Ontario) did not occur until after 1793 when the Canadian government abolished slavery. During this time some African Americans made it to Canada entirely on their own. Two decades later, between 1817 and 1822, a major wave of African Americans arrived in the area of Windsor, Ontario and established such communal settlements as Dawn, Oro, and Wilberforce.

John Brown's house in Akron, Ohio has a permanent exhibit showing Brown's significance as a symbolic hero and martyr of the antislavery movement.

Harriet Beecher Stowe's book, *Uncle Tom's Cabin,* was patterned after Josiah Henson (1789-1883), one of the leaders of the Dawn settlement. Born on a Maryland plantation on June 15, 1789, Henson was a slave for forty-one years. As a child he saw his father beaten and his family sold away. By circumstance he was sold to be with his mother, and in 1830, his family escaped to Upper Canada (Ontario) via the Underground Railroad. His familiarity with the Scriptures and his gift of oratory soon saw him recognized as a Methodist Episcopal preacher. In 1841 Henson moved his family to Dresden, Ontario, to establish a refuge for incoming slaves. Through his leadership an industrial school, the British American Institute, was founded to assist slaves in attaining training in the trades. He continued to work as an agent for the Underground Railroad.

Henson seemed to buy into the fame that followed him as a result of his efforts, but he did not wear it. His popularity gave him opportunity to travel around America and even to Britain where he met many celebrities including Queen Victoria.

Despite his fame, he maintained a steady concern for those in need. Henson and Hiram Wilson, who was connected to the American Anti-Slavery Society, were instrumental in raising sufficient funds to set up a commune with the assistance of the American Quakers. For some runaway slaves the Dawn Settlement was viewed as the last station on the Underground Railroad. Reaching their goal produced feelings of joy and gratitude.

The southern African Americans who made it safely to Canada did not always meet with utopian conditions. Public reception was sometimes negative, even hostile. Residents did not take kindly to the establishment of what they perceived to be colonies of ignorant, untrained foreigners whose lifestyle might negatively impact on existing social and moral conditions. Canada's record with slavery is therefore not impeccable. Although Canadians liked to boast that slavery had never existed in the country, to the contrary, many Aboriginal people lived in just such a state. Slavery also existed across Canada under British rule, and these numbers rose swiftly when the Loyalists arrived, bringing their slaves with them.

Mayhew Cabin and Historic Village and John Brown's Cave, Nebraska. Visitors may travel down the underground cave to better understand what the remarkable flight from slavery entailed.

The establishment of African American communes in Ontario was motivated by the way the new immigrants were regarded in the province. African American children were forced to attend separate schools, and their parents could find only mediocre jobs to support their families. Josiah Henson did his best to accommodate new arrivals. In 1840, money raised in England by Henson and his colleagues allowed the purchase of 300 acres of land on which the Dawn Commune would be built. Residents were to become farmers, and raise corn, wheat, oats and tobacco for sale to points south. Other industries such as a sawmill, a grist mill, a brickyard, and a rope factory were also developed. By the end of the decade the various Dawn enterprises were worth about $11 000.

And, of course, there were problems. A mortgage of $4 000 encumbered the commune so that its ownership was transferred to the board of the American Baptist Free Mission Society and Henson was relieved of his unofficial management position. His successor, the Reverend Samuel Davis, stayed only a short while and was replaced by John Scoble, a friend of Henson's. It was hoped that by working together the two men would be able to alleviate the financial pressure the colony was facing, but to no avail. Bills were simply not being paid. During the five years between 1847 and 1852, the financial records of Dawn were investigated six times. With Henson around, his unofficial word always carried the day. Henson, though gifted as a speaker, was not a financial manager. The low point of the commune was when John Scoble took Henson to court over a mortgage matter. Scoble won the case, and remained at Dawn until it folded in 1868. Halfway through the life of the colony, Henson moved to St. Catharines, Ontario, where he lived out his life.

Dawn's demise was unfortunate, because it could have provided a meaningful alternative lifestyle for former slaves who successfully managed to make their way to Canada. Unfortunately the clash of individuals with strong personalities, though talented, proved to be too much.

Today, visitors can make their way to Dresden, Ontario to visit the remains and rebuilt exhibits of the Dawn Settlement. Uncle Tom's Cabin is onsite, as is Josiah Henson's home and grave, and a half dozen 19th century buildings.

These monuments stand as a testament to the final Canadian station of the Underground Railroad.

> *The southern African Americans who made it safely to Canada did not always meet with utopian conditions.*

For Further Reading

Hill, Daniel G. (1981). *The Freedom Seekers: Blacks in Early Canada.* Agincourt, ON: The Book Society of Canada.

Hill, Lawrence. (2007). *The Book of Negroes.* Toronto, ON: HarperCollins Publishers.

Jackson, James S., and Margot Y. Jackson. (1983). *At Home on the Hill: The Perkins Family of Akron. Akron, OH:* The Summit County Historical Society.

Pease, William H., and Jane H. Pease. (1963). *Black Utopias: Negro Communal Experiments in America.* Madison, WI: The State Historical Society of Wisconsin.

Schlels, Paula. (June 16, 2002). *Halfway to Freedom.* Akron Beacon Journal, A1, A10-11, A16.

Stowe, Harriet Beecher. (2008). *Uncle Tom's Cabin.* New York: Oxford University Press.

Yount, Lisa. (1997). *Frontier of Freedom: African Americans in the West.* New York: Facts on File, Inc.

http://www.pbs.org/wgbh/aia/part4/4p2944.html
http://www.nationalgeographic.com/index.html
http://www.nps.gov/history/nr/travel/underground/

Women's Commonwealth

McWhirter House, Belton, Texas.

The garden of Martha McWhirter's home in Belton, Texas.

Several early North American communes were initiated and operated by women – like the Shakers and the Women's Commonwealth – and they were very successful.

Origin of the Women's Commonwealth in Belton, Texas, is accredited to Martha White McWhirter (1827-1904), originally from Gainsboro, Tennessee. Martha was only eighteen when she married George McWhirter who took his young wife to Bell County, Texas, to farm. Martha gave birth to twelve children before her husband left her to join the Confederate Army. After he died in 1887, his army service provided Martha with a generous pension even though they did not live together and were never officially divorced. Martha's inherited pension was a real asset when it came to running the Women's Commonwealth commune.

In 1867, Martha McWhirter was a loyal member of the Methodist Church in Belton, Texas. One day, while walking home from an evening of religious services, as McWhirter later testified, God had spoken to her and gave her "a kind of Pentecostal baptism." McWhirter interpreted the experience to mean that she was to become sanctified or separated unto God by giving up marriage. She further interpreted God's message to mean that she was being punished for being married by the death of two of her children and her brother through illness. McWhirter shared her experience with other unhappy wives in her weekly prayer group, and they jointly came to the conclusion that they would be better off without marriage. When the local Methodist Church heard of the women's experiences, they sympathized with them, but McWhirter would have none of it. She and her colleagues censured the church's interpretation of sanctification and made up their own. They even started their own weekly services, and the community nicknamed them "the Sanctified Sisters."

The doorway where bullet holes remain to this day marking the spot they struck the McWhirter house.

George and Martha McWhiter House. National Register of Historic Places plaque located on the front of the house.

By 1877 the McWhirter home had become a kind of haven for unhappy or abused women and Martha McWhirter's husband, George, left after Martha accused him of flirting with a hired girl. He moved to an apartment above a store he owned and never returned to the marriage. In the meantime a number of women moved in with Martha who decided to form a female organization known as the Women's Commonwealth. The group started their financial base with the twenty dollar savings of one of the women who was a local schoolteacher.

McWhirter shared her experience with other unhappy wives in her weekly prayer group, and they jointly came to the conclusion that they would be better off without marriage.

By the end of the 1870s the commonwealth women realized that they would have to become financially independent of their husbands if they wanted to control their own lives. This philosophy seemed to attract additional members, so that by 1883 the Women's Commonwealth was made up of forty-two women, many of whom brought their children with them when they joined. Every member took part in the responsibility of raising the children. Communal income was earned in many different ways; the women cut and sold cordwood, took in laundry, and did housework for their neighbors. The women scrimped and saved and in 1886 bought the Belton Central Hotel that was in foreclosure. They also purchased other property that was in foreclosure, much to the embarrassment of the men who owned the property. In 1892 the Sanctified Sisters purchased a second hotel and offered $500 to a railroad company if they would build a spur through the town of Belton instead of bypassing it. This arrangement greatly benefited the Women's Commonwealth because it both increased their hotel clientele as well as providing the women with ready access to a shipping outlet for their produce.

McWhirter was not opposed to males joining the commune, but made it clear that there would be no cohabitation. Some husbands who had lost their wives to the commonwealth tried unsuccessfully to get them back through various actions. However, when two brothers, Matthew and David Dow, joined the Women's Commonwealth, the community had had enough. Gossip went wild, and one day some of the disgruntled husbands became very angry. On February 13, 1880, a group of these men surrounded the McWhirter house, fired warning shots at it, and burst in. They seized the Dow brothers and beat them, then left as quickly as they came. Court action against the brothers resulted in the brothers being declared insane. However, the asylum to which they were sent refused to admit them because they were obviously quite sane. The Dow brothers remained within the commune for many years, but always fulfilling servile roles.

Belton Texas. This building was originally a three-story *Opera House* located near Belton County Courthouse. Martha McWhirter's name appeared on the cornerstone of the Opera House.

Martha McWhirter was an energetic personality. She gave speeches on women's rights, visited a Shaker colony for additional ideas on communal living, and presided over local matters. Life in the commune was not without its moments of leisure; the women engaged in painting, music, and reading. A reading circle was so successful that the commonwealth was able to donate 350 books to the Belton Library. All jobs were changed once a month so no one grew too weary of a particular responsibility. The system worked well so there was virtually no internal jealousy about anyone being favored over the others.

By 1898 the Sanctified Sisters had built excellent community rapport and garnered strong support for their activities.

By 1898 the Sanctified Sisters had built excellent community rapport and garnered strong support for their activities. There was no hostility against them, so when they announced that they were relocating to Washington DC, their neighbors begged them not to leave. Reasons for their move are not exactly clear. Some observers conjectured that the sisters wanted to retire to a less demanding lifestyle. Others suggest that the women wanted to live in a more culturally attuned community. Nonetheless, when the Sanctified Sisters moved to Washington, they continued to live much as they had in Belton.

Martha McWhirter died in April, 1904, and although observers predicted that the commune would dissolve after her death, it did not. The new leader, Fannie Holtzclaw, oversaw day to day operations, always looking out for the group's best interests. By 1910, however, only eighteen members were left, four years later the group divided peacefully with half of them remaining in Washington and the other half relocating to a farm in Maryland. Martha Scheble, the last remaining member of the Women's Commonwealth died in 1983 at the age of 101, her estate valued at $250 000.

The Women's Commonwealth owned and operated the *Central Hotel* as it was circa 1886-1900.

In many ways the Women's Commonwealth broke new ground in relation to women's rights and independence. As suffragettes, the Sanctified Sisters participated in many related activities, thanks in part to the vision and leadership of Martha McWhirter.

A visit to the Belton Museum will provide visitors with an abundance of information about the Women's Commonwealth. The McWhirter house is also available for tours by appointment.

For Further Reading

Chmielewski, Wendy E. (1993). Heaven on Earth: The Women's Commonwealth, 1867-1983. *Women in Spiritual and Communitarian Societies in the United States.* Wendy E. Chmielewski, Louis J. Kern, and Marilyn Klee-Hartzwell, eds. Syracuse, NY: Syracuse University Press, 75-88.

Fogarty, Robert S., ed. (1980). *Dictionary of American Communal and Utopian History.* Westport, CN: Greenwood Press.

Kitch, Sally L. (1993). *The Strange Society of Women: Reading the Letters and Lives of the Women's Commonwealth.* Columbua, OH: Ohio State University.

http://www.texasescapes.com/ClayCoppedge/Sanctified-Sisters.htm

www.tshaonline.org/handbook/online/articles/fmcax.

Zoar

Zoar Meeting House, 1853, now the United Church of Christ. Zoar Village is situated in Tuscarawas County, Ohio.

Nothing much new to report here; once again members of yet another German Separatist group, much like Amana, travelled to America in the 19th century to find religious freedom. Hard workers, great gardeners and cooks, the people of Zoar ended up living very much like the rest of their American communal counterparts. True, they followed a charismatic leader, Joseph Bimeler (1778-1853) to America, but when he died no gifted orator/preacher took his place. In all, Zoar lasted from 1817 to 1898, for a total of 81 years.

It all began in Württemberg, Germany with the trances of a Swiss prophetess named Barbara Gruberman who fled her native land to take refuge in Germany. Gruberman immediately aligned herself with the Separatist movement in Germany whose members were being punished for their "deviant" beliefs. For example, they rejected the office of clergy and refused to practice Holy Baptism, Confirmation, and Holy Communion (the Eucharist). They also withdrew their children from state schools. They suffered cruel punishments, consisting of floggings, imprisonments, and having their children taken away from them. Gruberman quickly assessed the situation and urged the Separatists to head for America where they might find physical and spiritual freedom.

Gruberman died before the journey started, and the group chose Joseph Michael Bimeler as their leader. In 1817, Bimeler, a weaver by trade, led 225 followers to Philadelphia where a contingent of Quakers awaited them. Once on American soil, the Separatists pooled their funds, took a loan from the Quakers, and purchased 5 500 acres of Ohio land for $16 500. Several families remained in Philadelphia to earn money to pay for their passage, and fifty men and 104 women followed Bimeler to Ohio. It was a long and difficult trek, but dreams of creating their own special utopia kept the group moving at a fairly fast pace.

As the colony took shape Bimeler created special rules for his people to follow. Women, for example, could become voting members of the organization, but if they married out, they would have to leave the commune. Individuals who applied for membership could be admitted, but they would have to donate all of their worldly goods to the commune, and serve a period of probation. This ... had legal implications when the society later dissolved.

This three-and-a-half story frame *Zoar Hotel* (1833) photo was taken prior to its restoration.

... celibacy would be the norm ... financial footing. He argued ... mouths to feed if there was not ... later, both marriage and pro- ... ng one of the first to marry. ... been assigned to take care ... rry her. Thus a marriage cer- ... ting that marriage was not ... , but it was permissible.

... ed an unexpected harvest of ... exavated in their neighbor- ... worth $21 000 to build part ... ucts to canal workers, they ... land. They also farmed, built ... mill, and took up gardening. ... olen factory, looms for weav- ... cider press, and an 80-room ... ient in terms of having their ... ers, tailors, and wagon mas- ... ley was reported to have vis-

The society adopted a seven-point star as a community symbol. The star represented the star that stood over the birthplace of Jesus Christ at Bethlehem, representing peace and goodwill toward all people.

When children were born in Zoar, they remained in the care of their parents until they were three years old. After that they were placed in dormitories and regarded as communal responsibility.

Boys were raised in one dormitory and girls in another. In 1832 the commune adopted an official name, "The Society of the Separatists of Zoar," with their membership growing to include 500 individuals. The society adopted a seven-point star as a community symbol. The star represented the star that stood over the birthplace of Jesus Christ at Bethlehem, representing peace and goodwill toward all people. The group deemed the number seven as sacred. The name "Zoar," meaning "place of refuge," was taken from the Old Testament to commemorate Lot's (Abraham's nephew) city of refuge.

Zoar Store (1833) restored from 1970-1980 sells reproductions of nineteenth century objects, rather than the usual "souvenirs."

The famous geometrically-shaped *Zoar Garden* (1835) which was kept in almost perfect condition.

The Zoar Hotel brought in a geat deal of village income and unexpectedly became a very strong factor in the commune's demise. By 1835 the hotel had become a very popular place to visit, and this trend had its consequences. First, the hotel offered some workers the opportunity to hold cash in their hands, and some of them took to pilfering from the till. Second, the steady influx of visitors with their message of freedom outside the commune influenced many to try their hand at independence. Third, sometimes men from outside communities visited the hotel and discovered that young Zoarite women were desirable mates. They courted the women and married them, taking them away from village life.

Another factor contributing to the desire to leave the commununity was Bimeler's death. No one with Bimeler's strong-will followed in his footsteps to take charge of Zoar's spiritual life. This meant that the commitment of the next generation to the commune weakened, and they found it quite easy to leave the community.

Daily activities at Zoar were a bit different than those of other agricultural communities of the time. Members lived in family units, cooking their own meals using produce from the communal garden as well as sustaining themselves on chicken and eggs. Other items were obtained from the central warehouse. The Zoarites did not consume pork, salt, tea, or coffee, nor did they use tobacco. They drank cider, beer, and water. Breakfast was slated for 7:00 a.m., dinner at noon, and supper at 6:00 p.m. Work assignments were meted out by the colony board and included enough of a variety of responsibilities so that no one found it difficult or boring to carry out their assignments.

Zoar was first of all a religious commune. On Sundays members were expected to attend three religious services with men sitting on one side of the church and women on the other. The congregation sang hymns in German and Bimeler would deliver extemporaneous sermons on a variety of subjects related to morality and Christian obedience. Members were expected to live according to the roles outlined by their leader, and except for music, leisure activities were quite limited. A brass band of ten members sometimes entertained Zoarites. The band played both religious and secular music, both locally as well as in surrounding communities. The commune had no library, and aside from reading Bimeler's sermon notes, no literature existed in the colony.

The Blacksmith Shop (1834 – reconstructed 1972) is one of the ten restored buildings at Zoar where costumed interpreters tell the history of the site.

An unusual Zoar feature was their carefully honed garden, called the Garden of Happiness. The garden was designed according to the model outlined in the last biblical treatise, the Book of Revelation. A unique spruce tree representing everlasting life was placed in the centre of the garden, and a circle of twelve juniper trees was planted to represent the twelve apostles. A dozen narrow pathways reached out from the centre of the garden to symbolize pathways to heaven. A wide variety of flowers and fruits were planted in the garden, a greenhouse was added and the whole enterprise was cared for by a special gardener. Today the Ohio Historical Society maintains a garden onsite similar in design to the original one.

Bimeler held all property in his own name, and when he became aware of his soon demise, he named a successor, Jacob Sylvan. After Sylvan's term ended a series of managers took over Bimeler's role. Notes from Bimeler's sermons were gathered and printed and read in church services. For thirty-five years after

> In 1827, the people of Zoar reaped an unexpected harvest of funds when the Ohio-Erie Canal was excavated in their neighborhood.

Bimeler's death, the membership gathered on Sundays to hear someone read Bimeler's sermons, and then it was all over. In 1898 the members voted to dissolve the society, and property assets were divided with regular members receiving half shares in communal property and probationers receiving fifty acres of land and $200 each. Those involved in the society's industries received a share of those businesses.

Today several descendants of the original Zoarites still live in the village of Zoar that is open to public visits. Some of the village homes are privately owned while others are the property the Zoar Village State Memorial that operates the site.

The site is well worth a long visit.

For Further Reading

Carpenter, Delburn. (1975). *The Radical Pietists: Celibate Communal Societies Established in the United States Before 1920.* New York: AMS Press.

Gutek, Gerald, and Patricia Gutek. (1998). *Visiting Utopian Communities: A Guide to Shakers, Moravians, and Others.* Columbia, SC: University of South Carolina Press.

Nordhoff, Charles. (1993). *American Utopias.* Stockbridge, MS: Berkshire House Publishers.

Morhart, Hilda Disachinger. (1981). *Our Zoar Story.* Strasburg, OH: Gordon Printing.

Ohio Historical Society. (1987). *Zoar: An Ohio Experiment in Communalism.* Columbus, OH: Zoar Historical Society.

Sutton, Robert P. (2003). *Communal Utopias and the American Experience: Religious Communities, 1732-2000.* Westport, CN: Praeger.

http://www.museumsusa.org/museums/info/1156905neo-hioamishcountry/p/zoar.htm

http://en.wikipedia.org/wiki/Zoar,_Ohio

Epilogue

What Can We Learn From These Idealistiic Pursuits?

As the search for a more desirable form of society continues in various localities of this continent, a number of related questions arise. Is the utopian dream an illusive phenomenon or can it be realized in some form? Of the models developed so far, is there one that stacks up well against failed models? After several centuries of experimentation, can one identify guidelines to assist in the building of an improved form of social organization? Is every devised communal lifestyle doomed to fail? Are people really not suited to communal living? Is utopia an inevitable pursuit but an unrealizable dream?

Undoubtedly these questions have been raised by dreamers and utopian designers many times in the past but satisfactory answers appear to be elusive. This reality has not stopped the quest to invent a more satisfactory form of idyllic living, and it likely will not impede such efforts in the future. Every generation produces new groups of inventive thinkers who will undoubtedly search for that elusive metaphoric pot of gold.

Two Kinds of Dreamers

Diligent researchers have found that there are two kinds of utopian thinkers – those who want to escape from what they perceive to be societal shortcomings, and those who would like to reform society. Although make-over-minded innovators can potentially benefit society as creators of alternative thought patterns, escapists tend to have limited interaction with their fellow citizens. Reformers, on the other hand, remain attached to society in selected ways and constitute a more immediate and practical avenue for considered change. The idyllic experimenters described in this book represented both orientations and their stories will hopefully stimulate appreciation for their efforts, and even serve as encouragement for social inquiry.

The tendency to conceptualize idealized lifestyles is probably as old as humankind. Some scholars draw attention to the Biblical account of Adam and Eve who lived in the Garden of Eden as the first planned utopia. We all know that their experience did not turn out very well. Other scholars make reference to Plato's (427-347 BC) *Utopia* as a model for idealized living, but, of course, it was never really tested. One thing proponents of utopian ideals are agreed on is the hope that one day, at some moment in history, the chaos of the world will be overcome and all forms of social evil will be eliminated. In the meantime, every effort should be undertaken to attain as many characteristics of an idyllic lifestyle as possible.

Envisaged forms of utopian lifestyles tend to take various shapes, depending on timing. These include belief systems that drive them, leadership styles, and availability of preferred sites. Community opposition and/or support for such projects can also be a strong factor in the success or failure of the experiment. Historically, communal utopias have been without strong local support, probably because of the unique ways they perceived that life should be lived. Their deviances from established societal ways tended to threaten their neighbors. This observation can be substantiated by public reaction to some of the experiments previously described. On a more positive note, it is useful to mention that leaders of various historic utopian experiments were often in contact with sister projects in the interest of sharing ideas. This was quite evident in the second section of this book.

Historial Roots

Historians, theoreticians, and academics have all had a share in wanting to explain the reasons why the challenge of creating an idyllic lifestyle is so often undertaken. The reason appears to be imbedded in the very essence of human nature. Here is a sample of historic philosophical musings on the subject.

In the strictest academic sense, the term "utopia," is most likely based on the writings of Thomas More (1478-1535), who was knighted by King Henry the eighth for service to the Crown, yet later beheaded because he would not endorse Henry as Head of the Church of England. In 1516, More coined the term "utopia" by making it the title of a book which compared England to a mythical island by that name. The term utopia has been popularized in literature ever since, although too often in a negative manner. Philosopher More portrayed a utopian society that was plentiful in creature comforts, but not necessarily in individual freedom, obviously basing his argument on the observation that no community can function without rules. In his satirical portrayal of utopia More regarded the sexes as equal. Everyone had something to do, there were no lawyers, no one went to war, and the aged were respected. Now that is a dream in which everyone would like to take part.

Most children, and those adults who were once children, are probably familiar with Jonathan Swift's (1667-1745) novel, *Gulliver's Travels,* and while the intrigue of the novel for youngsters is its fantasy, Swift was really trying to imagine a Garden of Eden of his own. Since Swift frequently indulged in satire in his writings, his critics were not sure whether or not he was being serious about developing an earthly utopia.

A little more than a century later, H.G. Wells (1866-1946) also envisaged an imaginative, picture perfect society. Wells, a prolific British writer of science fiction, produced works that underscored his very strong faith in human nature. Wells perceived that human nature was basically good in essence and a improved social system could be created by rational human beings. Sadly, the more perfect society did not occur in Wells' lifetime as international wars continued to rage around the globe.

A North American example of optimistic utopian thinking came from the pen of Edward Bellamy (1850-1898). His novel, *Looking Backward,* represents the foray of writers from the New World who became interested in utopian thinking. Most people who enjoyed Bellamy's work of fiction probably never equated it with the underlying socialist measures he was proposing. Somewhat removed from the thinking of Karl Marx, Bellamy, who was trained in law and took up journalism, was essentially a social reformer. Writing on the heels of the great labor struggles of the 1880s, Bellamy promoted equal opportunity and the chance for an upgraded lifestyle for all Americans.

Eric Arthur Blair, an English author, better known as George Orwell (1903-1950), penned a book that found its way into libraries across North America. His novel, *Nineteen Eighty-Four,* depicted an idyllic collectivist society that limited the role of government. Orwell's main character in the novel portrayed the dangers of pervasive government because it constantly encroached on the rights of the individual. In Orwell's mind, less government implied a better society.

Still another example of idyllic dreaming came in the form of Lewis Mumford's (1885-1990) writings. An American historian of technology and science, Mumford was also optimistic about human nature. He believed that members of the human race could use electricity combined with various forms of mass communication to build a better world for people of all cultures. Needless to say, he too did not realize the fulfillment of this dream.

A Word From the Critics

Utopianism has also had its share of criticism. American theologian, Karl Paul Reinhold Niebuhr (1892-1971) denounced the notion that at some moment in history the chaos of the world would be overcome and social evil would be eliminated. He did not believe that a state of complete harmony could occur, given the past actions of nations. Niebuhr quoted from Psalm 2:1,4 (NIV) to give support to his skepticism about the possibility of establishing any form of utopia. It was vain thinking on the park of humankind. The psalmist states: "Why do the nations rage and the peoples plot in vain? The One enthroned in heaven laughs; the Lord scoffs at them." Niebuhr contended that if utopian dreams were harnessed to human actions, the historical record would show that they were a futile endeavor.

Sociologist Rosabeth Moss Kanter (1943-) has studied utopian societies for many years. A distinguished professor of business at Harvard University, she holds the Ernest L. Arbuckle Professorship at that institution. Kanter believes that order is the primary attraction to those who would like to form a utopian society, in contrast to what the founders of such societies visualize as a chaotic and uncoordinated world. In Kanter's words, formers of utopias seek meaning, control and purpose—improvement, but not perfection.

The Hutterite Example

Individuals who study utopian history sometimes wonder why so many of these communities have such a short life. Very few of them last more than three generations, and this would include Amana, the Harmonists, Shakers, and Zoar. Today, there are less than a half dozen Shakers, two of them fairly recent converts. At one time their communities comprised some 6 000 people. The esteemed award for longevity, if one was created, would go to today's Hutterites, a people of whom very little is known by the average public. From their Swiss beginnings in 1530 until they migrated to Russia in the 1770s, the Hutterite movement annually grew in numbers. After Catherine the Great died in 1776 and Russia began to militarize, great pressure to conform was put on incoming minority groups. The effect on Hutterites because of persecution saw their communal members dwindled to less than 100. Migration to North America during the 1870s gave them new impetous and their numbers began to increase, mainly due to a very high birth rate. Today their 45 000 North American adherents live in some 460 colonies. They are still increasing in numbers, but their birth rate has dropped significantly.

Two questions must be asked; "What is the secret of Hutterite success? Why have they endured while other communal efforts have failed?" There are at least two factors to take into account in explaining this unusual phenomenon. First, and this may surprise some folk, Hutterites operate according to a strong but orthodox belief system. They are essentially conservative Christians. Their quite literal interpretation of the scriptures, accompanied by the historic Anabaptist-propelled strong work ethic, have assisted in their success. With the exception of believing that communalism is Biblically-mandated, Hutterite theology differs little from that of North America's many mainline Christian denominations. Hutterites proclaim no unusual doctrines and their religious practices are quite orthodox. Most Anabaptist groups would find themselves on familiar ground in a Hutterite colony.

A second factor in explaining Hutterite success is their form of social organization. Political scientists would probably call it a form of limited representative democracy, but it does seem to work. Although only baptized males are allowed to vote on matters affecting colony life, all ruling offices are subject to election – including the minister, assistant minister, colony boss, German language teacher, and so on. Women are assigned to significant posts such as head cook or kindergarten teacher, and they are left alone to influence the way their husbands vote in informal ways. The system functions well; there is no room for dictators, heroes, celebrities, or prima donna in Hutterite society. If an individual does not measure up to his or her expectations, they can be removed from office – men by election, and women by political removal. These instances are always conducted by confrontation, discussion, and prayer.

And so to conclude; it would seem that any contemporary social group bound by a unified orthodox belief system, and willing to commit to working together with shared responsibilities, *could* follow the Hutterite model.

This kind of utopian arrangement may not appeal to many, but it is probably as close to an idyllic form of communal living as possible.

For Further Reading

Bellamy, Edward. (1951). *Looking Backward*. New York: The Modern Library.

Fogarty, Robert S., ed. (1980). *Dictionary of American Communal and Utopian History*. Westport, CN: Greenwood Press.

Hofer, Samuel. (1998). *The Hutterites: Lives and Images of a Communal People.* Saskatoon, SK: Hofer Publications.

Holbrook, Stewart H. (1957). *Dreamers of the American Dream*. Garden City, NY: Doubleday & Company.

Hostetler, John A. *Hutterite Society*. Baltimore, MD: The Johns Hopkins University Press.

Kephart, William M., and William W. Zellner. (1994). *Extraordinary Groups: An Examination of Unconventional Life-Styles.* Fifth edition. New York: St. Martin's Press.

Marty, Martin E. (2003). But Even So, Look at That: An Ironic Perspective on Utopias. *Visions of Utopia.* Furaha D. Norton, ed. New York: Oxford University Press, 49-88.

More, Thomas. (2008). Utopia. *Three Early Modern Utopias: Utopia, New Atlantis, and The Isle of Pines.* Susan Bruce, ed. New York: Oxford University Press, 3-129.

Mumford, Lewis. (2008). *The Story of Utopias.* www.Forgottenbooks.org

Peter, Karl A. (1987). *The Dynamics of Hutterite Society.* Edmonton, AB: The University of Alberta Press.

Wells, H. G. (1999). *A Modern Utopia. The Utopian Reader.* Gregory Clays and Lyman Tower Sargent, eds. New York: New York University Press, 312-319.

Utopian Pursuits

ee

topian Pursuits

 help of a friend, Ellen G. Starr,
ed area of Chicago in 1889. Its pur-
and downtrodden to develop an ele-
intain educational and philanthropic
ditions in the industrial districts of

as the name chosen for an 18th cen-
 went back to 1714 when two men,
ed the Separatist organization called
were persecuted for their beliefs but
f Barbara Heinemann, a prophetess
ann and her husband joined 800
s. Once there, she joined with leader
 religious communal villages, later

), was Bishop of Sarapul and Yelabug
dox Church in 2000. Ambrosius gave
lled them "Doukhoborski," meaning
 the Spirit of God. The Doukhobors
d "in the Spirit," not against it.

in print, originated in 1906 by Cyrus

Salvation Army near Holly, Colorado,
ting poverty. The commune became
ught conditions forced the fourteen
here. Amity was one of several such
Army leader, Frederick Booth Tucker.

-1720). In 1693, Jacob Ammann, a
egan to insist on stricter church prac-
idung) of church members who were
footwashing and the Holy Kiss, both

rituals that set the Amish apart from the Mennonites. The holy kiss is an expression of fellowship and brotherly love; washing one another's feet represents humility.

Amish (the), were originally a branch of the Mennonite Church, but broke with the main body in 1693. However, they still cooperate with Mennonites on relief work projects through the Mennonite Central Committee. The Amish gradually built a unique culture of their own which differs in ways from Mennonites. The 17th century Amish lifestyle (buggies, bonnets, and babies) annually draws millions of visitors to their communities in twenty American states and the province of Ontario.

Anabaptists is a term applied to a 16th century left wing group that originated in the Protestant Reformation. The word Anabaptist is a Greek term that originated in derision and means "rebaptiser." Following a strict interpretation of the New Testament, most of the forty Anabaptist congregations hold to a general core of spiritual values. They reject infant baptism (substituting adult baptism) and the Sacraments, preach pacifism, and separation of church and state. By 1525, Anabaptist congregations were spread across most of German speaking Europe.

Anabaptists were often fined or imprisoned for their acts of civil disobedience such as refusing to take public oaths, paying taxes, and the taking up of arms. By 1540, most of the early Anabaptist leaders had been either imprisoned or executed. Persecutions against the Anabaptists continued in various portions of Europe into the 1580's, but they persisted. Many of them, like Amish, Hutterites, and Mennonites migrated to North America to avoid persecution.

Aurora, Oregon, founded in 1855, was the second communal settlement originated by William Keil. The first was developed in Bethel, Missouri in 1844.

Back to the Landers is a label attached to a North American social movement that began in the 1960s. Disillusioned with what they termed the treadmill of middle class living, many young people migrated to rural areas to redeem the virtues of a simple lifestyle. Some adherents worked part time in nearby urban centres while others lived entirely off the land, dwelling in log cabins, growing their own fruits and vegetables, and burning firewood in place of using electricity. Many developed cottage industries and homeschooled their children.

Barr Colony (the). In 1903, a group of English immigrants known as Barr Colonists comprised the last great emigration scheme in English North American history. Some 2 000 Englishmen, women, and children emigrated to what later became known as Lloydminster, Saskatchewan, lured by advertisements of the good life posted by one Rev. Isaac Barr. Theirs is a story of good intentions but poor planning, suffering, and internal strife that perhaps unfairly vilified their leader, Isaac Barr, and exaggerated the virtues of his replacement, the Rev. George Lloyd.

Barr, Rev. Isaac Montgomery (1847-1937) was born in Hornby, Ontario, where his Irish father was a Presbyterian minister. Barr became an Anglican priest and served many charges in Ontario, Western Canada, and the United States. Inspired by Cecil Rhodes' colonization schemes in Africa, Barr placed alluring ads about the good life in western Canada that attracted hundreds of would-be English immigrants called Barr Colonists.

Beachy Amish are a 1927 breakaway group from the Old Order Amish by following the vision of Moses Beachy. Although they maintain the use of traditional types of clothing, the group is less conservative than the Old Order, and permits members to use electricity, telephones, tractors, and plainly painted automobiles.

Beachy, Moses M. (1874-1946) was a bishop in the Old Order Amish Church who attracted a personal following in 1927. Unlike the Old Order Amish, the Beachy Amish sponsor Sunday Schools, construct church buildings instead of using their homes for worship services, and are evangelical in theology.

Beissel, Conrad (1691-1768) established his own Separatist following of 300 participants at Ephrata, Pennsylvania, in 1732, emphasizing mystical communalism. Having emigrated to America from Europe, Beissel joined the Germantown Mother Church in Philadelphia but soon broke away after theological disagreements with local elders. He then formed his own organization.

Bellamy, Edward (1850-1898) penned *Looking Backward*, a novel that promoted equal opportunity and improved living conditions for all Americans.

Belton, Texas, was the location of the Women's Commonwealth, a female commune based on the doctrines of religious perfectionism, celibacy, and a unique form of Wesleyan sanctification. Founded by Martha McWhirter in 1866, the commune began with a small group of middle-class Protestant women who shunned marriage and became financially independent. They operated a series of successful industries in Belton, Texas, then relocated to Washington, DC where the last surviving member, Martha Scheble, died in 1983.

Benedictines are a 6th century Roman Catholic Order founded in Italy in AD 529 by Benedict of Nursia. Dedicated to spirituality and the consecrated life, the Benedictines include a number of orders such as Trappists. Monte Cassino, the first one founded by Benedict, is the most notable Benedictine community.

Bethel, Missouri, is the site of William Keil's first German Separatist commune. Established in 1844, and basically an agricultural enterprise, at its peak the Bethel membership of 650 was engaged in a variety of successful industries including the manufacture of world class leather goods. In 1855, Keil and a band of followers established a second successful commune at Aurora, Oregon. Both colonies folded shortly after Keil's death in 1877.

Bimeler, Joseph (also known as Joseph Bäumler or Bäumeler) (1778-1853) was the leader of a group of 18th century German Separatists known in America as The Society of the Separatists of Zoar. Persecution led the group to the United States in 1817 where they prospered. By the time of Bimeler's death in 1853, Zoar's accumulated wealth amounted to more than one million dollars. Two decades later, their net worth had tripled, but in 1898 the community voted to dissolve.

Blackmore, William (dates unknown) was a Commissioner appointed by the Government of British Columbia to investigate why resident Doukhobors preferred not to send their children to public schools. Blakemore held public sittings and delivered an informative report in 1912 pointing out that the Doukhobors feared public schooling would influence their children with values of militancy and materialism.

Bountiful, British Columbia is an unusual polygamist community that is part of the Fundamentalist Church of Jesus Christ of Latter-Day Saints. When the larger Mormon Church banned polygamy in 1890, a number of splinter groups arose to defend the practice. One such group, numbering 700 people today, was led by Winston Blackmore and Warren Jeffs, who set up a camp near Creston, BC. The settlement has often been in the news.

Branch Davidians. The Branch Davidians descend from a 1930s schism in the Seventh-day Adventist Church, led by Victor Houteff. The schism was motivated by Houteff's charge that the church had grown spiritually lax, and a new group, the Davidian Seventh-Day Adventists was begun in protest. In 1981 Vernon Wayne Howell (later renamed David Koresh) connected himself with the group after having been excommunicated from the SDA church in Tyler, Texas, for moral reasons. Two years later, armed with a new vision, he founded his own commune. In 1993, a raid by the United States Bureau of Alcohol, Tobacco, Firearms and Explosives ended with the burning of the Branch Davidian compound killing fifty-four adults and twenty-one children.

This group is not to be confused with the Koreshan Unity commune established by Cyrus Teed in Florida in 1894.

Brisbane, Albert (1809-1890) was a disciple of Charles Fourier who inspired the construction of forty phalanxes in the United States.

Brook Farm was founded in 1841 by Rev. George and Sophia Ripley, and fifteen other members, following guidelines set out by French philosopher, Charles Fourier. Brook Farm adhered to transcendental principles – individual freedom and humane relationships – and fostered the notion that Brook Farm could serve as a model to inaugurate a new communal social order. Brook Farm adherents perceived physical labor as uplifting – a condition of mental wellbeing and health. Even writers and poets who lived at Brook Farm spent at least a few hours a day in physical effort.

Brown, John (1800-1859) is probably the best-known supporter of the Underground Railroad which was designed to aid hundreds of Black slaves in their escape to Canada and northern non-slavery states.

Budget (the) is the most popular and widely read local weekly newspaper in several Ohio counties in the Heart of Ohio's Amish Country. Established in 1890, *The Budget* is favored by many Amish who subscribe to it as a means of keeping in touch with their relatives and friends in neighboring Amish communities.

Burning Bush (the) was a religious commune started in Texas in 1912 by a group of 375 disgruntled Wisconsin Methodists. Unsuccessful sister colonies were also begun in Louisiana, West Virginia, and Virginia. The Texas experiment operated a farm, cannery, and sawmill, but was sold by auction in 1919 because of unpaid bills.

Burning of Arms was an event that occurred in Russia on June 28-29, 1895, when 7 000 Doukhobors in southern Russia simultaneously set ablaze huge piles of rifles, pistols and swords. It was the first mass protest in history against war and militarism, and political reaction was swift. Doukhobors who participated in the burning received severe beatings and floggings and 4 600 were exiled to isolated areas. Many of them handed in their military reserve papers and refused to carry weapons or take an Oath of Allegiance to the Tsar. The event triggered Doukhobor migrations to Canada in 1899.

Cabet, Etienne (1788-1856), a Frenchman, conceived the concept of a secular commune based on shares. Several experiments were developed in North America by a group known as Icarians whose name derives from Greek mythology meaning "soaring high in adventurous flight."

Cannington Manor is located forty miles south of Moosomin in southeast Saskatchewan. The site was established in 1882 by Capt. Edward Pierce, whose plan was to develop an aristocratic agricultural community based on English Victorian society. The people who answered Pierce's ads, many of whom had considerable wealth, were carefully chosen from the better class families of England. Many rich families paid for their sons to become Pierce's protégés with the hope that they would become gentlemen tillers of the soil. The experiment lasted only a few years and dissolved due to economic failure.

Card, Charles Ora (1839–1906), often referred to as "Canada's Brigham Young," founded of the town of Cardston, Alberta, in 1887, as the first Mormon settlement in Canada. The Mormon migration to Canada was motivated in large part by strained relations the LDS Church was experiencing with the federal United

States government over the practice of polygamy. Card became the first president of the Alberta Stake of the LDS Church, the first stake established outside the United States.

Catherine the Great (1729-1796) was a German princess who became the autocratic ruler of Russia in 1762. One of her life achievements was to lure European farmers to Russia.

Chase, Warren (1813-1891) was a major mover and shaker in the founding of the Wisconsin Phalanx. This commune, named Ceresco, was modeled on the writings of French philosopher, Charles Fourier.

Chinese immigrants in Canada worked very hard and often risked their lives to help build Canada's railroad in the 1880s. When their task was completed, the Chinese found themselves in very difficult economic times, having to struggle with job discrimination, prejudice and racism, and personal attacks. When the railroad was completed, the Canadian government went to great lengths to keep additional Chinese immigrants out of the country, including the launching of an extremely expensive head tax on all Chinese immigrants.

Chinese immigrants to the United States were the first Asian immigrants to enter America beginning in the 18th century. Later, large-scale immigration was motivated by the California Gold Rush. Later laws such as the *Chinese Exclusion Act* forced the return of thousands of Chinese back to their homeland. In 1920 the Chinese population in America fell to a lowly 62 000, but today the Chinese make up the largest Asian population in the United States.

The first Chinese immigrants were fairly well received by the Americans, partly because they were wealthy, successful merchants, along with skilled artisans, fishermen, and hotel and restaurant owners, and partly because they had a strong work ethic. Like their Canadian counterparts, they were later subject to prejudice and racism and job discrimination.

Christian Community of Universal Brotherhood (CCUB) was founded in Russia in 1889, and in Canada became primarily a spiritual and economic organization of Canadian Doukhobors from the early 20th century until its forced bankruptcy in 1938. In its corporate form, it was an instrument that allowed the community Doukhobors to hold collective ownership of the lands as well as domestic, agricultural, and industrial facilities.

Church of Jesus Christ of Latter Day Saints (Mormons) was started by Joseph Smith who questioned the existence of so many different Christian denominations. He claimed that while he was searching for an answer, on Sept. 21, 1823, at the age of seventeen, an angel named Moroni told him that he had been chosen to translate the *Book of Mormon* which had been compiled around the 4th century.

Smith allegedly found some golden plates that he later translated into the *Book of Mormon* and it became the foundation for his new denomination.

Community of Christ – known from 1872 to 2001 as the Reorganized Church of Jesus Christ of Latter Day Saints (RLDS); is an American-based, international Christian church established in April 1830. The newly-established organization claims that its mission is "to proclaim Jesus Christ and promote communities of joy, hope, love, and peace." There are approximately 221 000 members of the church living in 50 nations. Unlike the larger Mormon denomination, the head of this church is always a direct descendant of Joseph Smith.

Community of True Inspiration is the historical name of the Amana Society founded in Iowa in the early 1800s by Christian Metz.

Dariusleut are a branch of Hutterites named after Dartius Hofer, one of their leaders in Russia. The word "leut" means people.

Dawn Settlement. In 1841, Josiah Henson, a slave who escaped to Upper Canada via the Underground Railroad, helped establish the Dawn Settlement at Dresden, Ontario, as a refuge for runaway slaves. The commune attracted many former slaves, but many of them returned to the United States after 1963 when emancipation was proclaimed. Others remained to build a significant Black community in southern Ontario.

de Alvarado, Captain Hernando (1518-1550) invaded the Indian pueblos of the American southwest in 1540.

de Boissiere, Ernest (1811-1894) was a French aristocrat who established a short-lived commune in Silkville, Kansas, in 1873 for the purpose of manufacturing silk.

Divine Spark. A key to understanding Doukhobor theology is their belief in a Divine Spark that exists in all human beings and connects them to God. Faith in the Divine Spark means that anyone and everyone, regardless of race, creed, age, or sex can contribute spiritual insights whenever worship services are held.

Doerfler, Father Bruno (1866-1919) was a Benedictine priest who established St. Joseph's Colony in Saskatchewan in 1902.

Doukhobors are a religious communal group who emerged in 18th century Russia as a Christian peasant reaction to the excessive opulence and ritualistic authority of the Russian Orthodox Church. Doukhobors practised a simpler form of religion, rejecting the literal Bible and any form of clergy. In 1899, a contingent of 7 500 Doukhobors emigrated to Canada to avoid persecution in Russia. They settled on the western Canadian prairies on Crown land and built fifty-seven communal villages. In 1912 they relocated to British Columbia because of the government's insistence that they take an oath of allegiance. After emigrating to Canada, three separate Doukhobor groups emerged – traditional community Doukhobors; Independents who compromised their faith by swearing allegiance to government; and, the Sons of Freedom, a radical protest group.

Drop City was a hippie haven established near Trinidad, Colorado, in 1965, but came to an abrupt end in 1973 when residents were evicted for not paying their bills.

Duncan, William was a Church of England lay missionary who built a religious commune called Metlakatla, among the Tsimshian Indians of British Columbia in 1886. The community became economically very successful and featured the largest cathedral west of Chicago and north of San Francisco. Duncan taught the Tsimshian Indians the Christian religion and British Victorian forms of law and government.

Duss, John (1860-1951) was a trustee of George Rapp's third commune called Economy. When the settlement began to suffer financially, Duss charged his fellow trustees with mismanagement, although it was he who spent money wantonly on travel. Heavily involved in music, in 1887 Duss' band toured the United States including providing a concert at the Metropolitan Opera House.

Eckerlin, Israel (1706-1758) was appointed as leader of Ephrata in 1740 by Conrad Beissel as the latter's successor. Five years later, thoroughly jealous of his colleague's economic success with Ephrata, Beissel took back the leadership.

Economy was the third commune initiated by George Rapp, a Separatist preacher from Würtenburg, Germany. Built in 1925, the community dissolved in 1905.

Emerson, Ralph Waldo (1803-1882) was a well-known American writer remembered for his influence in the transcendental movement of the mid 19th century. He, along with other similar thinkers with the same convictions, was drawn to the operations of Brook Farm which was designed in keeping with Charles Fourier's concept of a phalanx.

Ephrata Cloister, was a commune founded in 1732, that grew to include 300 participants. It was also one of America's earliest religious settlements. Led by Conrad Beissel, the community emphasized mystical spiritual knowledge rather than earthly rewards. Settled in unique European style buildings, Ephrata was stratified with a group of celibate brothers and sisters, and a congregation of married couples with families.

Farm, The was initiated in 1971 by Stephen Gaskin and his hippie followers. Gaskin, an instructor at San Francisco State College scheduled special night classes to address contemporary societal developments and thus gained a large following of disillusioned youth. A movement of 250 flower children soon developed, so Gaskin gathered funds from his followers and purchased 1 800 acres in Tennessee to found The Farm. At its peak, Farm residents numbered 1 500, but dwindled to around 125 today. The Farm operates a number of trendy, green-related industries.

Finney, Rev. Charles Grandison (1792-1875) was a famous religious Presbyterian revivalist who figured strongly in the 19th century Great Awakening. Sometimes called "The Father of Modern Revivalism," Finney did not attempt to start his own denomination, and never claimed to be the recipient of special revelation.

Flower Children or "anti-establishment reactionaries" were labels given to the flamboyant North American youth of the 1960s who were also called "hippies." They were often described as long-haired, radical-looking young people who dreamed of creating a society based on freedom, love, peace, beauty and simplicity. Many hippies wore flowers in their hair and dressed in second-hand clothing obtained from thrift and army surplus stores. They wore ponchos, bell bottoms decorated with patches and embroidery, tie-dyed shirts, leather sandals, bright colors and intricate patterns. Around their necks both sexes hung amulets, bells, seeds and trinkets to ward off evil and improve sexual performance. Many of them spurned city life and became part of the back-to-the land movement.

Fourier, Francois Marie Charles (1772-1837) was a major influence on 19th century transcendentalism, and a brilliant radical theorist, utopian socialist, mystic sensualist, and eccentric visionary. Fourier's social theory was based on the innate goodness of human nature on which basis he proposed the building of a new social order.

Fourier's plan was that large communes, or "phalanxes," each consisting of 1 620 members be constructed wherein members would enjoy association and harmony. Members would express twelve major passions and happily engage in gardening, arboriculture, light industry, operas, and sexual orgies. The New England transcendentalists eagerly embraced Fourier's reformist zeal, and several other American communities organized such settlements. In 1844, the Brook Farm Community in Massachusetts reshaped itself into a Fourierist organization.

Fox, George (1624-1691) was an English dissenter who has often been called the founder of the Religious Society of Friends, commonly known as Quakers.

Gaskin, Stephen (1935-) is a counterculture hippie icon best known for his efforts in co-founding The Farm, a famous spiritual intentional hippie community begun in 1971 in Summertown, Tennessee. Gaskin is the author of over a dozen books, a teacher, a musician (drummer), a semantic rapper, a public speaker, a political activist, and a philanthropic organizer.

Golden Lamb Inn (The) in Lebanon, Ohio, built by Shakers in 1803, is the oldest continuously operating business in the state.

Grant, Elijah (1808-1894) was the founder of the Ohio Phalanx patterned after a communal model formulated by French writer, Charles Fourier.

Greeley, Horace (1811-1872) was an award-winning journalist for the *New Yorker* and the *New York Tribune* addressing current events and the arts and literature in his columns.

Gruber, Eberhard Ludwig (1665-1728) was a cofounder of the Community of True Inspiration in Germany in 1714 along with Johann F. Rock. A contingent of their members migrated to America during the 1840s under the leadership of Barbara Heinemann and Christian Metz. Once settled, they organized the seven villages of the Amana Community in Iowa.

Grüberman, Barbara (dates unknown), a Separatist prophetess subject to visions and trances, was forced to leave her Swiss homeland for Germany where she influenced the group that eventually established the Zoar Commune in Ohio in 1817. It was Grüberman who first originated the idea of migrating to America, but she died before they left. Joseph Bimeler succeeded her as leader and led her followers to America.

Gubanova, Lukeria Vasilyevna (?-1886) was a Russian Doukhobor leader who taught Peter Verigin (Peter the Lordly) the principles of the Doukhobor faith. She led the Golden Age of the Doukhobors in Russia, 1864-1886.

Harmony was a communal town founded in Pennsylvania in 1805 by George Rapp, a Separatist preacher from Württemberg, Germany, the first of three communal colonies he initiated. The others were New Harmony in Indiana in 1814, and Old Economy in 1924, again in Pennsylvania.

Hawthorne, Nathaniel (1804-1864) was one of the leading writers of his time, and explored the concepts of individual responsibility, the importance of creative expression, and mankind's relationship to the natural world. He also at times delved into transcendental philosophy which influenced the origins of Brook Farm. His most famous work was *The Scarlet Letter*, written in 1850. Hawthorne was friends with and neighbor for a time to some of New England's popular intellectuals including Amos Bronson Alcott and his daughter Louisa May Alcott, Henry David Thoreau, and Ralph Waldo Emerson who was also prominent in the transcendentalist movement.

Heinemann, Barbara (1795-1883) was one of the movers and shakers behind the origin of The Community of True Inspiration. In 1818 Heinemann was "illuminated" with a sense of religious calling and subsequently recognized by the community as a prophetess. The community emigrated to America during the 1840s where, along with Christian Metz and Heinemann, helped founded the seven Amana Colonies in Iowa. After Metz died in 1867, Heinemann directed the religious affairs of the community of 1 600, but when she died, no spiritual successor was named. In 1932 the Amana colonies dissolved their commune and restructured themselves as a corporation.

Henson, Josiah (1789-1883) was an escaped slave and lay preacher who started a new life in Canada working as a farm laborer. In 1836, Henson and Hiram Wilson purchased 200 acres in Dawn Township in Ontario to build a self-sufficient commune for Black fugitive slaves. Josiah Henson's name became synonymous with the central character, "Uncle Tom" in Harriet Beecher Stowe's famous novel, *Uncle Tom's Cabin.*

Hill, Sam (1857-1931) tried unsuccessfully to establish a Quaker commune at Maryhill in Washington. Dedicated in 1926, Hill's mansion is currently the Maryhill Museum of Art.

Hippies is a label that originated in the 1960s to describe the lifestyle of "rebellious" North American youth who ascribed to a reactionary belief system that rejected the roles and functions of all North American institutions – political, social, and religious.

Holoboff, Anastasia (1885-1965) founded an alternative Doukhobor village near Calgary, Alberta, when she was rejected for the leadership role after Peter the Lordly died in 1924. Instead, Peter the Lordly's son Peter Petrovich (also known as Peter the Purger) from Russia was called to that office.

Hostetler, John (1918-2001) was raised in the Old Order Amish community but became a sociologist who penned the first definitive study of the Amish. Dismayed by inaccurate popular essays on the Amish, Hostetler published *Amish Life* (Herald Press, 1952) and *The Amish* (Herald Press, 1995), books still in print at his death in 2001. The combined sales of his books at the time of his death approached 850,000.

Hull House was a settlement house co-founded by Jane Addams in 1889 for the purpose of helping the helpless build responsible, self-sufficient lives for themselves and their families. The practice of neighbors helping neighbors became a cornerstone of the Hull House philosophy.

Hutter, Jacob (1500?-1536) was a hatter by trade, but chosen as minister of a Tyrolean Mennonite congregation. Disillusioned with the growing worldliness of the church, in 1530 Hutter broke away to form a new denomination today known as Hutterian Brethren. Like other Anabaptists of the time, Hutter was assigned a price on his head. On November 29, 1535 he was bound and gagged and taken to Innsbruck where he was tortured and interrogated. On February 2, 1536 he was condemned as a heretic and burned alive at the stake.

Hutterites (Hutterian Brethren) are followers of Jacob Hutter (see above). There are three main types of communal Hutterites: Schmiedeleut (Blacksmith people), Dariusleut (so named after their original leader), and Lehrerleut (teacher people). The Schmiedeleut live in Manitoba and the Dariusleut and Lehrerleut live in western North America – Saskatchewan, Alberta, British Colombia, Washington, and Montana.

Icarians were part of a nonreligious French social movement that followed the philosophy, teaching, and writings of Etienne Cabet. The Icarians were forced to leave France because of their political beliefs and immigrated to America in 1848. They first settled in Texas, then moved to Nauvoo, Illinois. Later they developed sites in Corning, Iowa, and Cloverdale, California.

Jansson, Erik (1808-1850) led a group of Swedish immigrants to the America Midwest in 1846 where they started a commune known as Bishop Hill. The commune reached its peak in 1859 with 800 people.

Japanese Hutterites have one colony in Owa, Japan, patterned after the lifestyle of North American Hutterites. The colony was built in the 1950s after a contingent of Japanese visited a colony in the United States.

Jeffs, Rulon Timpson (1909 -2002) known to his followers as Uncle Rulon, was the leader of the Fundamentalist Church of Jesus Christ of Latter Day Saints, a Mormon fundamentalist organization based in Colorado City, Arizona.

Jeffs, Warren Steed (1955-) was president of the polygamous Fundamentalist Church of Jesus Christ of Latter Day Saints (FLDS Church) from 2002 to 2007. While "President, Prophet, Seer, and Revelator" of the organization, Jeffs wielded both religious and secular power.

Jones, James Warren or "Jim" Jones (1931-1978) was the founder and leader of the Peoples Temple, which is best known for the November 18, 1978 death of more than 900 Temple members in Jonestown, Guyana.

Kant, Immanuel (1724-1804) was one of the most influential philosophers in the history of Western philosophy. His contributions to metaphysics, epistemology, ethics, and aesthetics have had a profound impact on almost every philosophical movement that followed him. Kant promoted the idea that doing good for others can sometimes visit the greatest evils upon them. This way of thinking provided the possibility of forestalling political utopianism and totalitarianism.

Kanter, Rosabeth Moss (1943-) is a soiologist who holds the Ernest L. Arbuckle Chair at Harvard University and specializes in the study of intentional communities.

Keil, William (1812-1877) was a mystical thinker who founded two major religious communal societies in Bethel, Missouri, and Aurora, Oregon.

Kibbutz, Kibbutzim-plural is a Hebrew word for a communal settlement(s) that is(are) dedicated to mutual aid and social justice. This is also a socioeconomic system based on the principle of joint ownership of property, equality and cooperation of production, consumption and education. Its underlying philosophy is founded on Louis Blanc's motto, "from each according to his ability, to each according to his need." The first kibbutzim (plural of "kibbutz") were founded some forty years before the establishment of the State of Israel in 1948. Today there are some 270 kibbutzim involving some 130 000 individuals scattered throughout Israel with memberships ranging from 40 to more than 1 000.

Koresh, David (1959-1993) was born Vernon Wayne Howell, and became leader of a communal Branch Davidian religious sect near Waco, Texas. Koresh's commune was destroyed by fire on February 28th, 1993 in Waco, Texas in a clash with local law enforcement officers.

Koreshan Unity Community was a religious cooperative community developed by Cyrus R. Teed in 1894 at Estero, Florida. In 1908 the population of Koreshan Unity peaked at 250, although Teed, who believed himself to be immortal, prophesied that its membership would reach millions. Koreshans practiced celibacy, men and women occupying separate living quarters. Their membership declined after Teed's death in 1908 and the site became a state park in 1961.

Lee, Ann (1736-1784), also known as "Mother Ann Lee," became leader of the United Society of Believers in Christ's Second Appearing, who originated within the Quaker movement. The method of worship Lee and her followers practiced was one of ecstatic dancing or "shaking", which dubbed them as Shaking Quakers. They were also celibate. A small number of Shakers migrated to America in 1774 where they successfully attracted as many as 6 000 adherents living in nineteen communes. Today, only a handful of Shakers remain.

Lehrerleut are a branch of Hutterites who derived their name from their reputation as teachers. The word lehrer means "teacher;" leut means people or literally teacher people.

Lloyd, Rev. George Exton (1861-1940) was the second leader of the Barr Colonists who located to the Saskatchewan prairies from England in 1903.

Rev. Isaac Barr was responsible for initiating the movement but was replaced when it became evident that his financial abilities were less than desirable.

Lloydminster, Saskatchewan, derives its name from the Rev. George Exton Lloyd, the second leader of the Barr Colonists. When the provinces of Alberta and Saskatchewan were created in 1905 and the 4th Meridian was selected as the inter-provincial boundary, the Village of Lloydminster was split in two. The Alberta portion of the divided community was incorporated as a village in Alberta in July 1906, while the Saskatchewan portion was incorporated as a town in Saskatchewan in April 1907.

Luther, Martin (1483-1546) occupies a very unique place in religious history as a monk who defied the Roman Catholic Church. Although Luther originally saw himself as a reformer within the Catholic Church, he was branded a heretic and asked to recant his views. In the end, however, he helped inspire the formation of the Lutheran Church and divided Christianity into two separate Christian camps, Protestantism becoming the second division.

Markova, Anna Petrovna (1902-1978) was the daughter of Doukhobor leader Peter Petrovich Chistiakov Verigin. During her life she played a large part in the early history of a Doukhobor women's organization. Arriving in Canada in 1960, Markova helped build bridges within the Doukhobor community as well as with the global community at large

McWhirter, Martha (1827-1904) founded a religious commune in Belton, Texas, known as the Women's Commonwealth. McWhirter's haven inspired women to leave their abusive husbands and along with their children undertake a new lifestyle. In 1866 McWhirter had a spiritual revelation that she interpreted as God calling her to "sanctify herself, filling her with purity and holiness." This experience justified her to leave her marriage and join with other women to form a commune known as the Womens' Commonwealth, but nicknamed "The Sanctified Sisters." The group became very prosperous and in 1899 retired to a large house in Washington, D.C.

Matthijs or Matthijsz, Jan (1500-1534) was an Anabaptist leader who, with Melchior Hoffman seized the town of Münster, Germany, in 1534 to establish a radical Anabaptist kingdom. After breaking into the city, the Anabaptists instituted a reign of terror and ordained apostles of revolution to preach throughout Europe. The communist paradise of Münster attracted thousands of Anabaptists from throughout Germany and Holland. Matthijs was killed in one of the early battles with troops who surrounded the city. Dictator Johan Bokelson took command of the city and issued the order that everything be held in common, including wives.

Metlakatla. In 1886, William Duncan, an English tannery employee and lay minister of the Anglican Church built the communal village of Metlakatla in British Columbia's Tsimshian Indian territory. After a doctrinal dispute with church authorities Duncan moved his followers to Alaska to rebuild his settlement. The US Congress granted him Annette Island and other surrounding islands which today comprise the only Indian reservation in Alaska. Duncan remained at the Alaskan settlement until his death in 1918, after which his commune dissolved.

Mennonites are a fellowship of Christian Anabaptist pacifists named after their 16th century leader, a former Roman Catholic priest named Menno Simons (1496–1561). Today there are 1.5 million Mennonites living in more than fifty countries, with their largest populations in Canada, the Democratic Republic of Congo, and the United States.

Metz, Christian, (1794-1867) was a leader of the Community of True Inspiration, a German Separatist group of 350 who migrated to America in 1842. They eventually purchased 26 000 acres of rich farmland in Iowa where they built seven communal villages known today as the Amana Society.

Miss Harmony was a shapely statue situated in a garden outside of George Rapp's living-room window as a symbol of peace and tranquility.

Molokans, are a 17th century Russian-derived protest religion, so named because they drank milk during fasts sponsored by the Russian Orthodox Church. The Molokans rejected the tsar's claim to Divine rule, and rejected all icons, orthodox fasts, military service and other practices, including baptism. They also rejected traditional theological beliefs such as the Trinity, the physical resurrection of Christ, and the literal existence of heaven and hell.

At the end of the 19th century there were about 500 000 Molokans in Russia. Three percent of them emigrated to the United States at the beginning of the 20th century. Today the Molokans are best described as a Biblically-centred religious movement consisting of some 20 000 adherents who worship in 200 Molokan churches, 150 of them in Russia. Some 5 000 Molokans regularly attend services in the United States, most of them living in the Los Angeles area.

Moon, Rev. Sun Myung (1920-) founded the Seoul, Korea-based Unification Church in the 1950s and led that institution to enormous wealth. The church's doctrine is a mixture of Christian, Confucian, and traditional Korean values, and the belief that Moon came into the world to complete the work of Jesus Christ. In 2004, Moon had himself crowned as the Messiah in a public ceremony. He is widely known for performing mass weddings of followers. Always in pursuit of wealth, Moon's church owns hundreds of properties and companies around the world, including the United Press International news agency.

Moravians are a theologically mainline Christian denomination that claims to be the first Protestant group in the world. The Moravians originated in ancient Bohemia and Moravia in what is the present-day Czech Republic. Their best-known reformer was John Hus (1369-1415), who was a professor of philosophy and rector at the University in Prague. Hus led a protest movement against many practices of the Roman Catholic clergy and hierarchy. He was accused of heresy, underwent a long trial at the Council of Constance, and was burned at the stake on July 6, 1415.

More, Sir Thomas (1478-1535), was a theologian highly favored by Henry VIII for writing a Defence of the Seven Sacraments, thereby repudiating Martin Luther's revisionist theology. Henry made More Speaker of the House of Commons in 1523 and Chancellor of the Duchy of Lancaster in 1525. Despite these favors, however, More refused to endorse King Henry VIII's plan to divorce Katherine of Aragón in 1527, so did not attend the coronation of Anne Boleyn in June 1533. This defiance made the king angry. More was later found guilty of treason and was beheaded on July 6, 1535. His final words on the scaffold were; "The King's good servant, but God's First." More was beatified in 1886 and canonized by the Catholic Church as a saint by Pope Pius XI in 1935.

Mormons is a more informal name for the Church of Jesus Christ of Latter Day Saints begun by Joseph Smith in 1830.

Mother Road of America – Route 66 – comprises a 2 448 mile highway that stretches from Chicago to Los Angeles. Writer John Steinbeck nick-named Route 66, "The Mother Road," and the name stuck. During the dust bowl days of the 1930s, an estimated 210 000 people migrated along Route 66 to California to escape poverty and settle in "the land of opportunity."

Route 66 helped facilitate the single greatest wartime manpower mobilization in the history of the nation. Between 1941 and 1945 the government invested approximately seventy billion dollars in capital projects throughout California, a large portion of which were in the Los Angeles-San Diego area. Every year travellers with an appreciation for nostalgia, travel along bits of old Route 66 to re-live the romance of this famous road.

Müller, Bernard (1788-1834) originally joined George Rapp's Harmonists at Economy, Pennsylvania, declaring himself Archduke Maximillian of the Stem of David and the Root of David. After a dispute with George Rapp, in 1832 Müller led a contingent of Harmonists to establish a short-lived commune called the New Philadelphia Society at Philipsburg, Pennsylvania.

Mumford, Lewis (1885-1990) promoted the theory that the invention of electricity and mass communication systems could assist in the building of a better world.

Münster or Muntzer, Thomas (1488-1525) was perhaps the most controversial figure of the German Reformation.Sometimes known as one of the founders of the Anabaptist movement and a fore runner of modern socialism, Múntzer also dabbled in the mystical spiritual realm. Historians have connected him to the

Peasants' war of 1525, and the Múnster Communal Kingdom that was officially founded later, both roles for which he got into trouble with civil and religious authorities. Múntzer, who tried to escape from arrest was caught, imprisoned and tortured to make him yield a full confession of all his misdeeds. He recanted, accepted Mass accoring to Roman Catholic tradition, and was behaded on May 27, 1525.

Nashoba Community was founded in Shelby County in 1825 by Frances Wright, a contemporary of Robert Owen. The commune featured an interracial membership based on Wright's view that slavery should be outlawed. Although Wright promoted the concept of free love, when her assistant, James Richardson, had sexual relations with several former slave members, Wright heeded public displeasure, lost interest in the project and abandoned it in 1830.

Nauvoo, Illinois, was the location where Mormon leader Joseph Smith settled his followers in 1839 after they were forced out of Missouri by religious persecution. Nauvoo soon became famous for its beautiful homes, fine shops, and its magnificent Mormon Temple. Soon, however, internal dissention, religious antagonism and the fear of Mormon political power exploded into a fury. In 1844 Joseph Smith and his brother were assassinated and the Mormons were forced to evacuate the city. The burning of the Mormon Temple in 1846 was the last recorded act of anti-Mormonism.

In 1849 Etienne Cabet and his Icarian comrades arrived in Nauvoo from France. They bought Temple Square and began a short-lived experiment in communal living. Soon minor disagreements within the community grew into open rebellion and the commune fell apart. Many Icarians left Nauvoo, but those who remained realized that the soil and climate of Nauvoo was much like that of their native France and suitable for the cultivation of grapes. Soon Nauvoo became noted for her fine wines. Cecil J. Baxter, whose father planted grapes and operated a winery in 1857, obtained a license to manufacture wine. Today the winery is operated by the fifth generation of the same family.

Niebuhr, Karl Paul Reinhold (1892-1971) was a prominent theologian who denounced the notion that a world free of chaos and social evil could be developed.

New Harmony, Indiana, was founded by George Rapp in 1814 as a second commune, following the establishment of Harmony in Pennsylvania in 1805. In 1824, Rapp sold the town to British industrialist, Robert Owen, who wanted to create a perfect society achieved by free education as well as the elimination of social classes and personal wealth. Rapp and his followers returned to Pennsylvania where he directed the construction of the town of Economy, his third commune.

New Melleray Abbey is a communal Cistercian (Trappist) monastery located in the rolling farmland south of Dubuque, Iowa. The thirty resident monks support themselves by farming and making wooden caskets and urns. As Roman Catholics, the monks of New Melleray profess the Rule of St. Benedict and are wholly orientated to a contemplative life of prayer.

Noyes, John Humphrey (1811-1886) was the founder of the Association of Perfectionists (later known as the Oneida Community) in Pitney, Vermont in 1845. Initially the commune became known for the manufacture of animal traps, but as the market dissolved, the community switched to manufacturing their famous Oneida silverware. Today, shareholders in the Oneida Corporation are descendents of the original communal population of 350 people.

Noyes, Theodore W. (1858-1946) was the son of John Humphrey Noyes who took over the reins of Oneida community after his father decided to retire. The move was unsuccessful because Theodore was an atheist who refused to live in the settlement, and lacked his father's talent for leadership. His policies divided the community and contributed to its demise as a commune in 1879. Oneida then became a joint stock company with shares being distributed to the commune's descendents.

Oberlin College. Both the college and the town of Oberlin were founded in 1833 by a pair of Presbyterian ministers, John Shipherd and Philo P. Stewart, who named their project after Jean-Frédéric Oberlin, an Alsatian minister whom they both admired. Oberlin attained prominence because of the influence of its second president, evangelist Charles Finney, after whom one of the College's chapels and performance spaces are named.

Old Believers are a Russian Separatist group who originated in 17th century Russia in opposition to new rituals established by Patriarch Nikon of the Russian Orthodox Church. They continue to use the older Church Slavonic translation of the sacred texts, including the Psalter, striving to preserve intact the traditional practices of the Russian Church. At first, because of religious persecution, the Old Believers found it necessary to move to the peripheral areas of Russia but later they immigrated to a large number of other countries including Canada and the United States.

Old Order Amish is another name for members of the mainline Amish community. Break-a-way groups include the Beachy Amish and the New Amish, who comprise a series of evangelical persuasions.

Oneida was a 19th century commune established in 1848 by John Humphrey Noyes, a former Unitarian minister. The commune operated for thirty-three years until Noyes was forced to leave the United States on charges of sexual misconduct. Succumbing to internal and external pressures, the Community disbanded in 1880 and formed a joint-stock corporation, Oneida Community Ltd. The company has achieved world wide recognition for the tableware it manufactures.

Ordnung is the name of a group of selected Amish men who make major decisions about Amish lifestyle in the local community which they reside.

Orwell, George (1903-1950) was a popular British writer who penned *Nineteen Eighty-Four,* a novel depicting an idyllic collectivist society.

Owen, Robert Dale (1771-1858) was a successful Welsh industrialist who devoted much of his profit to improving the lives of his employees. His reputation was enhanced when he set up a textile factory in New Lanark, England, and introduced shorter working hours, schools for children, and affordable housing for his employees. In 1824 he purchased the town of New Harmony in Indiana from George Rapp and set up an Owenite commune. The experiment collapsed a few years later because of mismanagement and because many of the followers he attracted had a limited work ethic.

Palliser Triangle is a label used to describe the near desert conditions of the southerly regions of southeast Alberta and southwestern Saskatchewan. During 1857 to 1860 Captain James Palliser (1817-1887) surveyed the area and pronounced it unfit for agricultural purposes because of its climate and soil. Though populated by European immigrants in the latter part of the 19th century, today the area has virtually been evacuated.

Patriarch, Nikon (1605-1681), Patriarch of Moscow, was of peasant origin, and in time became Patriarch of the Russia Orthodox Church. As head of the Church of Russia Nikon set introducing a series of Greek reforms, including revisions to service books and introducing new rituals. As a result, over the next century hundreds of opposing sects emerged in opposition to Nikon's reforms. These sects included Doukhobors, Molokans, and Old Believers.

Penn, William (1644-1718) was the English founder and "Absolute Proprietor" of the Province of Pennsylvania, an English North American colony that became the state of Pennsylvania. Penn became known as an early champion of democracy and religious freedom and was famous for making treaties with local Aboriginals and maintaining good relations with them. He was also involved in establishing the city of Philadelphia.

Peosta, Iowa is the site of an agricultural Trappist commune called New Melleray. Resident monks, who rise at 3:30 each morning, spend most of their time in prayer and worship. They also grow forests featuring a variety of hardwoods that they use to manufacture coffins and urns.

Pestalozzi, Johann Heinrich (1746-1827) was a Swiss educator who has often been cast as the forerunner of the Progressive Education movement in the United States.

Peter the Lordly Verigin (1859-1924) was the title given to a prominent Doukhobor leader named Peter Vaselievich Verigin. Verigin was the first Doukhobor leader in Canada when the group settled in Saskatchewan in 1899. After abandoning that province, Verigin helped them resettle in British Columbia where they built ninety communal houses in the name of the Christian Community of Universal Brotherhood (CCUB).

Peter Petrovich Chistiakov Verigin (1880-1939) was the son of Peter the Lordly Verigin and the second leader of the Christian Community Universal Brotherhood in Canada. Six weeks after Lordly's death, by Doukhobor custom, the communal Doukhobors held a mass meeting to select their new leader and the vote fell to Peter Chistiakov who was resident in Russia. Under his leadership a number of successful reforms were initiated in Canada including decentralization and increased productivity for the CCUB, expansion of the arts, and Russian language schools. When the Doukhobor commune was dissolved by government action in 1939, Verigin formed an alternative organization known as the Union of Spiritual Communities in Christ (USCC) which still operates today.

Phalanx was the name of a complex social unit invented by French philosopher, Charles Fourier in 1803. Each phalanx was to comprise three square miles and include 1 620 members, who were to reside in a dormitory-like buildings known as a phalanasteries – six-story buildings, each with a long body and two wings. In front of the building there was to be a parade ground with a courtyard inside the building.

The social makeup of the phalanx would consist of spontaneous associations of people, called groups who would form to do particular tasks. Each group would be made up of seven individuals, and five groups would constitute a series. Each series would be involved in specific work areas – for example, a garden series, an education series, and so on, until these series united to form a phalanx. Individuals would eventually belong to thirty or forty groups, and so fulfill their individual needs.

Although Fourier never lived in America, a half dozen phalanxes were developed there following his design. The best known were Ceresco in Wisconsin, and Brook Farm in Massachusetts. Both phalanxes operated for about six years.

Philipsburg Colony in Pennsylvania was begun in 1832 by a factional group of 250 dissident Harmonists led by Bernard Müller (also known as Count Leon) who had moved to the town of Economy the year before. Müller promoted himself as the Messiah and insisted that he had found the philosopher's stone which made it possible for him to turn metal into gold. Rapp was initially excited by Müller's announcements, but the two soon quarreled over several administrative issues such as celibacy. Müller accused Rapp of hypocrisy because Rapp spent so much time alone with a young woman named of Hildegard Mütschler.

The Philipsburg commune lasted only a year and Müller departed to start a new experiment in Louisiana. Many of his disillusioned followers joined William Keil's commune at Bethel, Missouri.

Pierce, Captain Edward Mitchell (??-1888) established a bourgeois Victorian commune in southeast Saskatchewan in 1882 along with an agricultural college aimed at teaching young bachelors to become farmers. His tuition fee of $500 to $1 000 per year attracted a group of remitance men and youth from wealthy British families who were more interested in parties and leisure than work. The experiment lasted only eight years.

Plato (428/427–348/347 BC) was a classical Greek philosopher, mathematician, and writer of philosophical dialogues. Plato founded the Academy in Athens, the first institution of higher learning in the Western world. He also helped lay the foundations of Western philosophy, natural philosophy, and science. His best-known work, written in 380 BC, is *The Republic*, which outlines Plato's concept of city-state governance. It is quite likely the first written attempt to elaborate an ideal form of society (utopia), and one of the most influential works of philosophy and political theory in Western thought.

Pleasant Hill Shaker Village is America's largest restored Shaker commune and is regarded as a national treasure. The village operated from 1805 to 1910, and at its peak the 3 000 acre National Historic Landmark was occupied by 500 individuals. Although still occupied by a few Shakers after its dissolution as a community, restoration of the village began in 1961.

Puritans was the name assigned to a group of 16th century Protestants whose extreme theological views led them to abandon the Church of England. The Puritans thought that the English Reformation had not gone far enough in reforming the doctrines and structure of the church. The Puritan objective was to purify the national church by eliminating every shred of Catholic influence. Many Puritans emigrated to the America in the 17th century where they sought to found a holy Commonwealth in New England. Puritanism remained the dominant cultural force in that area well into the 19th century.

Quakers began as a nonconformist movement in England in the early 1650s. Due to religious persecution, many adherents emigrated to America to more freely practice their religion. Traditionally George Fox has been taken to be the founder or at least the most important early figure in the Quaker movement, but modern scholarship suggests a more complicated picture.

On arrival in America the Quakers soon found themselves in conflict with Puritans of the Massachusetts Bay Colony who opposed their beliefs. Quakers were often imprisoned, their books were burned, much of their property was confiscated and they were banished from the area. Their darkened prisons featured terrible conditions, and they were deprived of food. Were it not for sympathizers smuggling food to them, they might have starved in their cells. They eventually departed for other areas of the American frontier.

Rapp, Frederick Reichert (1775–1834) was the adopted son of George Rapp and chosen heir to the Harmonist leadership. An architect and stonecutter by trade, during his term of office the Harmonist village of Economy was transformed to feature finely proportioned buildings, quaint and charming gardens, and tantalizing labyrinths.

Frederick Rapp was a talented poet, an artist, and a musician. While in charge of the village of Economy, he gathered a worthy collection of paintings and created a museum of Indian relics and objects of natural history. He also composed many fine hymns. He was an energetic and skillful businessman who successfully represented the colony in its external affairs

Rapp, Johann Georg or George (1757-1847) was recognized as a Separatist preacher at an early age. He believed in the individual's power of direct communication with God and the right to interpret the teachings of Jesus in a personal way.

Very quickly experiencing opposition from religious forces including spending time in prison, Rapp left Germany for Pennsylvania in 1803 where he eventually established three successive communal towns – Harmony, Pennsylvania in 1805, New Harmony in Indiana in 1814, and Economy, back in Pennsylvania in 1824.

Reorganized Church of Jesus Christ of Latter Day Saints is the former name of a little-known remnant of the Mormon Church that Joseph Smith established in 1830. Renamed the Community of Christ in 2001, the Reorganized Church has a membership of 221 000-members and claims that a direct descendent of Joseph Smith has always been the president of the organization.

Republic (The), was Plato's written conception of what an ideal society should look like.

Reunion Tower, Dallas TX, was named in honor of the former Icarian settlement of La Reunion established in 1848. The fifty-story tower Reunion Arena was completed in 1980 at a cost of twenty-seven million dollars, and is topped by a three-level geodesic sphere that houses a restaurant, observation deck and revolving lounge. Fully illuminated at night, an elevator trip to the top of the tower takes sixty-eight seconds. The restaurant at the top of the tower revolves every fifty-five minutes.

Ridley, Bishop Nicholas (c.1500–1555) was an English Bishop of London, who was burned at the stake during the English Reformation because of his "heretical" beliefs. Every October 16, Ridley's role is commemorated in the Calendar of Saints in some parts of the Anglican Communion.

Rigdon, Sidney (1793-1876) founded a short-lived commune at Kirkland, Ohio, then joined Joseph Smith's Mormon Church. When Smith was assassinated, Rigdon became a candidate for the leadership of the Mormon Church. When Brigham Young was appointed leader, Rigdon led a faction of members to Pittsburgh, Pennsylvania, to start a short-lived reactionary organization.

Ripley, Rev. George (1802-1880) was an American social reformer, Unitarian minister, and journalist who identified with the philosophy of transcendentalism. He was the founder of the short-lived Fourierist utopian community, Brook Farm, in West Roxbury, Massachusetts.

Ripon, Wisconsin, also known as the Wisconsin Phalanx (or Ceresco), was established on May 27, 1844, as a phalanx settlement based on Charles Fourier's version of an ideal community. The foundation for the settlement was initiated by an advance party of nineteen men and one boy. Later, a larger group arrived, led by Warren Chase who had been inspired by Fourier's principles of social philosophy.

The Wisconsin settlers named their new community named Ceresco after the Roman goddess of the harvest, and located it in a valley nestled between two hills. Before long, the community became home to more than 200 idealists. They constructed several community owned dwellings called long houses, one of which still stands on its original site.

Rock, Johann Friedrich (1678-1749), a saddle-maker, was one of the co-founders of the Community of True Inspiration, later known as Iowa's Amana Society.

Roosevelt, President Franklin D. (1882-1945) repealed *The Chinese Exclusion Act* in 1943.

Rousseau, Jean Jacques (1712-1778) was a major writer and philosopher of the 18th century Enlightenment. His book, *The Social Contract,* written in 1762, influenced political thought during the French Revolution and later the development of modern political and educational thought.

Route 66, an official highway in the U.S. System, is known as the Will Rogers Highway after the late great humorist. More informally, it is also known as the Main Street of America or the Mother Road.

One of the nation's original highways, Route 66 was established on November 11, 1926, but its road signs did not go up until the following year. The original highway encompassed 2 448 miles, and ran from Chicago, Illinois, through the states of Missouri, Kansas, Oklahoma, Texas, New Mexico, Arizona, and California, before ending at Los Angeles.

Ruskin Cooperative Association was founded by Julius Wayland (1854-1912) in 1894 at Cave Hills, Tennessee, with the chief industry of publishing *The Coming Nation,* a radical newspaper dedicated to espousing the benefits of practical socialism. In 1893 the depression formed the evacuation of the 200 residents to seek accommodation elsewhere.

Russian Orthodox Church. Also known as the Orthodox Christian Church of Russia, this organization is a body of Christians who constitute the Eastern Orthodox Church under the jurisdiction of the Patriarch of Moscow. Dozens of sects left the church during the 17th century when Patriarch Nikon initiated Greek reforms.

This particular denomination is often said to be the largest of the Eastern Orthodox churches in the world and second in size only to the Roman Catholic Church, numbering over 135 million members worldwide. The denomination comprises 29 262 parishes with 203 bishops, 804 monasteries, and 87 theological schools

San Francisco's Chinatown, established in the 1840s, is the oldest and one of the largest Chinatowns in North America. Today, with a population of over 100 000, it is a centre for the study of Chinese history and culture, and offers many venues for the arts, film, music, photography, and literature.

Sanctified Sisters (the) were started by Martha McWhirter in Belton, Texas, in 1866 after she was the recipient of a vision encouraging her to leave her marriage and establish a commune for abused women. Soon the McWhirter House became a haven for women whose marriages had gone sour with no possibility for divorce. The Sanctified Sisters became financially independent by operating a series of businesses including a popular hotel. They also sold surplus eggs and butter, hired out as maids and cooks, took in home laundry, and cut and peddled firewood. The group relocated to Washington DC in 1899 where the commune eventually dissolved.

Schmiedeleut are a branch of Hutterites whose name derives from the art of blacksmithing. Schmiedt means "blacksmith;" leut means people, so literally blacksmith people.

Scoble John (1799 - ??) was a British politician and abolitionist in Western Canada. Scoble helped form the British and Foreign Anti-Slavery Society and from 1842-1852 served as its secretary.

Seventh Day Adventists comprise a religious denomination established by Ellen G. White in 1863. Numbering sixteen million members worldwide, Adventists are known for their philosophy of wholesome living and insistence that Christians should worship on Saturday instead of Sunday.

Shakers are an 18th century religious group from England who immigrated to America in 1774, following their leader, Ann Lee. Formally known as the United

Society of Believers, they were also called Shaking Quakers and broke away from the main body of Quakers because of their use of ecstatic dance in worship. At the height of their history they numbered 6 000 people living in nineteen communes. Today only a handful of Shakers remain.

Sifton, Clifford (1861-1929) was Canada's Minister of the Interior from 1896 to 1905. A successful lawyer and committed politician, Sifton dedicated himself to turning the Canadian West into a premier agricultural area by populating the area with land-hungry European immigrants.

Silkville, Kansas, was a commune established in Kansas in 1873 by a French aristocrat Ernest de Boissiere. The experiment lasted only a few years, but the silk produced by the community was fine enough to win an award at the Philadelphia Exposition. Unable to attract sufficient workers, de Boissiere donated his assets to the Odd Fellow's Grand Lodge of Kansas for the purpose of establishing an orphanage, then returned to France. Today the site is privately owned.

Simons, Menno aka Simonszoon (1496-1561) was a Dutch Roman Catholic priest whose Anabaptist followers are known as Mennonites.

Smith, Hyrum (1800-1844) was the older brother of Joseph Smith, Jr. and a leader in the early Latter Day Saints movement. In 1847, he was assassinated at Carthage, Illinois, along with his brother, Joseph.

Smith, Joseph (1805-1844) was the originator of the Church of Jesus Christ of Latter Day Saints in accordance with a vision he was a recipient of on September 21, 1823. He was assassinated at Carthage, Illinois, in 1847 along with his brother Hyrum.

Society of Separatists of Zoar, also known as Zoarites, was the name adopted by a German Separatist commune in Ohio. The commune operated from 1817 to 1898.

Sons of Freedom (or Sons of God) emerged as a radical subsection of the 7 500 Doukhobors who migrated to Canada in 1899. In 1903 more then 1 000 Sons of Freedom staged an unsuccessful protest march at Yorkton, Saskatchewan, to denounce their stand against militarism and government regulation.

Spirit Wrestlers is a name assigned to the Doukhobors in Russia by Archbishop Ambrosius. He accused the Doukhobors of wrestling *against* the Spirit of God. The Doukhobors adopted the name, insisting that they wrestled in the Spirit of God, not against it.

Starr, Ellen Gates (1859-1940) co-founded Hull House with Jane Addams in Chicago.

St. Joseph's Colony, Kindersley, Saskatchewan. The first Roman Catholic administrative and pastoral structures for this vast community were established during the missionary period in the prairie west of Canada. Parishes, dioceses and archdioceses were formed later, when the Catholic population increased with the arrival of settlers from other parts of North America and Europe. At the time of Saskatchewan's entry into Confederation in 1905, the entire province was part of one large vicariate which was administered as a mission of the Diocese of St. Albert in Alberta. As the Catholic population of the province increased, the diocesan territories were changed to meet the needs of the people.

St. Joseph's Colony, near Balgonie, Saskatchewan, is an example of a religious-based settlement established near the end of the 19th century in the Canadian West. It was established in 1886 under the direction of Roman Catholic Bishop Alexandre Tache.

Stowe, Harriet Beecher (1811-1896) is best known today as the author of *Uncle Tom's Cabin*, which helped galvanize the abolitionist cause and contributed to the outbreak of the Civil War. *Uncle Tom's Cabin* sold over 10 000 copies in the first week and was a best seller in its day. After the publication of the book Stowe became an internationally acclaimed celebrity and popular author. Stowe wrote in an informal conversational style, and presented herself as an average wife and mother.

Sudeten Germans were a group of 300 immigrants who chose Saskatchewan and British Columbia as their new home following extensive international negotiations aimed at saving them from Nazi concentration camps or death. Their unfortunate lot was to be Germans living as a minority in Czechoslovakia among Czechs and Slovaks in a country created out of the treaties following World War I. The Social Democratic Party in their homeland lobbied the national government to meet its promise of fair treatment for minorities.

Suitcase Immigrants is a label ascribed to Canada's first generation immigrants who were not certain that they wanted to stay in the new land so they "kept their suitcases packed" in order to be ready to return to the homeland.

Summertown, Tennessee is the location of The Farm, a hippie commune established by Stephen Gaskin and his followers in 1971. At its peak The Farm attracted 1 500 utopians, and its present membership is around 125.

Swift, Jonathan (1667-1745) penned *Gulliver's Travels*, a fantasy novel about idyllic living.

Tache, Bishop Alexandre (1823-1894) was an Oblate Roman Catholic priests who became the first Archbishop of St. Boniface in Manitoba. He presided during the period of Catholic immigration to the West.

Tarasoff, Koozma (1932-) is a well-known Doukhobor writer and photo-journalist living in Ottawa, Ontario. His best-known work is *Plakun Trava: The Doukhobors*.

Teed, Cyrus Reed (1839-1908) founder of Koresh community in Florida, changed his name to Koresh. In the autumn of 1869, Cyrus had what he later referred to as an Illumination that awarded him the philosopher's stone, and thereby the ability to change lead into gold.

Teed's vision also explained the nature of the universe was revealed to him. According to Teed, the earth is enclosed and people live on the inside. He called this Cellular Cosmology, following Isaiah 40:12, and thus Koreshans often used the phrase, "we live on the inside."

Trappist Monks, are a group of devoted Roman Catholics who operate a communal monastery in the rolling farmland south of Dubuque, Iowa. The 30 resident monks support themselves by farming and making wooden caskets and urns. As Roman Catholics, the monks profess and are devoted to the Rule of St. Benedict which means that they spend most of their time in prayer and meditation.

Tsimshian Indians, living on the northwest coast of British Columba were the target group for William Duncan, an Anglican lay missionary who built a religious commune among them in 1886.

Tubman, Harriet (1822-1913) was born and raised a slave for thirty years. After her escape she was active in the Underground Railroad, assisting in the freedom quest of some 300 slaves.

Uncle Tom's Cabin was written by Harriet Beecher Stowe in 1852 and instantly became a bestseller. Publication of the book, describing slavery in America, made Stowe an internationally acclaimed celebrity and influenced the beginnings of the American Civil War.

Underground Railroad (The) was begun around 1780 and assigned the informal name of Underground Railroad in 1831. Its purpose through a series of established "stations," (safe houses) was to assist slaves in escaping to Canada and several non-slavery states.

Union of Spiritual Communities on Christ (USCC) was a replacement Doukhobor institution designed to take the place of the Christian Community of Universal Brotherhood (CCUB) when the latter was forced into bankruptcy by the Canadian and British Columbia governments in 1939. Its organizers believed that if a physical commune was no longer possible, the concept of a spiritual commune should be maintained.

Utopia, Ohio, is located in Clermont County, and in 1844 was patterned after Charles Fourier's concept of phalanx – an ideal type of settlement. After a short time the commune failed and was sold to John O. Wattles, the leader of a group of spiritualists. On December 12, 1847 the Ohio River overflowed to the point that nearly everyone in the commune's largest building drowned. Of 165 people attending a festive occasion, only fifteen survived.

Van Leiden, (van Leyden) Jan (1509-1536), was a radical Anabaptist leader at Münster in Westphalia, Germany. Originally a tailor, then a merchant, and later an innkeeper, he liked to act the part of the biblical King David. Van Leiden was in many ways a highly gifted man, but his conceit and his self-love betrayed him. He became an influential man with a large and devoted following, and when he founded an Anabaptist government at Münster, he became king of the "New Jerusalem" with absolute supremacy for more than a year.

Verigin, John J., (1921-2008) succeeded his great grandfather, Peter the Lordly, as Doukhobor leader in 1959 after Peter Chistiakov (Peter the Purger) died. At that point John J. Verigin became "honorary chairman" of the Union of Spiritual Communities in Christ.

Verigin, Peter Petrovich, also known as Peter the Purger or Peter Chistiakov Verigin (1881-1939) succeeded his father, Peter the Lordly, as leader of the Christian Community of Universal Brotherhood in 1924 when his father was killed in an explosion that rocked the train on which he was a passenger.

Verigin, Peter Vasievich, also known as Peter the Lordly (1859-1924) was the first leader of the Doukhobors in Canada, arriving here in 1902. He died in 1924 when an explosion rocked the train on which he was riding.

Verigina, Evdokia Gregorevna (dates unknown) was Peter the Lordly's wife in Russia. The marriage was dissolved when he moved to Canada in 1902.

Wabash River (The) in Indiana was the site of New Harmony, the second communal second town built by the Harmonists under the leadership of George Rapp. In 1924 the town was sold to British industrialist and philanthropist, Robert Owen.

Wallis, Michael (1945-) is a big fan of America's first major highway and commemorated it in a book called, *Route 66: The Mother Road.*

Warren, Josiah (1798-1874), a follower of Charles Fourier, founded the commune of Utopia in Ohio in 1844.

Wells, H.G. (1866-1946) was an English author best known for his work in the science fiction genre. Wells is sometimes referred to as "The Father of Science Fiction." Wells was an outspoken socialist and a pacifist, and his later works became increasingly political and didactic.

Western Canadian Drybelt is a label ascribed to the semi-arid regions of southeast Alberta and southwest Saskatchewan. Heavily settled by European immigrants during the first decade of the 20th century, the area soon proved to be too desert-like to grow crops. As a result many farmers lured to the region by false advertising, were faced with bankruptcy and loss of property. During the decades that followed hundreds of farms in the area were abandoned.

Whittaker, James (1751-1787) was a major organizer in the Shaker movement. It was he who arranged to feed Ann Lee when she was imprisoned, by smuggling wine and milk to her by placing the stem of a pipe though the key-hole of her cell door.

Wilson, Hiram, (1803-1864) received his theological degree from Oberlin Theological Seminary in 1836. That same year, he was given twenty-five dollars by Rev. Charles Finney to travel to Upper Canada and observe the situation of fugitive slaves there. He returned to Canada the following spring as a delegate of the American Anti-Slavery Society and began raising and borrowing money in order to establish an educational institute for fugitive slaves. By 1839, Wilson had established ten schools and recruited fourteen teachers, most of whom were Oberlin graduates.

Women's Commonwealth, Belton, Texas was the official name of a female commune founded by Martha McWhirter in 1866 after she was the recipient of a vision. Nicknamed the "Sanctified Sisters" the group comprised married women who left their husbands and operated several very successful businesses in Belton, Texas. In 1899 the group relocated to Washington, DC where they eventually disbanded.

Women in the Wilderness, more popularly known as the Society of Women in the Wilderness, was originated in 17th century Germany by Jakob Zimmerman, but led in America by Johannes Kelpius. On arriving in Pennsylvania the group lived in caves like hermits and encouraged private study of ancient manuscripts and meditation, waiting for the millennium. As the group began to interact with mainstream society and their leader died, their membership gradually dissolved.

Wright, Frances (Fanny) (1795-1852) was a friend of Robert Owens who purchased George Rapp's second commune at New Harmony, Indiana. Wright visited New Harmony and was immediately converted to Owen's philosophy, so much that she decided to form her own co-operative community. In 1825

Wright purchased 2,000 acres of woodland near Memphis, Tennessee and formed a community called Nashoba. She then bought slaves from neighboring farmers, freed them, and gave them land on her settlement. When her marriage dissolved, Wright became and advocate of free love. She also developed her own dress code for women which included bodices, ankle-length pantaloons, and a dress cut to above the knee. This style was later promoted by feminists such as Amelia Bloomer, Susan Anthony, and Elizabeth Cady Stanton.

When Wright died in 1852 her ex-husband managed to gain control over her entire property, including her earnings from lectures and the royalties from her books. At her request, Wright's tombstone in Cincinnati, Ohio, reads: "I have wedded the cause of human improvement, staked on it my fortune, my reputation and my life."

Young, Brigham (1801-1877) was chosen as successor to Mormon leader, Joseph Smith, when the latter was assassinated in 1844 at Carthage, Illinois. On August 8, of that year, Young and the Twelve were sustained by the membership to lead the Church of Jesus Christ of Latter Day Saints (Mormon). Young remained President of the Church until his death in 1877.

Ziegler, Abraham (1756-1834) bought the Town of Harmony from founder George Rapp with four other Mennonite families for $100 000 in 1915.

Zoar, Ohio, is a small community in Tuscarawas County founded in 1817 by a group of German Separatists led by Joseph Bimeler. The resultant community adopted the name, "The Society of the Separatists of Zoar." The word Zoar was taken from the Old Testament citing the place where Abraham's nephew Lot went after the destruction of the sinful cities of Sodom and Gomorrah. The Zoar community operated from 1817 to 1898, and several descendents of the original group still reside in the village.

Zwingli, Ulrich (1484-1531) was a well-known proponent of the Protestant Reformation in Switzerland. Zwingli's theological views were based on a single principle – if the Old or New Testament did not say something explicitly and literally, no Christian should believe or practice that belief. This was the foundation for his opposition to the sale of indulgences. Despite Zwingli's conservative stance, several Anabaptist leaders, George Blaurock, Conrad Grebel, and Felix Manz accused him of compromising his position as a reformer of the Roman Catholic Church. Zwingli died at the age of forty-seven in a battle with Swiss Canton armies.

About the Authors

John W. Friesen, Ph.D., D.Min., D.R.S., is a Professor in the Faculty of Education at the University of Calgary where he teaches courses and conducts research in teacher education and Indigenous education. An ordained clergyman with the All Native Circle Conference of the United Church of Canada, he is the author, co-author, or editor of more than fifty oooks including:

Profiles of Canadian Educators. (edited with Robert S. Patterson and John W. Chalmers). D.C. Heath, 1974;

Rose of the North. Borealis, 1987;

Introduction to Teaching: A Socio-Cultural Approach. (with Alice L. Boberg), Kendall/Hunt, 1990;

When Cultures Clash: Case Studies in Multiculturalism. Detselig, 1993;

You Can't Get There From Here: The Mystique of North American Plains Indians Culture & Philosophy. Kendall/Hunt, 1995;

Pick One: A User-friendly Guide to Religion. Detselig, 1995;

Perceptions of the Amish Way. (with Bruce K. Friesen). Kendall/Hunt, 1996;

The Community Doukhobors: A People in Transition (with Michael M. Verigin). Borealis, 1996;

The Real/Riel Story: An Interpretive History of the Métis People of Canada. Borealis, 1996;

Rediscovering the First Nations of Canada. Detselig, 1997;

First Nations of the Plains: Creative, Adaptable and Enduring. Detselig, 1999;

Aboriginal Spirituality and Biblical Theology: Closer Than You Think. Detselig, 2000;

Legends of the Elders. Detselig, 2000;

Sayings of a Philosopher. Detselig, 2005;

What's Your Church Like? Compared to Nine New Testament Models. (with Virginia Lyons Friesen). Xulon, 2007.

Canada in the Twenty-First Century: A Historical Sociological Approach. (with Trevor W. Harrison). Scholars' Press, 2010.

Virginia Lyons Friesen, Ph.D., earned a Diploma in Early Childhood Education at the University of Calgary and a Certificate in Counseling from the Institute of Pastoral Counseling in Akron, Ohio. She served as a Sessional Instructor with the Department of Communication and Culture at the University of Calgary from 2001 to 2010, and has co-presented a number of papers at academic conferences. She currently serves as Director of Christian Education at Morley United Church on the Stoney (Nakoda Sioux) Indian Reserve.

The Friesens have co-authored the following Temeron/Detselig titles:

In Defense of Public Schools in North America, 2001;

Aboriginal Education in Canada: A Plea for Integration, 2002;

We Are Included: The Métis People of Canada Realize Riel's Vision, 2004;

More Legends of the Elders, 2004;

First Nations in the Twenty-First Century: Contemporary Educational Frontiers, 2005;

Still More Legends of the Elders, 2005;

Even More Legends of the Elders, 2005;

Legends of the Elders Handbook for Teachers, Homeschoolers, and Parents, 2005;

Canadian Aboriginal Art and Spirituality: A Vital Link, 2006;

Western Canadian Native Destiny: The Cultural Maze Revisited, 2008; and,

And Now You Know: 50 Native American Legends, 2009.

The Friesens' website is **drsfriesen.com.**